My Autobiography

being jordan
My Autobiography

Katie Price

JOHN BLAKE

Published by John Blake Publishing Ltd,
3, Bramber Court, 2 Bramber Road,
London W14 9PB, England

www.blake.co.uk

First published in paperback in 2005

ISBN 978 1 84454 132 4

British Library Cataloguing-in-Publication Data:

A catalogue record for this book is available from the British Library.

Design by www.envydesign.co.uk

Printed in the UK by CPI Bookmarque, Croydon, CR0 4TD

13

For my mum Amy, Paul, Daniel, Sophie;
my son Harvey, my nan, my late granddad
Harvey and all my friends and fans who
have believed in me all the way

CONTENTS

	This is why ...	ix
	Prologue	xiii
Chapter One:	Meet the Family	1
Chapter Two:	A Narrow Escape	7
Chapter Three:	First Love	17
Chapter Four:	Sparky	35
Chapter Five:	Becoming Jordan	43
Chapter Six:	Here's Looking at You, Kid ...	57
Chapter Seven:	Oh, Teddy, Teddy!	63
Chapter Eight:	My Gorgeous Gladiator	73
Chapter Nine:	Pit-stop Pin-up	83
Chapter Ten:	I Did it My Way: The Story of My Surgery	89
Chapter Eleven:	Formula 1 Love	99

Chapter Twelve:	Nightmare in Germany	113
Chapter Thirteen:	Poptastic	119
Chapter Fourteen:	Torn Between Two Lovers ...	131
Chapter Fifteen:	From the Heart	141
Chapter Sixteen:	Posh?	153
Chapter Seventeen:	Falling Apart	163
Chapter Eighteen:	A Bit of All Dwight	173
Chapter Nineteen:	Footballers' Wives	183
Chapter Twenty:	La-La Land	189
Chapter Twenty-one:	Monte Carlo Misery	195
Chapter Twenty-two:	Bunny Girl	205
Chapter Twenty-three:	Oh Baby	215
Chapter Twenty-four:	All By Myself	225
Chapter Twenty-five:	Pop Idol	233
Chapter Twenty-six:	Single Mum	251
Chapter Twenty-seven:	Hello Harvey	257
Chapter Twenty-eight:	The Bombshell	265
Chapter Twenty-nine:	The Only Way is Up	269
Chapter Thirty:	Back to La-La Land	275
Chapter Thirty-one:	The Big C	281
Chapter Thirty-two:	Return of the Pop Idol	293
Chapter Thirty-three:	Lover Boy	299
Chapter Thirty-four:	Jungle Fever	309

THIS IS WHY...

I've been called a slapper, a tart, a man-eater; a woman who is so desperate for male attention she will do anything to get it.

I've been told that I'm a freak; that I'm addicted to plastic surgery; that I've mutilated my body because I hate how I look.

I've been described as unstable, insecure, out of control; a drunk.

It has been claimed that I'm obsessed with fame and will do anything for publicity.

Worst of all, they say I'm an unfit mother.

Journalists write about me as if I'm a dumb bimbo. Yes, I'm famous for my boobs. So what? Modelling is just my job, and there's more to me than that. There's a person inside this body.

So who am I? The Jordan of the tabloids who doesn't

seem to give a toss and only cares about fame and partying? Or Katie Price, the successful model and single mum who is trying to make the best of things?

Now you can make up your own minds. This is my story, and I've held nothing back: not the parts I'm ashamed of, nor the things I regret. It's all here. My life is in your hands. Judge for yourself.

ACKNOWLEDGEMENTS

A huge thank you to my mum for everything, but
especially for giving up her job to look after Harvey
(even though you do wind me up at times!) and for helping
me with this book; Daniel for my website and for always
supporting me and to Sally, Clare, Michelle and Roxie for
always being there to pick up the pieces...and to Rebecca
and Maggie for their help with this book.

Visit my official website at:
www.jordanfanclub.co.uk

PROLOGUE

MAY 2005 – SUSSEX

It was two o'clock in the morning and, as usual, I was having trouble sleeping – a certain person had just woken me up.

'Hey, Pete.' I gently shook his arm, wanting him to wake up and share this moment with me, 'The baby's moving again!'

I grabbed Pete's hand and placed it on my bump, right where the baby was wriggling around. Now the baby was getting bigger there was hardly any room for him to move, but he still managed to be extremely busy in there and keep me awake at night.

'Wow!' Pete said, as we both felt the baby moving. 'What was that?'

'I think it's our baby, Pete!' I couldn't resist teasing him.

'I meant what part of our baby was it!'

'His foot, I reckon.'

We looked at each other and grinned. Then Pete said, 'I still can't believe that we're having a baby.'

'Well you'd better,' I laughed. 'There's only a few weeks to go!'

Pete lay back down next to me, putting his arms around me, enfolding me with his warmth and making me feel so safe and loved. God, I loved this man! Loved him with all my heart. We've been together for a year-and-a-half and it has been the most wonderful, magical time of my life. I had dreamed of meeting someone like Pete but I had never thought my dream would come true. I closed my eyes and thought for the millionth time how lucky I was – I was having a baby with the man I loved and we were getting married. And it was going to be the fairy-tale, full-on, Disney-style wedding that I had always fantasised about having. I had found my happy ever after.

I stroked my tummy, whispering to the baby, 'You've got the best daddy in the world and we all love you so much and your brother's going to love you too.'

Then I felt a sudden, sharp pang of sadness as I remembered how lonely, how desperate and abandoned I had felt when I was pregnant with my first son, Harvey. I remembered what it was like not having a partner to share the excitement of seeing the baby in the scans, not being able to confide my anxieties about the birth to the baby's father, not having anyone to hold me at night and tell me that they loved me and that everything would be all right. And I remembered what it was like going into labour and not knowing if Dwight, the father, would even bother to turn up to see his newborn son. As if sensing my bad thoughts, Pete kissed me, murmuring, 'Love you, Katie.'

'Love you too,' I whispered back.

All my life I have been looking for love. I longed to meet a man I could fall in love with completely, body, mind and soul. A man I could commit to totally, a man I could respect and trust, a man who would love me for myself, a man I could marry and spend the rest of my life with, a man who would be the father of my children and a father to Harvey. I'd almost given up hope of ever meeting him, resigning myself to getting love where I could, never feeling satisfied, always feeling restless, knowing that I hadn't yet found 'the one.'

There has been no shortage of men in my life. Some of them I even thought I was in love with and one I convinced myself that I wanted to marry. Now I look back and realise that it was just infatuation and my own insecurity. I thought I needed them, thought I couldn't survive without the relationship and I let most of them treat me like shit. I wasn't even in love with the father of my child but I still hung around long enough for him to walk all over me and treat me like crap, he even failed to support me while I was pregnant with our child ... but you'll read about that later in the book.

I had a couple of relationships after Harvey was born, even though my priorities had shifted completely. By then I had someone in my life who needed me and depended on me more than I needed any man. But I still wanted the reassurance of having a man hold me in his arms and tell me that he loved me, to tell me how much he wanted me, especially when I received the heartbreaking news that my baby was blind. But the men – or rather boys – I had chosen to be with were never going to be anything more than a stopgap, even though I told one of them that I loved them too. Deep down, I didn't really mean it. The words came easily but I hadn't given away my heart. I was still waiting for that man who was so special that I would never want anyone else.

Then I met Peter and my life changed forever. I wanted him with an incredible, overwhelming intensity from the moment he walked into the room. The time we spent together in the jungle sealed my fate: I wanted him like I have never wanted anyone else. I was certain that he was 'the one', the man I had been searching for all my life. I fell passionately, hopelessly, madly in love with him – a love which has only deepened and grown stronger the more I have got to know Pete and the closer we have become. In the past, I have fallen for men quickly and dramatically and then fallen out with them just as suddenly. But I guarantee that's not going to happen with Pete.

It's not just about his looks – though to me he is the best looking man I have ever been with – or have ever seen – with his handsome face and his beautiful hazel eyes. And, of course, he has the most gorgeous body – in all departments! Let's just say that I'm a very, very lucky girl! Sexually, I have definitely found my match.

I love Pete for himself – his warm, loving personality, his strength of character and his cheeky sense of humour. I love the fact that he's so passionate and open about his feelings and he makes me feel wanted. I hate being with men who never open up and tell you how they really feel, who are too afraid to show any emotion. Pete knows me better than any other man ever has. He knows how to deal with me and as a result he keeps me on my toes. I could never wrap him around my little finger as I admit that I've done to quite a few of the other men I've been out with. He's totally honest and, if I ever lied to him, he'd walk and he'd find someone else in an instant. But I've no need to lie to him and I've got no secrets from him. For the first time in my relationship history I have met a man who is my equal.

Very fortunately for me, I was 'the one' he'd been searching for; otherwise I really don't know what I would have done. And now we are together, I cannot imagine life without him. He's my best friend, my lover and my soul mate. And I can't wait to say that he's my husband!

But that's another story ... As for what happened in my life before I found Pete, I don't regret a thing – not the good, the bad or the ugly. I truly believe I had to go through all those highs and lows, all those crazy times, all that heartbreak, pain, rejection and bad sex to recognise the real thing when I found it. Now I've found him, I'm never going to let him go ...

CHAPTER ONE

MEET THE FAMILY

My family are the most important people in my life. I love them all to bits. Through the bad times and the good times they have always been there for me, especially my mum. It is something the press has managed to twist over the years. The way some journalists have described my background, you would think I had the most miserable and unstable childhood, which couldn't be further from the truth. Yes, my real dad finally walked out on the family when I was three, but I had hardly seen him anyway so he was no loss to me. After that my mum fell in love with Paul Price and, although I've never called him Dad, I definitely see him in that role. He and Mum got married when I was nine and they have the strongest marriage of anyone I know.

My real dad, Ray Infield, met my mum Amy at school. They were childhood sweethearts from the age of fifteen.

They had some happy times together and were deeply in love, but Ray couldn't be relied on. He was a bit of a playboy, incapable of being faithful to one woman, and, after they were married and Mum was pregnant with my brother Daniel, Dad just left, claiming he was depressed and couldn't handle fatherhood. When Daniel was born he returned for a while, leaving again when his son was nearly a year old. My poor mum, I really feel for her; I know only too well what it's like to be abandoned by the father of your child. Fortunately she could handle it, and I take after her in that respect: I'm strong and independent and, while I've often fallen for the wrong type of man, I can pick myself up again.

Dad claimed to have had a nervous breakdown, and he and Mum ended up seeing a counsellor. The bottom line was that my dad wanted to be with Amy, but he also wanted to be free to do *what* he wanted, *where* he wanted, *when* he wanted – and to see *who* he wanted. Because my mum loved him so much she put up with all of this, but she wasn't happy about it. Then one of my dad's friends told Mum that he'd been seeing a sixteen-year-old girl. Can you imagine how she felt with a young baby, trying to hold together a failing marriage?

She and my nan discovered where the girl lived and met her parents. They were horrified that Ray was seeing their daughter, especially when Mum told them she had a baby. They all agreed to confront the couple. So one night my dad walked into the house with his young girlfriend to be greeted by my mum, my aunt and my nan. 'Oh,' he said. 'I've been caught out.'

'That's it!' shouted Mum, and she took the house keys from him.

A couple of months passed and Mum tried to get on with her life, but she was still irresistibly drawn to Ray; even after all he had done, she still loved him. They decided to make a fresh start, to buy a new house and give their marriage another go. I'm pleased they did, because I was the result. Ray stayed until I was three, but I barely saw him. He was an antiques dealer and was away most of the week on buying trips; at the weekend he would be down the pub or playing golf. He wasn't an important person in my life. I had all the stability and love a child could want from my mum and my grandparents.

By now my mum had met Paul Price, who worked for my dad. Whenever Dad returned from one of his trips, he'd give Paul money to take Mum out for dinner. Ray wanted to do his own thing, play cards and snooker, without having Mum on his case. But he couldn't have imagined the consequences! Paul fell in love with Amy. Whenever Mum went out with her friends, he would turn up as well and he was forever calling at her house. As she says, he started to grow on her.

As they got closer, Paul told my mum that Ray was seeing other women on his trips away. Mum was horrified. By now she'd had enough. My parents split up, this time for good, but Ray still owned part of the house. One day Paul said to him, 'What will it take for you to be out of this house and Amy's life forever?' Ray named his price, Paul paid him and he left. As Mum says, she was bought and sold in a lounge.

Given her stormy first marriage, it's not surprising that

Mum has been so tolerant of some of my relationships with men. She knows what it's like to be passionately in love with someone, even if they are treating you badly. Her story turned out happily and she is now with a man who gives her all the love and stability she deserves. Perhaps there is hope for me yet.

I don't blame my unsuccessful relationships with men on the fact that my dad left when I was three. Yes, I can be insecure in relationships; I do need constant reassurance; I need the man to tell me that he loves me, to give me cuddles, to say I look good; but I don't think it's because of my dad. I didn't feel abandoned when Ray left; in fact, I can honestly say it didn't affect me. Paul has always been there for me. And, although he and Mum moved house lots of times, she always kept me and my brother at the same schools so we wouldn't feel disrupted. We had a stable family life. When Mum gave birth to my half-sister Sophie, I was twelve and I couldn't have been happier. As far as I was concerned my family was complete.

My dad was free to see us whenever he wanted. Usually we'd spend alternate weekends with him. As I got older I started to get the feeling that he favoured my brother over me. The two of them would do father–son things like go fishing together, but he didn't really make much of an effort with his daughter. When he met another woman, he would often leave me with her and go down the pub. Not exactly an ideal father figure. Gradually our visits grew fewer, and by the time I was a teenager I rarely saw him.

I don't feel any bitterness – when he remarried in 1988 I was one of the bridesmaids – but I haven't seen my real

4

dad for two years. We have gone our separate ways now, and we don't know each other. My brother still sees him, and my mum and Paul are friends with him. I was upset when his second marriage broke up and he went off with another woman. Shay, his wife, sold a hurtful story to the papers saying he'd gone off with a Jordan lookalike who was only two years older than me. It was cheap and nasty, but I just shrugged it off: she became just another in the long line of people who had used their connection to me to make a bit of money.

CHAPTER TWO

A NARROW ESCAPE

I'd always wanted to be a model; either that or a pop star – or both! I can almost hear you thinking, She must think a lot of herself. But I don't. I've just always been a bit of an exhibitionist. I love showing off and being the centre of attention. Modelling gives me the perfect chance to do that. It's not that I think I'm God's gift, but I know I'm not half bad looking, and I know how to work it. Mum reckons I get my exhibitionist streak from her mother. One of her many jobs was as a topless mermaid at an exhibition. She had to lie behind a fish tank with only her long red hair to preserve her modesty. She was one of the more popular attractions, but got the sack for smoking – just like me she could never obey rules.

Let's face it: I was never going to be a brain surgeon. But I've probably earned more money than anyone else from my school. I was only eighteen when I bought my first house, and how many people do you know who have done that? Now I own two houses with a fair bit of land, a couple of flats, several very nice cars, including a Range Rover and a Bentley, and three horses. I'm in the position where I can pretty much have what I want. I didn't get all that by being a dumb bimbo. I've done very well out of being a model, but success didn't just fall into my lap. I've worked for everything I've got.

I was eleven when I enrolled for a series of modelling lessons, and believe me they were anything but glamorous. For two hours a week I would have to strut my stuff up and down a tiny studio surrounded by mirrors, pretending to be on a catwalk, with Tina Turner's 'The Best' blasting out. The classes were run by a former model. Typically for a child, I remember thinking that she couldn't really have been a model because she looked so old – in truth she was probably only in her thirties.

I laugh about the experience now, but when you're young and naïve you really think, Yes! This is it. I'm going to be a model because I'm doing these lessons. I *will* get spotted. One day I *will* be famous. In reality, if anyone had videoed these amateurish modelling classes I would have been more likely to appear on *You've Been Framed*. They were well dodgy.

Then, when I was thirteen, a proper job did come up: modelling for Joe Bloggs jeans. I had to go to the shopping centre in Brighton – not a very exotic location, I admit – and pose with a group of girls in jeans and T-shirts. Then we were taken to a local park to do some more shots, this time on horseback. It was a revelation to me, and I absolutely loved the whole experience. It gave me a real taste for modelling and I knew I wanted more. I knew inside that I was good at it, and when everyone saw the pictures they thought the same. It was such a great feeling.

I'd got on really well with the photographer who had done the shoot. He had made the whole session a real laugh, and I felt relaxed posing for him. A few days later he called my mum and said that I should seriously think about modelling, that I had a lot of potential and could go far. He said that he could help because he had an agency in London. He was very convincing. He showed Mum his portfolio and it looked totally legit. He seemed completely trustworthy, and so we trusted him. We thought he was a professional photographer. As it turned out, we couldn't have been more wrong.

He arranged with Mum to do more pictures of me. He said he could get me into catalogues. Great, I thought. Katie Price, you're going somewhere!

Every week, Mum would take me to his house and then leave me alone with him. He convinced her that if she was in the same room as me it would put me off, so she'd go and walk the dogs or have a cup of tea with his mum. He still lived with his parents, and his so-called studio was his bedroom. That should have alerted us straight away. But Mum and I had never been to a professional studio before, so to us a couple of lights, a backdrop and a big camera looked like the business. And of course he looked normal and was very charming. But then, paedophiles don't wear badges advertising who they are. They are clever and manipulative; they know how to make children trust them. When I think of what might have happened, I feel sick.

So I became his model and I really enjoyed it. At first he took pictures of me in my own clothes. He particularly liked me to pose in my black velvet skintight catsuit – no prizes for guessing why. Or he liked me to dress up as a schoolgirl – not that hard, as I was one. Then he started to take pictures of me being cheeky, sticking my tongue out at the camera, or sucking a lollipop and looking saucy. When he showed Mum and me the contacts, we just thought I looked as if I was having fun. We didn't realise that the whole cheeky schoolgirl look was fuelling his depraved sexual fantasies.

He kept saying that he could get me lots of work, he just needed more pictures for the agency. And I was happy to model for him, as it was a laugh to go to his house after school. I liked him, he let me be as lippy and cheeky as I wanted. There were a few strange things about his behaviour, like the fact he always offered me a milkshake every session, even though I told him I didn't like them, but I thought nothing of it.

After a while the schoolgirl look wasn't enough for him and he started to get more extreme. He wanted me to pose in lacy underwear and he got me to wear suspenders and stockings. He didn't get me to do any explicit poses – everything was covered up even if it was with lacy underwear – but I did have to wear high heels and red lipstick. I must have looked atrocious – a little girl dressed up to look like a woman. It was all done under subdued lighting, me standing with my hand on my hip looking straight at the camera. At the time I thought it was 'arty'. I didn't really think anything of it – it's not as if he had me lying spreadeagled in crotchless knickers with my legs wide open. It all still seemed like a game.

One day I went round as usual to do a shoot and he introduced me to a woman. Like him, she seemed perfectly ordinary, nice even. He said that she was his stylist, there to help him get a new look with me. This time he wanted to try something different: he wanted me to pose wearing a wet shirt with nothing on underneath. Suddenly this didn't feel like a game any more. I didn't want to show off my body in front of these people. I felt really uncomfortable with the idea, and for the first time I was quite frightened. I was alone with them – my mum had gone off for a walk with the dogs – and there was no one else in the house.

'No,' I said, 'I don't want to. It'll be too cold.' Well, I had to think of something!

'Don't worry,' he replied, 'we'll use warm water.' It was horrible, both of them standing really close to me trying to get me to do something I didn't want to do. And they were very persistent, joking at first and then getting cross. The woman was the most persuasive, saying it would make a really good picture, and didn't I want to be a model? She told me I had to learn to take direction, that they knew what was going to look right, how he had done all these pictures of me, how I owed him one. But thank God I am stubborn and strong-willed because I didn't give in; the more they tried to talk me into it, the more I refused. After a while they gave up.

I couldn't face doing any pictures with them. I felt really freaked out, so I said I would wait outside for my mum to come. Typically she was late – she always was – so I had to sit outside in the freezing cold for what seemed like hours, willing her to come and rescue me. Suddenly he came outside. My heart started pounding – I didn't want to be with him. He apologised and said could we just forget about what had happened and pick up next week where we left off. I nodded without saying anything. I'd already decided I wanted nothing more to do with him. Then he leaned towards me and said, 'Don't I get a kiss goodbye then?'

I could smell the coffee and stale cigarettes on his breath, and could see where the saliva had dried at the corners of his mouth. My skin crawled at the thought of having any contact with his lips. I took a step backwards. 'No way,' I said. All I wanted was for my mum to come and take me away; all I could think of was that I was alone with him, and he was bigger than me.

Fortunately for me, at that moment a group of school kids went by. He gave up and went back into the house. At the doorway he called out, 'See you next week then.' I didn't answer.

My mum finally turned up and I ran and got in the car. 'You look terrible,' she said. 'What's the matter? Why are you outside?'

'I don't feel very well.' I couldn't bear to talk about what had happened until we were back home safely. But when I recounted what had happened to my mum, she told me not to be so silly. She shrugged off the whole incident saying that I was being oversensitive.

I always, always say that parents should believe their kids when they say an adult has tried to make them do something they don't want to. I know I will always believe what my son tells me, however unlikely it seems. Perhaps this stems from an incident which is one of my earliest memories: me and two of my friends were sexually assaulted when we were six years old in a local park. My mum was sitting with her friend close by while we played hide and seek in the bushes. Suddenly a man appeared and promised to buy us an ice cream if we let him touch us. He lined us all up, exposed himself and bizarrely began his assault by licking each of us. Then he touched us. I think we all knew it was wrong, but we were paralysed with fear. When you're that young you tend to go along with what an adult says. Thank God some older children saw what he was doing, because I don't think he would have stopped otherwise. I rushed to tell my mum, but by the time she ran to where we were he had disappeared. She called the police but I don't think they ever caught him. It makes me shudder to think how vulnerable children are.

Mum was totally taken in by the photographer. He seemed so plausible that she was convinced I was being an over imaginative teenager. She changed her mind a few days later, however. He rang to ask me to do more work, but I refused to speak to him and said I never wanted to see him again. He kept on calling. Every day he would ring and I think my mum started to feel unsettled, thinking that it wasn't normal for a grown man to be pestering a thirteen-year-old in this way. Eventually she told him that she wanted to go and see his agency and pick up some pictures of me. He gave her an address in London; we went up at the weekend and couldn't find it anywhere. When he rang again and she challenged him about it, he just said that she must have got the wrong street. That's when she told him in no uncertain terms to stop ringing us.

And that was it, or so we thought.

It was a couple of years later that we heard a knock on our door one evening. On the doorstep were two female child-protection officers who wanted to talk to us about the photographer. They came and sat down in the lounge with my mum, Paul and me. They looked very serious, and told us that he was in prison for indecent assaults on young girls and for taking pornographic pictures of them. Apparently he'd been doing it for years. He was a known paedophile who had been operating under fourteen different aliases. They asked if he had been in contact with me. He hadn't, thank God. They said he was going to be released in the next couple of weeks and that they had wanted to see me because his prison cell was plastered with pictures of me. I felt frightened then – I was older and I now knew all about men like him who preyed on young girls. They told me that if he tried to contact me I must call them straight away.

Then they told us all about him. He had been taking pictures of young girls just like me but he had been drugging them. Then, when they were unconscious or too out of it to know what was happening, he had been putting them in pornographic poses. He had hundreds of pictures. He had been putting the drugs into milkshakes. I hated those drinks, and every time he had offered me one – and he did at every session – I had said no. That is what had saved me: if I had accepted those drinks, I would have ended up like all the other young girls. I felt so sorry for them, but also

relieved that it hadn't been me. I had had a lucky escape –
that experience has probably scarred the other girls for life.
I was shaken up, but also angry. How dare this pervert think
he could get away with ruining young girls' lives? What a
sick bastard.

CHAPTER THREE

FIRST LOVE

You might imagine that my experience with the paedophile photographer would have put me off modelling for life, but I wasn't going to let a pathetic pervert stand in the way of me and my dreams. If I had done that, he would have won and I wasn't going to let that happen. I knew that modelling was something I could succeed in.

So my granddad, who was a keen amateur photographer, took a series of pictures of me which I put together in a portfolio. Looking back through those pictures makes me cringe. I was going through a phase when I always wore my hair scraped back in a bun, with one long strand hanging down. *So* not a good look. In some of the pictures, I'm posing in a swimming costume and flesh-coloured tights; in others I am wearing some of my nan's glittery tops. No wonder I looked so stiff and uncomfortable – as if I had a poker stuck up my arse! I don't think I would have made it on to the front cover of *Loaded*. But at the time I thought I looked pretty good.

I kept pestering my mum to take me to London to see some modelling agencies. Finally she gave in. We traipsed round to all the big names like Models 1, Elite and Storm with my portfolio. God, they must have wanted to laugh when they saw the pictures. I felt very self-conscious when I saw all the other wannabes – they looked so sophisticated and glamorous, and they all towered over me. There I was, fourteen years old, sat next to my mum and my brother, feeling like some kid from the sticks. The answer from all the agencies was the same: I was too short, and should wait until I'd grown some more. One even said my legs were too bandy! In other words, I was being rejected. I felt crushed.

But I had pinned all my hopes on modelling, and hadn't given much thought to what I would do if it didn't work out. Up until the age of fifteen I'd been a fairly good student who always did her work and always obeyed her teachers. I was bright, so there were any number of possibilities open to me. I probably could have done quite well academically – my brother Daniel certainly did – but when I met my first boyfriend I went off the rails completely, and my school work went out the window. I stopped being the sweet naive Katie who loved spending time with her family, and turned into the teenager from hell.

It was all the more upsetting for my mum because I had never been difficult before. I never went out without telling her where I was going, and I never went out clubbing. I wasn't even allowed to go to the local youth club because my brother got fed up of some of the lads trying to chat me up. I was a bit of a tomboy and I spent all my free time swimming, doing gymnastics or up at the stables riding. I'd been horse-mad since the age of seven. My bedroom wall was plastered with pictures of ponies and every single pencil case, rubber and pen I bought before I discovered pop music and boys had to have a picture of a horse on it. A friend of my mum's taught me to ride when I was seven and from then I dreamed of owning a horse of my own. However, back then it seemed impossible, something way out of my league because we weren't a particularly well-off family. Mum and Paul worked hard to bring us up and riding is an expensive hobby.

Then, when I was eleven, I found out that you could get horses on loan – you don't own them, you just pay for their keep. Straight away I was on at my mum and Paul and I begged them to get me a pony. When I saw Star advertised in the local paper I convinced them to get him for me on loan. He was a New Forest pony and eighteen years old. He was the shabbiest, scruffiest little beast you could imagine but I absolutely loved him. I spent all my free time looking after him, going for rides and entering him in shows. I wasn't one of those stuck-up horsey types, though – I never had the right kit and, whereas all the other little girls' ponies were clipped and groomed to perfection, Star looked a bit ropey. But I didn't care.

By the time I was fourteen I was keen to get another horse. By, then and I'm not being arrogant, I was a very good rider and I needed a horse that could offer me more of a challenge. I had a Saturday job working in a fabric shop

19

and was able to save up a little bit of money myself. Once again Mum and Paul came up trumps and this time I got an ex-racehorse on loan.

Then, when I was fifteen, an ex-racehorse was advertised for sale for £500 – his name was also Star. To my delight Mum agreed to buy him for me. It wasn't the best purchase – he was lame more times than I could ride him and he ran up a fortune in vets' bills but I adored him. If you'd asked me to choose between a boyfriend and a horse back then I'd definitely have gone for the horse!

Even now riding is one of my passions. When I was young, I could only afford the *Only Fools and Horses* type of horses; now I buy the Mercedes of the horse world. I've got three gorgeous animals and they are the business. Riding gives me space to think. I love being on my own with my horse, surrounded by fields. I sing to myself and talk away to the horse – about my dreams, and my problems. It sounds completely mad but galloping wildly is a great escape when things are getting you down. And, as you'll find out, there have been lots of times in my life when I've needed to escape.

But back to fifteen-year-old Katie ... I fancied one or two boys at school but I'd only ever gone as far as kissing. I was pretty innocent. I was, however, starting to get interested in clothes and was developing my own unique style. Even at that age I loved outrageous outfits – the tighter and more revealing the better. In fact, when I was given some money to buy some clothes for a family party, I shocked my mum completely by getting a tight leather skirt and matching leather top. I started wanting to look different. I had my eyebrows dyed jet black and wore bright red lipstick. Well, I certainly stood out then! My mum could cope with my weird dress sense; it was my first boyfriend she couldn't be doing with.

I met Jeff up at the stables where I kept my horse. I was just fifteen and he was ten years older than me. In fact, it was his horse that caught my eye first. She was gorgeous – a magnificent black mare called Greta – but her owner was certainly no looker. His face looked as if he'd been around the block a few times. He looked hard with his deep-set eyes and a thick nose. I was impressed by his size: he was well over six foot, with good biceps. But he had no six pack, I'm afraid – just a bit of a beer gut. All in all, not a catch in the looks department. It certainly wasn't love at first sight.

But we got talking because of the horses, and I found I liked him. At first he came across as being quite shy, and he wasn't very good at dealing with people. Later I was to find out just how bad he actually was with people, but I was young and I enjoyed having an older man to flirt with, even one that did seem a bit odd. He had this horse that I loved, and a car. I suppose he seemed quite flash to me – a proper man compared to all the boys I knew from school.

When my mum met Jeff she took an instant dislike to him. She thought there was something very strange about him, and she certainly didn't think he was someone I should get involved with, especially given the age gap. But it was partly down to her that we became so close. She used to take me to the stables and wait while I fed and mucked out my horse, but she was always telling me to hurry up. So after a while Jeff offered to pick me up from school and take me to the stables and then Mum could collect me. Typically, though, she was always late picking me up, so in the end Jeff started taking me home as well. But he started dropping me off later and later, and during those car journeys and the hours spent at the stable we began to get closer.

We would go off driving around Brighton in his turquoise XR2 just listening to music, sharing a drink and a bar of chocolate. Pretty sad, I know, but when you're fifteen just being in a car with a man can seem quite adventurous. I remember one track that we played over and over again: 'Stay' by Eternal. Even now when I hear that song it makes me shudder, and not because it triggers happy memories. Similarly, whenever I meet someone who is wearing Obsession by Calvin Klein, I get a wave of nausea: that's what Jeff wore, and what started out as a casual flirtation with an older man nearly destroyed me.

I soon discovered that Jeff had plenty of time on his hands as he didn't have a job. He always seemed to have money, although I never knew where it came from. I gradually discovered that he was a bit of a dodgy character and I wondered just what he was capable of.

But I knew nothing of his dark side when we met and after a couple of weeks flirting at the stables he became my first serious boyfriend. Your first love is something you should be able to look back on and feel a bit misty eyed and nostalgic over. I remember how Jeff treated me and feel physically sick. My friends at school were all giggling about the boys they fancied; I was about to get involved with a man who would abuse and batter me.

It all started off so innocently. We would spend our time together either riding or sorting out the horses at the stables.

The fact that my mum didn't approve somehow gave our relationship an added thrill. Even Jeff's mum took against us, after initially letting us stay at her house together. In fact, she threatened to throw battery acid in my face if she caught me round her house again. But I think she was seriously disturbed. Like mother, like son – as I was about to find out. I felt as though everyone was against us because they didn't understand true love. I was only fifteen, what did I know? I soon fell in love with Jeff. He was like a drug and I had to be with him all the time. I didn't care about anything or anyone else. My school work started to suffer; I switched off and answered the teachers back. I earned a reputation as a naughty girl and would regularly be sent out of the classroom for bad behaviour. The head teacher called my mum and Paul in to see him because he was so concerned. But it had no effect on me: all I could think about was Jeff.

Even so it was three months before we shared a proper kiss. One night we were playing cards and I decided to go for it. So I jumped on him in a flirty play-fight way. As we lay struggling on the floor, we started to kiss passionately for the first time. I did find it a real turn-on. I liked the feel of the stubble on his face, and he kissed me like a man who knew what he wanted.

Two months later I was ready to go further. I wanted to prove how much I loved him, so I decided I would sleep with him on my sixteenth birthday. I had gone to see E17 in concert with my best friend Claire, and after the gig I phoned my mum and pretended I was spending the night at her house. Instead Jeff picked me up and took me back to his flat. He had obviously guessed what was on my mind because as soon as we walked into the flat he started kissing me and caressing me all over. Then he pulled off my jeans and led me to the mattress on the floor. No man had ever seen me naked before and I'd never seen a man naked before, so I felt quite shy and self-conscious and, in spite of his efforts, I kept my top on. I knew I was about to lose my virginity and was half excited, half petrified. I was so innocent that I didn't know what to expect: girls at school who had lost theirs always made out it was some great experience without exactly going into details.

My first time was painful, short and not particularly pleasurable, which isn't unusual. I enjoyed the kissing and the caresses but when Jeff entered me it really hurt. The act itself didn't last long, and when he finished he just rolled off me. He didn't say anything tender or loving. There was no 'How was it for you?' I just lay there and thought, Is that it? The earth definitely hadn't moved. I felt dirty, impure and sore and I wished I had waited until we got married.

But the next day I was back in my school uniform, sitting in class and convinced that I must be in love. I felt like a woman now, surrounded by little girls.

Some time after that Jeff ended up in prison for non-payment of fines. When I went to court to see him being tried, his probation officer took me to one side and advised me not to have anything to do with him, that he was no good. But I've always been terrible at taking advice: if someone tells me not to do something, nine times out of ten I'll do it. So I told him that I loved Jeff and I wanted to stand by him. The probation officer just shrugged his shoulders and walked off. I could tell that he thought I was mad. Even though I was only sixteen Jeff had taught me to drive and that day, when Jeff was led down to prison, I drove home on my own without a licence in a car that wasn't insured. I was paranoid that the police would pull me over. Jeff was dragging me into his world and I was powerless to prevent him.

Mum couldn't bear the fact that I was seeing him. She tried everything to stop me. She banned him from coming to our house and we had endless bitter rows about him. Usually I'm very close to my mum and would never do anything to hurt her, but I refused to listen. Like a typical stroppy teenager, I couldn't see why she didn't like him. At her wits' end she even phoned social services to see if they could give her some help in dealing with me. But as I had just turned sixteen I wasn't exactly high priority and they were unable to help.

Jeff wasn't inside for long – just a few weeks. One day I drove to visit him at Lewes prison only to discover they'd moved him to the Isle of Sheppey. I was in such a rush to get inside that I'd left the dog in the car, with the keys in the ignition. To my horror the dog managed to lock the door. At any other time it would have been funny; as it was I nearly burst into tears. I was stranded in the prison car park in the pouring rain with a car I shouldn't be driving anyway. In desperation I trudged up the road to a garage and luckily one of the lads came back and opened the door for me.

Visiting your boyfriend in prison isn't really what you expect to be doing when you fall in love, is it? We should have been going clubbing or taking romantic walks along the beach, hanging out with friends – anything but this. But we were in our own closed world. I never saw any of my friends.

25

I was cutting myself off from my family and I thought this was what I wanted. By the time Jeff came out of prison I had left school and we ended up moving in together. My mum was devastated, but there was nothing she could do.

I thought I was so grown up keeping house for my boyfriend. I tried to convince Mum that I was doing the right thing and that the flat was great but, when she came round to see me, she was shocked at how seedy the place was. And it was – I just refused to see it. There was no sofa, just a single bed, and my clothes were all in a suitcase as there was no wardrobe to put them in. The contrast with my mum's house could not have been greater. She is the most house-proud person I know and has always created a wonderful home for her family. Looking back, I realise that Mum was in torment: one part of her was desperate to get me out of this situation and back home safe; the other knew it wouldn't do any good. She couldn't force me. I had to discover for myself that my relationship with this man was wrong.

As soon as I moved in the rows started. Shy Jeff turned out to be a violent, possessive bully. He was eaten up with jealousy, convinced that I fancied other men. There was one time when we were at a petrol station and some guys drove up and were staring at me. Jeff jumped out of the car and screamed, 'Who are you looking at? Do you want a fight?' It was terrifying to watch. Another time some bloke gave me a lift back from the stables, where his wife kept a horse. When Jeff found out he went ballistic. He stormed up to the woman claiming that her husband was having an affair with me.

Although his moods scared me, I thought he was just being manly and protective and that because he got so wound up he must really love me. But soon he started to become violent towards me. It was mainly after he had had a few drinks that the arguments would kick off, and after that it wouldn't be long before he would push me around. It was always over the same thing: that I fancied other men, that I looked at other men, that I wanted to sleep with other men. I'd be pleading with him to calm down, that it wasn't true, that I only fancied him – anything to stop him hurting me. But it made no difference. He'd grip my arms so tightly I'd be covered in bruises; he would slap my face; then he'd go into a frenzy and start ripping up my clothes, saying that I was a tart and that I dressed provocatively to attract other men. It was crap – I was just a typical sixteen-year-old in jeans and a T-shirt. I hardly ever wore make-up because he made such a fuss when I did. He especially hated my white swimming costume. He said it made me look too virginal and he was obsessed that it might be see-through. He told me he would spy on me when I went swimming to check that I wasn't wearing it. He didn't, and so I got a brief moment of power over him when I wore it to go swimming. I was glad that it did go see-through.

He wanted to keep me all to himself, locked away from everyone. He even threatened to scar my face so that no other man would ever find me attractive again. Then he tried a different tactic. He told me that I had caught VD from him, and that if I slept with another man I would give it to him. Worse than that, if I didn't tell the man I had this disease and he got it, I could be done for murder. Oh, and I could die as well. I was so innocent that half of me believed him. I was terrified, which is of course exactly what he wanted. He had me completely in his power.

27

The arguments always ended the same way: us having sex to make up. Often it was quite violent sex, but he was my first lover and I didn't know any different. The only thing Jeff ever seemed to worry about when we had sex was that I didn't see or touch his bum, as it was covered in pimples. I was so into him that I just thought it was sweet, that he was self-conscious. Now I'd run a mile if someone showed me an arse like that!

Then Jeff insisted that we have sex in all sorts of places, even up at the stables. I think he enjoyed the idea that someone might see us. I just thought that this was what happened in a relationship, and gradually I started to enjoy taking risks too. Having sex with him also made me feel like I had power over him for a change. Sometimes I'd even dare to wind him up, saying that I was going to leave him. He would be on his knees begging me not to go. Then I'd let him have sex with me. It wasn't healthy, but I was powerless to stop it. I couldn't imagine what I would do without him.

Even so there were many times I'd have to phone my mum after a row and beg her to come and rescue me. Often I'd be standing at the bottom of the road waiting for her wrapped in just a towel because Jeff had ripped up all my other clothes in a fit of jealousy. It was always such a relief to get into her car and feel safe and normal again. She would drive me home, I'd get some fresh clothes and we'd talk. She would tell me that I couldn't carry on like this. I knew my mum was going through hell, but I still couldn't leave him.

After I left school I didn't do much for a couple of months, so I was with Jeff all the time, except when I had my Saturday job working in a fabric shop. We would look after the horses, go riding and generally doss around together. Sometimes we'd call on some of his mates he knew from prison, but we never saw any of my friends. My best friend Claire had met him, but just like my mum she took an instant dislike to him. So it was just me and Jeff.

I was so caught up with him I couldn't think about my dreams of becoming a model. I left school with a few GCSEs and no real idea about what I wanted to do. Nursing was the first thing that came into my head. It was either that or be an air hostess or a policewoman. It might sound a bit mad but I think it was the uniforms that attracted me – well, it definitely wasn't the money! Also I am quite practical and good at dealing with people. I got a job working in a home for old people. All I can say is that people who nurse full-time deserve a medal. It is such incredibly hard work and so badly paid. I had to do everything for the patients: feed them, wash them, take them to the toilet, clean up after any accidents. I'd have to sit with them when they were dying, which really upset me, and I even had to lay out dead bodies. When I look back I think it was too much for someone of my age to deal with. The only good thing about the job was that it got me away from Jeff.

I was growing to hate his jealousy and cruelty. One day my horse Star became lame – as an ex-racehorse he was more prone to injuries. Jeff told me that I would have to have him put down, that there was nothing that could be done to save him. Miserably I agreed. The day the vet came to put him down was one of the worst of my life. Jeff told me to brush him to make him look as if he was worth more. He was going to be sold for dog meat. I was crying as I groomed him for the last time. I could tell that Star knew where he was going, because it was really difficult to get him into the horsebox. I felt as if I was betraying him and I was heartbroken. Jeff showed no emotion.

I had to drive us everywhere even though I didn't even have a licence because he was nearly always drunk. I used to hate him drinking because, even though he was jealous when he was sober, when he was drunk all the arguments would start. He would also spend a lot of time at Moulsecoomb, a big council estate in Brighton, and I'm sure that he was going there to get drugs. I dreaded him coming home after a visit there because he'd be up all night, and quite manic.

After a few months in the flat we moved out of Brighton and into a tiny cottage in Hurstpierpoint, a small village near the nursing home where I was working. Again I tried to impress my mum and make out that Jeff was looking after me, that he loved me really. But she was horrified when she saw the state of the place. It was a right tip with hardly any furniture, and was in need of a good clean. Her visit didn't get off to a good start because she didn't have the address and had to knock on a neighbour's door to find out where we lived. The neighbour pointed out our cottage and said she had heard us rowing, a lot. We'd only been there a couple of days. I tried to convince Mum that everything was all right, but my heart wasn't in it. Increasingly I knew I couldn't stay with someone who treated me like this. I couldn't go on living in fear, always wondering what kind of mood he was in, always tiptoeing around him, afraid of triggering off yet another row, yet another slap or punch. But I had one more disturbing experience to go through with Jeff.

30

Above: My first set of wheels! Me aged seven months.

Below: On holiday in Spain, pictured here with my big brother Daniel.

Above: Already learning how to look sultry for the camera!

Below: With Daniel, in our trendy matching stripes. My mum is behind, keeping an eye on us.

Above: I began my sun worshipping at an early age.

Below: A family holiday at my Uncle Henry's villa in Marbella. It was Uncle Henry who designed and built the Brighton Marina. *From left to right*: My Grandad, Harvey; me aged 9; Uncle Henry; my Grandma, Esther and brother Dan.

Some wonderful 80s hair from the family album!

Above: Mum and Paul's wedding in 1989. I think I got more than my fair share of confetti.

Below: A family portrait (*left to right*) Me, Daniel, Paul and Mum.

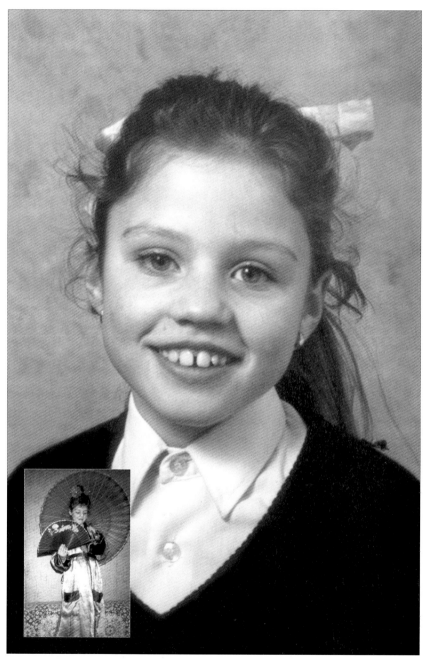

Little angel Katie Price, aged eight. *Inset*: Having fun dressing up – my pink cocktail umbrellas finished off the costume nicely.

I started modelling when I was very young. Although this is a good picture of me, it was taken by a photographer who turned out to have a sinister side.

Above left: Another early modelling shot.

Above right: Never shy of skimpy outfits, here I am with my friend Spud, all dressed up and ready to go to *The Rocky Horror Show*.

Below: An early picture of me in the days when my preparation for a shoot was mousse, mascara and bit of lip gloss.

Brotherly love from Danny.

My period was late. I told my friend Claire and she said I'd have to take a test, so on my way home from work I called in to a chemist and bought a pregnancy kit. I was praying that it would be negative. I didn't want to do the test when Jeff was around so I waited until he went out to deal with the horses. It was dark and raining outside. My hands were shaking so much I could hardly open the packet. I think I already knew what the result would be as my stomach and boobs felt unusually bloated and tender. All the same, when the blue line appeared it was a shock. I knew there was no way I wanted to have Jeff's baby. For a start I was much too young, and God knows what kind of father he would have been if his treatment of me was anything to go by.

When he returned that night, I told him I was pregnant. He was delighted. I suppose he thought it proved what a big stud he was, and he would think that I was well and truly trapped with him now. Little did he know that I had no intention of going through with the pregnancy.

I told him I wasn't sure what I wanted to do, and that I really didn't want my mum to know as I knew she would be really upset. But when she came to pick me up after yet another argument, he said to me, 'I hope you're going to tell your mum the good news.'

I felt sick. I turned round to him and said, 'If you tell my mum, that's it forever for us.'

He didn't like me threatening him, so he replied, 'If you go with your mum now, I'll tell her.' But there was no way I was staying with him, so I left the house. He followed me out to where Mum's car was, opened the passenger door and said to her, 'Amy, Kate's got something to tell you.' I told Mum to ignore him, that he didn't know what he was talking about. But he went ahead and told her. I screamed at him, telling him I hated him and that we were finished. Then I pushed past him, got in the car and slammed the door shut. Mum asked me if it was true. I tried to deny it but I was too upset and burst into tears.

'There's no way you can keep the baby, Kate,' she told me, totally shocked by what she had heard. Sobbing, I agreed. All I wanted to do was get away from Jeff and have my life back. I decided then and there I was going to leave him.

A few days later, back home with my family, I started bleeding and having stomach cramps. Mum took me to the hospital where they scanned me. I was having a miscarriage. I didn't say anything to Mum but I suspected Jeff had caused it. A few days before I told him I was pregnant he had punched me in the stomach after one of our rows. By then I was feeling so numb I was glad it had happened. For once, his violence had done me a favour.

Jeff couldn't accept it was the end and bombarded the house with phone calls and letters begging me to come back. But now I was safe with my family I had no intention of going back into his world. My stepdad went round to the cottage with a mate to pick up my stuff – well, anything that hadn't been ripped up by Jeff. He even managed to get some money out of him to pay for the operation I needed after the miscarriage.

Unfortunately that wasn't the last of Jeff. One day he went round to where I worked and tried to see me. He was screaming and threatening; everyone was terrified. We called 999. It took eight policemen to restrain him. I looked on in horror as he battled with the officers, shouting abuse and ranting. He looked like a madman, a monster. I couldn't believe I had ever loved him. All I cared about now was that he was out of my life. My six-month nightmare was over. I was going to make the most of my freedom.

It was all so sad. In spite of how he treated me, I had loved him completely. But it wasn't a good introduction to having relationships with men. Though the physical scars were quick to heal, my time with Jeff had damaged me emotionally and left me feeling vulnerable. Worst of all, he has not been the only man to treat me badly. He started a pattern which has been hard to break.

For a while I thought the only good thing about Jeff was that he hadn't sold a kiss-and-tell story when I became famous. But a couple of years ago he gave in to the money. Ironically it showed him up more than me and by then it was too late to hurt me. It just confirmed what I had always thought of him: he was a sad, pathetic loser.

CHAPTER FOUR

SPARKY

I stuck it out at the nursing home for about a year. I would do my shift and then go out with my friends, wanting to forget about what I'd had to do during the day. Now I was rid of Jeff I just wanted to enjoy myself and make up for all those months of misery. Soon, though, I decided I needed a break from work while I waited to hear whether I'd got a place on a training course to be a nurse. I planned to go on holiday and then temp. I went to Tenerife with my family and had a great time. It was the start of my obsession with having a tan, ideally all over – I don't want any strap marks. I love lying out in the sun, and the hotter it is, the better. Luckily for me I go brown really easily and never burn. Forget what the magazines try and tell you about white skin being sexy: tanned flesh wins hands down. Pale is definitely not interesting. When I can't have the sun, I hit those sunbeds or that St Tropez bottle straight away.

I had the odd flirtation during this time, but nothing serious. I did meet a gorgeous surfer – well, he was actually something in property, but when I met him he was surfing. I was down on Brighton beach one day with my mum, my nan and my sister watching the World Surfing Championships and I had been eyeing up this good-looking guy with a fantastic body. Suddenly he saw me watching him and, after we'd engaged in a bit of heavy-duty eye contact, he strolled up and asked my mum if he could take me out. I think Mum nearly fainted with relief – at last, someone who looked half decent. He was called Kieran and I went out with him for a couple of weeks. It was nothing serious, just a bit of fun. He was clean cut, had a convertible and a nice flat, and was the complete opposite to Jeff. But, just as I was beginning to like him, he started lying to me. He would claim that he couldn't see me because he was going out. I didn't believe him and when I'd drive past his flat it was obvious he was in. I don't know what he was up to, but I didn't like it.

Then, one day, he asked me to do this really weird thing. He told me to lean over the sofa so I was practically on all fours, then he got on my back and started pushing against me making me bend my knees up and down. What the hell was that all about? Also when we were in bed together I would lie on my front wearing my T-shirt and knickers, and he would lie on my back. He'd start rubbing his body against me, whispering and groaning – probably trying to wank himself off. I thought, Stuff this, just because I won't have sex with him doesn't mean he has to get all kinky. So I got shot of him pretty quickly. Later I found out that he tried the same thing on with my friend Lucy. It just goes to show that appearances can be deceptive; at least I could laugh about it and move on.

Modelling was still my ambition, but in the meantime I had to get a new job. It was as a receptionist in a business centre. It wasn't the most exciting work in the world, but it certainly beat wiping someone's bottom. I got a new boyfriend as well, Gary Bolingbroke, a twenty-three-year-old electrician and general Jack the Lad. At first, Gary seemed like a massive improvement on Jeff. He turned out to be a right shit though, finally selling some ridiculous story to the papers about how he had turned me into Frankenstein's monster, making me obsessed with plastic surgery and getting me into kinky sex. What bullshit. Once I split with him I never gave him a second thought. I'm only writing about him now to set the record straight.

It was a Saturday night and I was out clubbing at The Event in Brighton. I was in an exhibitionist mood and was dancing on stage in a skimpy pink dress with my friend Roxie. When Gary strolled over to ask us if we wanted a drink, my first impressions were positive. He was quite good looking; he seemed like a laugh and he definitely had the gift of the gab. After flirting and dancing together for the rest of the night we swapped numbers. I went home hoping that he would call me.

When he rang the next day I was really excited. I should have been more choosy, but I think I was just glad that someone who seemed normal was showing an interest in me. Being with Jeff had dented my confidence. Unfortunately, as I was to discover, Gary was no man to make a girl feel good about herself. While Jeff had used his fists to control me, Gary's speciality was the put-down.

For our first date we met up with my friend Roxie and Gary's friend Mitch at a pub near my house. Then we went back to his place. I had no intention of sleeping with him, and he didn't try anything on even though we spent the night in the same bed. The two of us arranged to meet the following evening and he took me to a pub outside Brighton. It seemed an odd choice, seeing as there are so many places to go to in the city. I found out later that it was because he already had a girlfriend and he obviously didn't want anyone to see us together. He finally told me about her after we'd been out on a few dates. I was furious and told him he'd have to choose between the two of us. He kept saying he would tell her and then he didn't. But late one night he was put in a position where he had to do something. We were just pulling up at his place and there she was waiting outside with her mum. She didn't look happy. Gary, coward that he was, just put his foot down and drove off, but not before she saw us together. 'That's it then,' I told him. 'It's make-your-mind-up time – her or me. What you're doing isn't fair on either of us.' He chose me. I was pleased at the time, but looking back now I wish he hadn't. His ex-girlfriend's mum even phoned my mum in the middle of the night to warn her about Gary's womanising ways: she told her that he was a two-timer and bad news. My mum told me, but once again I didn't listen to her.

On the plus side he could be a laugh, and at least he seemed like a normal lad. He also hung out with a group of mates who weren't like the dodgy characters Jeff associated with. We'd go round to each other's houses and go down the pub. I got on well with his family and gradually mine began to like him, even my mum. I was besotted with him, especially as I knew I hadn't got him where I wanted him and it made me want him more. I was a bit surprised that he never wanted to take me out clubbing with him. Later I realised it was because he wanted to go out on his own on the pull. I should have known that, if he was capable of two-timing one girlfriend, he was capable of two-timing me.

I wouldn't say he was the greatest lover I've ever had, but our sex life was OK. His speciality was the quick shag. He was really into football and we tended to have sex during the commercial breaks, while the match was on – that's how quick he was! But we were much more adventurous than I'd been with Jeff. One night we got back from clubbing with some mates and played strip poker. When we were all naked we jumped into the car, drove up to Devil's Dyke, a local Brighton beauty spot, and had sex there in front of each other. We didn't swap partners or anything, we were just pissed and having a laugh. But even now I do enjoy the thrill of having sex outdoors. I think it's really boring to make love in a bed all the time. I do like a bit of experimentation.

Another time Gary and I were driving over to my mum's for dinner and we were early. So we stopped off in a park, stripped off and started having sex. We were in mid-shag when there was a knock on the window and this bloke said, 'When you've finished your business can you leave? I'm waiting to lock up the gate.' I was extremely embarrassed, but we just giggled and carried on.

Whereas Jeff had hated me looking too sexy because he was so paranoid I'd go off with someone, Gary definitely appreciated it if I made an effort. I started buying sexy underwear and enjoyed showing off my body. But I didn't always take sex seriously. One time I put on all this leather gear – a tight leather basque and long black boots – and decided to wind Gary up. I marched into the bedroom and ordered him to call me mistress and lick my boots. He was on his knees, looking a bit freaked out. 'Do you really want me to?' he asked in a quivering voice. I was trying not to laugh, and pretending to be this cruel dominatrix. Eventually I got him to lick them. It didn't turn me on at all – bondage doesn't really do it for me – I just wanted to see what I could get Gary to do.

Looks-wise he was a lot more attractive than Jeff, with a much better body. I did think his willy was a bit of an odd shape though: when it was erect the end was a bit bent. This was when I began to realise that willies come in all different shapes and sizes! The only thing I didn't like about Gary's body was the wart he had on his balls. He was always trying to cover it up, and when I asked what it was he told me it was a cyst and he was going to get it removed. I didn't believe a word of it. He played football and his nickname on the pitch was the warthog. I expect his mates had seen his balls in the shower and named him after that. Looking back at our relationship and how he ended up treating me, it now seems like a really appropriate name for him.

But our sexual antics aside, he told me that he loved me and I believed him. That has always been my biggest weakness. Once someone shows an interest in me, I think they must be all right. And who doesn't want to be loved? I told him I loved him too, and I did. I had fallen for him in a big way. I just prayed he wasn't going to hurt me.

Pretty quickly – much *too* quickly – we moved in together. At first I was blissfully happy, but it wasn't long before Gary started to show a different side. For a start he was incredibly unreliable and would never come home at the time he said he would. Whenever he went on a lads' night out he was always really late back. He just expected me to wait in for him like I had no life of my own. Then every Saturday after he had played football, he would ring and tell me to order us a curry and that he'd be back soon. He would eventually roll up drunk at three in the morning, and sometimes it wouldn't be until eight o'clock the next morning. What the hell had he been up to all that time? I began to suspect that he was being unfaithful to me – I could just never catch him at it.

His behaviour started to make me feel insecure about myself. I became desperate for him to prove that he loved me. I was only seventeen and had already been damaged by my relationship with Jeff. I needed to feel loved and secure. But Gary was too much of a lad who mainly cared about himself and his fun. He made me feel jealous and paranoid – a horrible combination.

It didn't help that he was constantly making fun of my dream of becoming a model. He was always boasting that his ex-girlfriend had been a Page 3 girl. Then he would turn round and taunt me saying that I'd never make it because my boobs weren't big enough. While his comments hurt me, I want to make it clear that I never went on to have my boob jobs because of anything Gary said. I had the surgery for myself and no one else. Even without Gary's comments I'd never been happy with the size of my boobs. But, when I saw his ex, I thought, Stuff it, if she can make it, so can I. She was attractive, but nothing special, and I didn't think her boobs were that impressive. I tried to ignore Gary and kept my dreams alive.

CHAPTER FIVE

BECOMING JORDAN

At least at work people were more supportive. Because I was sitting down all day answering the phones and typing, I could afford to take more trouble over my appearance and I got compliments all the time. People were always saying that I was wasted being a receptionist there and that I should be a model. One of the girls in the office in particular kept on at me to give it a go. She put me in touch with a good friend of hers, who was a keen amateur photographer, and said she would love to take some pictures of me.

So one lunch hour in the summer we all nipped down to Hove beach. We found a nice quiet bit because I didn't want the whole world watching, but as soon as I stripped off to my bikini bottoms I realised that I was being ogled by a gang of builders working nearby. I tried to ignore the wolf whistles and just concentrate on looking good in front of the camera. We quickly did some snaps, very natural ones of me in my

43

bikini, and topless ones too. My hair was blowing all over the place in the wind, and I was hardly wearing any make-up as I only knew how to put on mascara and lipgloss. I didn't need any ice cubes for my boobs though, because in that breeze anything would stand to attention.

The photographer knew about a modelling agent called Samantha Bond, so we sent some pictures to her and some to the *Sun*. I received a letter back from the paper a few days later saying I wasn't what they were looking for at that time, which was very disappointing; but then Samantha Bond wrote back and said she wanted to meet me.

I was so excited, and so was everyone around me – everyone except Gary. When I told him about the letter he barely cracked a smile and became really sarcastic, saying that I'd never make it as a model, but if I was going to try then good luck to me. I ignored his hurtful comments and the following week, in June 1996, I went up to London to meet Sam. I took along my mum for moral support. It was amazing walking into her office. The walls were covered with pictures of girls, some in bikinis, some topless, all gorgeous. I had never seen so many pairs of naked breasts before, and I did wonder what I was letting myself in for. But then I saw a picture of Jo Guest up there. Jo was a very successful Page 3 girl and I thought, Wow, I'm meeting her agent.

Our attention was then caught by ten models waiting in Sam's garden to do an audition for a calendar. We thought they looked stunning. Sam saw us looking at these girls and I was totally gobsmacked when she said I was more beautiful than any of them. It was an amazing compliment.

Sam was so nice – very down to earth and friendly – and

we hit it off straight away. She was in her forties and reminded me of Goldie Hawn. She had been a model herself so she knew the business inside out and, after we had chatted for a while and she had looked through my portfolio, she said she wanted to take me on. I was over the moon.

But then she said I had the perfect looks for glamour modelling. I was shocked. 'No way,' I told her. I associated glamour modelling with the kind of stuff that ends up on the top shelf, all crotchless panties and legs open. I definitely didn't want to do that. Sam assured me that it wasn't at all what I thought, and I wouldn't have to show everything. So I told her I wouldn't go further than topless, if it was all right with her. I remember telling her that my ultimate ambition was to be a pop star and that I hoped the modelling would help to get me there.

As we left her office and walked back along the Kings Road I was on cloud nine. Everywhere I looked I could see beautiful women, as so many of the leading model agencies have their offices around there. I could hardly believe that I was going to be joining them – little me in my tight black trousers, black-and-white top and horrible clumpy shoes. I couldn't wait to get home and tell Gary that he was wrong. I was going to be a model.

When I broke the news I could tell that he didn't really believe me, but my family more than made up for him – they were delighted. The following week Sam called saying she had castings for me in London. I didn't even know what a casting was, but I didn't want to ask her and show myself up. I had to go along to a number of different studios where lots of other girls were auditioning for underwear and swimwear catalogues, and calendars. It was a bit like a conveyer belt: one girl would go in, pose, have a Polaroid taken, then it was on to the next. All the other girls had professional photos of themselves to show off; I still only had the pictures that my granddad and Jacqui had taken.

It was all such a new experience, but I loved it. For that first week Gary came with me and, even though he spent a lot of time eyeing up the other girls, it was good to have a familiar face around. After that, though, I used to go up on my own; the only downside was my terrible sense of direction as I tried to find my way around London – I was always getting lost, and it's not like I was at the stage where I could afford to keep people waiting ...

I had only been with Sam for two weeks when I got the call that was to change my life forever. I was in London for a casting when she rang to say that one of her girls hadn't been able to make a Page 3 shoot. I could hardly believe my ears when she went on to ask me if I wanted to do it. I couldn't say yes quickly enough. My God, I thought, I'm going to be famous. I felt dizzy with excitement and anticipation.

Sam told me that I was going to have to think of a different name to use because doing Page 3 can stop you getting other work. I could hear her asking round the office for suggestions. The only name I could think of was Emily – it doesn't exactly scream glamour model, does it? Fortunately, after some frantic brainstorming, Sam's assistant Paul came up with the name Jordan. It was different and I liked the way it sounded. So I said yes. It didn't seem possible that I would make it into the *Sun*; after all, they had turned me down when I'd sent in pictures of me on the beach. I couldn't wait to prove them wrong.

Sam told me that the photographer was a man named Beverley, who turned out to be Beverley Goodway, the legendary Page 3 photographer; I was shaking with nerves as I made my way to his studio, but hugely excited at the same time. This could be my big break and I really didn't want to mess it up. When I got to the address Sam had given me I nearly didn't go inside at all. It was a run-down office block which looked very uninviting. I rang the buzzer, pushed open the door and walked up the stairs. I saw a man sitting behind a desk in a dingy-looking office. I really hoped he wasn't the photographer as he didn't look at all friendly. I told him I was looking for Beverley and he just pointed upstairs. When I got to the studio door I was still feeling apprehensive as I thought the location would be much more sophisticated. When I walked into the studio I remember seeing the walls covered with hundreds of pictures of topless girls and my first reaction was, Oh no, this looks some kind of porno den! What have I let myself in for? And there was Beverley waiting for me. I don't know what I was expecting – maybe someone young and trendy in leather trousers – but he was easily in his fifties and looked more like my granddad.

He was great, though, and put me completely at my ease by chatting away and offering me a cup of tea. Then he took me through to a dressing room filled with bags of underwear and bikini bottoms. There was every possible design and colour of G-strings, thongs, knickers and French knickers. There were frilly ones, lacy ones, cotton ones,

47

satin ones, silk ones, PVC ones, rubber ones, leopard-skin and fur ones. It was like a girl's paradise having so much underwear to choose from. Beverley was very laid back and just told me to get undressed, put on a G-string and meet him back in the studio.

I took off my clothes and after sifting through the mountains of underwear I decided on a pink G-string – it's my favourite colour so I was hoping it would bring me luck. I stood in front of the mirror for a minute, just trying to get my head together. Go for it, girl, I told myself, this is your moment. As I walked back into the studio trying to look completely at home in just a G-string, a pair of stilettos and a smile, I was determined not to show any nerves. I wanted to look confident and succeed. So when Beverly told me where to stand in front of the camera I posed as if I'd been doing it for years. As the camera started clicking and he started firing comments at me like 'Great! Hold it there! Fantastic!', suddenly I didn't feel nervous at all. I felt on fire with the thrill of it all. I loved it.

At that stage I didn't even know any of the tricks of the trade like how you can breathe in and stand a certain way to make yourself look as slim as possible without showing too much rib cage. But Beverley still thought I had done a really great job. And so did the *Sun* because, as soon as they saw the pictures, they phoned Sam Bond and told her they wanted to book me for a whole week of Page 3. The idea was that I would do a striptease across the week to promote Demi Moore's new film *Striptease*. I'd start the week wearing a corset, suspenders and stockings and every day remove one item so that by the end of the week I'd be naked and in the same pose as Demi, lying stretched out on the floor with my arms and legs strategically placed.

It was an amazing moment when I opened the paper for the first time and saw myself. I went out and bought loads of copies of the paper and spread them all out just gazing at my photo in astonishment. The phone didn't stop ringing with friends wanting to know whether it really was me. I was on such a high. I was only just eighteen, and there I was: famous. Looking back I can see that it wasn't such a big deal, but at the time I was ecstatic.

My mum didn't tell anyone at work about my modelling; although she was pleased for me, I think she found it a bit embarrassing, but you can't exactly keep something like that a secret. Several of her colleagues had met me and, even though I was modelling under a different name, they still recognised me. So, after I'd appeared in the *Sun* for three days, Mum went into work and had a bit of a surprise. She switched on her computer and I appeared in all my Page 3 glory. One of her colleagues had made me into the company screensaver! In the end, she had to laugh it off.

If Mum was slightly embarrassed, my brother took it a step further and told me, when I started modelling, that I was ruining the family's name! I suppose it was hard for him as a young lad – he was bound to come in for a lot of stick about me. He is more than OK with what I do now, though, and actually runs my website.

Gary, on the other hand, quickly changed his tune. Once he saw me on Page 3 he loved taking me out, having me on his arm, showing me off to all his friends like a trophy. But he was starting to take me for granted and it annoyed me. He was due to go to Tenerife on holiday with his mates and I didn't want him to go because I knew he would be unfaithful. I begged him not to, but he took no notice. Even though I had made it to Page 3, I still felt insecure.

While he was away I had loads of sessions on the sunbed so I could look my best for when he returned. Then I found out that they were holding auditions for *Blind Date* in my area. I was so annoyed with Gary for going away without me that I decided to audition for the show. I made my mum come along with me. I never thought that I'd be selected, but I was chosen to be a picker. Of course, a few days later the producers found out that I was a Page 3 girl and they said I couldn't be on it, and that story got in the papers. When Gary returned from holiday he saw the article and was furious with me. But I didn't say anything. I was beginning to think that maybe I didn't need a cocky electrician in my life. I had other things to think about.

Within just a few weeks I became a regular Page 3 girl. Beverley was the main photographer and I loved working with him. Even now I would love to go back and do a session with him, he was such a nice man. When you're modelling it is so important to build up a rapport with a photographer. If you don't get on with them, the pictures might look OK but it won't have been a good experience. Beverley and I worked really well together and he appreciated the fact that I always wanted to experiment and try new poses. I wasn't like some of the other girls who would just turn up and expect to be told what to do like some other models. I always had an opinion on how I wanted a shoot to look. I still do –

it's one of the things I pride myself on. I instinctively know what's going to work and what's not.

We would have such a laugh doing the pictures, trying out different poses and props: sometimes we'd get the wind machine out for that seductive hair-blowing-out-behind-you look; or we'd try the ice cubes to perk up my boobs; or the water spray, for that glistening come-and-get-me look. He had different backdrops for the shoots, such as the seaside, or a sunset. The great thing about his studio was that he had a mirror behind his camera so you could check out how you looked, which I liked. He is the only photographer I've ever worked with who does that. I guess the others think it will make you too self-conscious.

Even so, I look back on my early Page 3 days and can't believe my appearance. Nowadays I'll have spent hours having my make-up applied before a shoot so that it's absolutely perfect. Someone will have spent ages on my hair, putting in new extensions, colouring it, washing it and styling it. My nails will have been manicured and painted. I'll have shaved and plucked all the crucial areas – and I mean *all* (thank you, Gillette!) Every part of me will be in perfect shape. I probably won't have eaten for hours to make sure my stomach is as flat as possible. Back then, I didn't have any help so I had to do my own hair and make-up – and I really didn't have a clue. I would just wear tons of mascara (so my lashes ended up looking like spiders' legs), layers of dark lipstick and some well-dodgy lipliner. I didn't wear any foundation, powder or blusher, and in those days they didn't airbrush the pictures afterwards. As for my hair, it was wild and all over the place. I have naturally curly hair and I didn't do anything with it – just a quick wash and blow-dry and a bit of mousse. I was still my natural colour, which is chestnut brown. Nowadays it's long and straight – with the help of hair extensions – and the colour changes according to what I'm doing. But one thing will never change: I hate having curly hair.

A shoot with Beverley would usually take about two hours, but before I could get started I would always need something to eat, usually because I had driven up to London without any breakfast. So Beverley would nip out to the deli and get me two jacket potatoes with cheese and onion and a smoothie. He would always say, 'I can't believe you eat so much and look like you do.' But back then I never worried about how much I ate, even right before a shoot. Let's face it: the waif look is out when it comes to glamour modelling. Who wants to see a skeleton posing? In any case, I'm lucky because I can eat what I want and not put on weight, although I am now more conscious of my stomach when I'm modelling.

People always assume that because you're a Page 3 girl you must be raking it in, but the truth is that when I began modelling I was hardly paid anything. I think I started out on about £60 an hour for the shoots. Typically I'd be doing one every two weeks and, by the time you've taken away your tax, travel expenses and the agent's cut, you're not really left with very much. So I was still trying to juggle my Page 3 work with my receptionist job; it wasn't easy and was causing resentment from some people. After about a month of doing both jobs, something had to give. I couldn't keep taking time off for shoots, so I took a gamble and went into modelling full-time.

At first it was hard to make ends meet. I was constantly having to ask Sam Bond for advances to tide me over, and I would make the £70 she gave me last ages. Fortunately it was a move which paid off. Within a few weeks I had landed a great job posing for a calendar, a topless shoot in Arizona. Models are always desperate to get these gigs because the money is fantastic. I was on location for two weeks and was paid £1,500 – more money than I'd ever earned from a job before. Unfortunately it turned out to be a miserable time. One of the other models didn't stop picking on me and telling me how incredibly lucky I was to have got the job – I think she was just jealous because she'd been in the business such a long time and she didn't think I deserved to get this break so quickly. In the end I had to tell the organiser to keep us apart because I was close to slapping her.

It was my first time away from home on my own, and I really missed my family. I was so unhappy I even missed Gary, but when I returned home he didn't appear that pleased to see me; I couldn't help wondering what he had been up to while I had been away. It seemed the more successful I became, the more my relationship with Gary deteriorated. I think he was jealous that I was doing so well and that I was the centre of attention whenever we went out. On top of that, his mates at work were always making comments about me and taking the piss out of him for dating a topless model. I told him to ignore them, but he got more and more wound up. I was so proud of myself for doing well that I just wanted to go out and have a good time. He was really dragging me down.

One evening, Tony Blair was down in Brighton to give a

speech at an Italian restaurant. I had just started making a name for myself as a model and they asked me along with Gary. He was in a foul mood from the moment we got there. I was just listening to Tony Blair's speech like everyone else, but Gary went mad and started saying things like, 'Look at you arse-licking, watching him and thinking you're so important because you've been invited here.' I was desperately trying to get him to shut up. When we got home, it was worse. He started pushing me into the corner of the room. 'You're not going to last as a model. I don't know why you're bothering, you're nothing special. And why are you acting like you're ashamed of me?' He was trying to make out that I thought I was better than him, when I was never like that. I was hurt and confused by the change in him; what had happened to the easy-going lad I thought I knew? In retrospect, I don't think he could cope with the fact that I was becoming famous, and I think he felt threatened by my success.

His comments became more and more negative. He couldn't bear to see me happy or getting so many modelling jobs. He grew even more unreliable about coming home when he said he would, and even more evasive about where he had been. Then one day he went to work and left his phone behind. I had to know if he had been seeing anyone else, so I accessed his voicemail messages. Sure enough there was a message from a girl. She didn't say very much but it was obvious from her tone that she and Gary were more than just friends. I was furious. When he got home that night I confronted him about the message. Of course, he denied everything, and we had a blazing row.

I should have been brave enough to get him out of the flat there and then; I wasn't, and we carried on living together. But I didn't think I could trust him an inch and you can't build a relationship on that. One night, fuelled by alcohol, I decided to see how far he would go. My friend Clare was round at the flat and we'd all been drinking for hours. I had this horrible plan hatching in my head to prove what a shit Gary was. So I told him and Clare that I would find it a real turn-on if they kissed. Clare wouldn't at first but I insisted. Gary didn't bat an eyelid. As I watched them snogging on the sofa, I started to feel a burning rage build up inside me but I couldn't leave it there.

'Stop!' I called out. 'Now I want Clare to give you a blow job.' Clare was shocked but so incredibly pissed that I think she would have done anything I asked. Gary couldn't have looked happier. As she started going down on him, I thought I would explode with jealousy. But I remained eerily calm and watched it to the end. Then I stormed off to bed and wouldn't speak to either of them. Gary had shown his true colours. If he could behave like this in front of me, God knows what he was capable of when I wasn't there. All right I had encouraged him, but he hadn't thought twice. Looking back I don't know what possessed me. I suppose it was my own insecurity coming out. True I was only young but I probably had gone too far and I got more than I bargained for. I knew then that we would split; it was just a question of when.

CHAPTER SIX

HERE'S LOOKING AT YOU, KID ...

I was becoming a proper glamour model. I had seen all the other girls tottering around trying to look important in sky-high heels, with great long acrylic nails and Filofaxes tucked under their arms. Whenever they met up with each other they would all do the air kisses and 'darling' business. I thought, There's no way I'm going to end up being like that, but before I knew it I was doing exactly the same. Nowadays I've ditched the nails and the Filofax; but the 'darling' bit and air kisses – they're essential tools of the trade.

After a few weeks on the *Sun*, I met Jeany Savage, a photographer with whom I was to work a lot over the years. Sam Bond told me I should audition for her, but when I first went to her studio I couldn't stand the woman – she was so bossy and rude. I sat on her sofa with three other girls, hoping she would pick me, but she marched in and straight away said, 'I don't like your fucking hair or your nails, they'll have to go. Let's have a look at your book. No, you're not right for me.' Talk about telling it like it is! She made me feel terrible. I had spent two-and-a-half hours travelling up to see her, only to be told I wasn't good enough. She was probably right about the hair and nails, though. I ditched the false talons and started to get extensions for my hair. My curls were history.

I thought I was never going to work with her, but the next time we met she changed her tune and wanted to use me. We argued a lot during shoots over what I should wear and how I should pose, but we'd always get there in the end. At least she listened to my ideas and took them on board. I hate it when photographers ignore what I think and just order me about as if I haven't got a clue. I don't tell them how to point their cameras or what lens to use. I know what angles I look best in and what positions are going to look good. I have to be comfortable; if I'm not I know it will show on my face. When they don't listen to me, I do get the hump.

I always say to them, 'OK, let's do your thing first and then we'll do mine, then we can decide what looks best.' When you're doing different positions in a shoot the photographer will take a Polaroid so you can check how the pose looks, and nine times out of ten they have to admit that I'm right. Even when I started out I had strong opinions. I'm not just an empty-headed model who has to be told what to do. I know what works and what will sell.

I've always loved creating my own poses. I like to tease and get into provocative positions that look naughty – just as well, I suppose, in my line of work! After nine years in the glamour-modelling business, I've probably covered just about every position and look there is, from bondage to girly. I definitely love the girly look, all pinks, whites and baby blues in all kinds of tiny, tempting outfits – hot pants and cropped tops, corsets and G-strings, high heels and ankle socks. Whatever I'm doing, I want to make an impact, to make the person stop turning over the page and look at me.

I'm often asked what I think about when I'm posing. I think journalists are hoping I'll come out with some full-on sexual fantasy and, yes, sometimes I do like to imagine there is someone there who I'd like to be watching me. I suppose deep down I do get a thrill from knowing that men are turned on by what I'm doing. Doesn't every girl want to know that men find her attractive? But I don't really think about that when I'm modelling. I'm too busy concentrating on the job, on looking good, on breathing in just enough to keep my stomach flat, but not so much that I'll show off too many ribs. I'm worrying about my hair being in place. And of course I'm perfecting my Jordan stare. While I'm looking at the camera I try and imagine I'm gazing way into the distance at a sunset – for some reason that seems to give me the perfect challenging, come-and-get-it-if-you-dare look in my eyes. And I'm very proud of my pout, which I achieve by pretending I'm blowing bubbles very gently.

What I do is called glamour modelling, which makes me laugh because if people knew what went on at a shoot they wouldn't think it was glamorous at all. You won't find me sipping champagne and lying back on some gorgeous sofa. I'll be having a cup of tea surrounded by piles of clothes and shoes and probably arguing about what I will and won't wear. The clothes the stylists get in are supposed to fit me but they often don't so they'll have to be pinned. Everyone is rushing around, and there is often tension because shoots cost a lot of money and people want to get them finished on time. For magazine shoots I'm probably booked all day – ten till six – and, believe me, that is a long day. I know people will think it's just normal working hours, but modelling is extremely tiring.

I'm definitely a studio girl; I hate modelling on location. Beach shoots in the Caribbean may sound exotic, but they never are. I can't stand being photographed on a beach: my eyes are sensitive and start streaming in the sun, which isn't a good look. And I hate being cold. At home I always have the central heating on full blast, so my worst shoot was with Jeany when she made me pose for hours on the seashore in Brighton, and it wasn't even summer. I was absolutely frozen. It's hard to ooze sex appeal when you're freezing your tits off. I had a few things to say about that, believe me. Put me in the studio, give me a baked potato and the right clothes, get the shoot done quickly and I'm a pussy cat!

On the whole I've always got on well with photographers, apart from that traumatic experience with the paedophile when I was thirteen and then another unfortunate encounter with someone in Brighton. Before I made it to Page 3, a photographer called Jeff Kaine took a series of photos of me naked. They were supposed to be tasteful and not too revealing – in other words my bits weren't supposed to be on show. Little did I know he managed to get some more revealing ones. Later, when I was starting to make a name for myself as a model, I discovered he'd sold them to a men's magazine. Ironically I worked with him again in 2003. I really didn't want to, but he was the photographer booked to do my calendar with me and my manager insisted that I went ahead with the shoot. The pictures turned out well, but I'll never forgive him for what he did.

After a few months in the *Sun*, the work started pouring in. I was bombarded with offers to pose for other tabloids. A lot of the other models I met had switched to an agent, who I'll refer to as Jenny, who seemed to be promising extremely good deals on the work. I was very happy with Sam Bond but I thought I should give Jenny a go as everyone who met her was very impressed by her promises.

We met up and I liked her. She was much more over the top than Sam, but by then I was getting used to all the 'darling this' and 'darling that' which seemed to go on in the modelling world. Straight away she fixed me up a deal with the *Sun* which on the face of it looked great – at least, it was more money than I had been getting, but it wasn't as good as it seemed.

She was also the woman who introduced me to the footballer Teddy Sheringham. I had fancied him for ages, ever since seeing him on *They Think It's All Over*, and it certainly made watching football with Gary a lot more interesting when Teddy was playing. Whenever I read a paper I would always check the sports pages to see if he was in there. I told Jenny about my crush on him and she said she could fix it for me to meet him. She promised it would be discreet and no one would ever find out. But, as I was to discover, Jenny said a lot of things. The problem was, some of them were wishful thinking.

CHAPTER SEVEN

OH, TEDDY, TEDDY!

I feel a mix of emotions remembering my brief encounter with Teddy: regret at what might have been, and anger at the way the press treated me. The tabloids loved having me pose for them, but they wanted to tear into my private life as well. No areas of my life were off-limits to them. I was a glamour model, therefore I was fair game. They seemed blind to the fact that what they printed had consequences, and that people might get hurt. In the summer of 1997 it was the turn of Teddy and Jordan to come under their spotlight.

I was in Jenny's office one day when she finally got hold of Teddy's number through one of her contacts. Straight away she said I had to call him. As we weren't alone – there were a couple of other people there, including the footballer John Scales – I really didn't want to. It would be nerve-racking enough calling a total stranger; with an audience it would be even worse. But they all joined in with Jenny, urging me to do it. In the end I thought, Why not, I've nothing to lose.

I think he must have been expecting me to call because he didn't seem that surprised to hear from me. He sounded lovely, but I told him I felt too embarrassed to talk properly because I was in a room full of people who were all listening in. I promised to call him later that night. I felt quite nervous, and also a bit guilty because of Gary, but it didn't stop me ringing Teddy later when Gary was out of the flat. We had a very relaxed conversation and arranged to meet in Essex for a drink. I put the phone down and I couldn't believe my luck. I was going on a date with Teddy Sheringham!

I didn't tell anyone except Jenny what I had planned. First of all I had to get the right outfit for the night. I didn't have a clue whether I should dress up or down as I didn't know what we were doing or where we were going. In the end I thought, I *am* a glamour model, I should look like I've made an effort. So I went along to Karen Millen and bought a see-through, skintight, leopard-skin dress. Looking back I can't believe that I wore such an outfit. Then I spent hours at the hairdresser's having my hair blow-dried straight.

As I sat on the train to Essex, I kept wondering what he would think of me. Would he fancy me as much as I fancied him? I started to feel all flustered, I really wanted him to like me. I had arranged with Sue, a make-up artist I knew who lived near Teddy, to do my make-up. While I was round her house I phoned Teddy and he told me where to meet him. Even with Sue making such a good job of my face I was starting to feel uncomfortable about my outfit. I just didn't know what a footballer would expect me to wear. Worst of all, my hair was starting to go curly at the sides and I hate it when it does that. A bad hair day was the last thing I needed.

When I was ready, Sue gave me a lift to meet Teddy. My heart was pounding when I saw him drive up in his blue Mercedes. He really was gorgeous. But straight away I thought I was overdressed: he was just in jeans and a sweatshirt. Then, as I got into his car, I dropped my bag and everything fell out of it. I felt hot with embarrassment, but Teddy was so sweet and really put me at my ease. He leaned over and gave me a kiss, and I could tell that he really was a charming, down-to-earth guy. He said we were going to a hotel bar to meet one of his best friends.

When I saw how casually they were dressed I realised that I had overdone it, but there was nothing I could do as I hadn't got any other clothes to wear. I stuck out like a sore thumb, and looked as if I was going clubbing. We had a drink at the bar and then went on to a pub. I had a few drinks to relax me, but I didn't get drunk. I was enjoying being with Teddy too much, and I wanted to be aware of everything.

The evening passed quickly. I could tell that Teddy was attracted to me, and I had no doubt that I fancied him. I was having a great time flirting and chatting, and I thought I could really fall for him. Suddenly I looked at my watch and realised that I had missed the last train home. I thought it would sound totally pathetic if I told this massively successful footballer that I had come by train; but I was relieved that Teddy didn't want me to go home yet. He said we should return to the hotel and get a room there. Unfortunately it was fully booked, and Teddy was too much of a gentleman to throw the 'Do you know who I am?'

routine. Luckily another guest overheard our problem and offered us his room so long as Teddy autographed some things for his son. Of course Teddy agreed, and then it was just the two of us alone together in the hotel room.

Much as I fancied him, I had no intention of having sex with him on a first date; but that didn't mean we couldn't get close. We both stripped to our underwear. While my dress had been a disaster I had no need to worry about what was underneath it: I was wearing a sexy matching bra and knickers set in black lace.

Immediately we got into bed together and started kissing passionately. I remember thinking, Wow, what a fantastic kisser. I had butterflies just from that kiss. He was obviously desperate to make love and kept breaking away from kissing me to explore my body with his hands and his lips, but I wasn't having it. It's not that I wasn't tempted, of course – my God, he was turning me on – but I resisted. He kept saying, 'Just relax,' and tried to continue his travels down my body, but I kept pulling him back to my lips.

After a while he got the message, and we kissed and cuddled for the rest of the night. I kept thinking, What am I doing? What about Gary? But then I'd feel Teddy's lips on mine and I forgot about everything else. I didn't want the night to end.

I don't think either of us got much sleep. The next morning Teddy had to go to football training so he dropped me off at the station and promised to call. All the way home I had that lovely tingly feeling you get when you really fancy someone. I kept smiling to myself on the train, looking at all the commuters and thinking, If only you lot knew who I've just been with. Little did I know that they were about to find out in the worst way possible.

I couldn't wait to see Teddy again. I thought I'd already fallen in love. Gary was furious that I hadn't told him where I'd been, but I just said I'd spent the night at a friend's house. His track record of staying out all night without telling me where he was meant that I didn't feel like I had betrayed him.

As soon as Gary left the flat, I was on the phone to my agent. I was so thrilled by my first date with Teddy, I couldn't wait to tell her all about it. She wanted to know everything, even down to the details of what I'd worn in bed. I was so happy, I told her exactly what had happened. I then spoke to Teddy and we arranged to meet in a couple of days. It really seemed like there was a definite chance we could get together; the chemistry between us was strong, and I couldn't stop thinking about him.

A day or so later I was doing a shoot when Jenny phoned me. She sounded hysterical with excitement. 'Oh my God, darling, you're not going to believe this! You're on the front page of the *Sun* tomorrow!' I didn't know what she was talking about and then she told me it was to do with the night I had spent with Teddy. I couldn't believe what she was saying. Barely able to reply with the shock, I said, 'But it can't be. I haven't told anyone about what happened.'

'Don't be silly, you must have done,' she said. 'You wait till you hear the headline.' She must have been the most insensitive person in the world because she just didn't understand how upset I was. I couldn't believe my ears when she read it out to me: ON MY BED, TED!

I felt sick to my stomach. I knew Teddy would be horrified,

and so was I. And what the hell would Gary think? Jenny just went on and on saying how exciting it all was, as if I should have been pleased to have my private life splashed across the paper for everyone to read, pleased that everyone would think that I was a right bitch.

I couldn't bear to be with Gary when the story broke, so I made up some excuse and went back to my mum's. That's it, I thought, I'll have to split with him now. Even though I knew I wanted to, I lay awake all night worrying about how he would react. But my biggest concern was what Teddy was going to think of me.

The next day at half past six in the morning, Gary came storming into the house and up to my bedroom, holding the paper in one hand and screaming, 'What's all this? What have you been up to?' It's a good job Mum and Paul were there because I really thought he was going to hit me. Then he threw the paper down on the bed and ran out of the house in a fury, shouting, 'That's fucking it, you just wait!'

With shaking hands I picked up the paper and started reading. The words swam in front of my eyes; it was like a nightmare. Every detail of our night together was down there in black and white. Worst of all there were pictures of me alongside the story as if I had told it – one was even of me holding a teddy which had been taken ages ago, but which of course looked as if it had been specially shot to go with the story. Teddy was going to think I'd done a kiss and tell. I was in pieces. Later that week there were even pictures of the little boy we'd met in the hotel holding Teddy's autograph and telling his story about how he had met us in the hotel lobby with his dad. It seemed as if everyone wanted a piece of us.

The story destroyed any chance I had with Teddy. He didn't want to know me after that. He didn't return my calls and, when I finally got through to him and tried to explain that it wasn't me who had gone to the papers, he put the phone down on me, saying, 'Don't bother.' Obviously he believed that I had stitched him up and that our night of passion had been a set-up all along. I was so hurt. I had really liked him, and I hated the fact that he would think I was the kind of person who would do that sort of thing. But there was nothing I could do about it. Jenny promised to send a letter to Teddy explaining that I had nothing to do with the story getting into the papers, but I'm not sure if she ever did. I was desperate to set the record straight, but whenever I saw him out in London he just looked right through me as if I didn't exist. If he reads this book he will finally know the truth.

If the story hadn't blown up in the press, who knows? I would love to have given it a go with Teddy, and I definitely would have dumped Gary straight away. As it was, I tried to pull myself together and carried on with Gary. I didn't even have the energy to argue with him. I admitted that I had spent the night with Teddy, but said nothing had happened. Part of me hoped that he would change his ways now he could see what kind of men were attracted to me – men like Teddy who were way out of his league. Don't mess me about, I thought. If someone like Teddy Sheringham was interested in me, I wondered who else would be. It sounds bad when I say it like that, but you have to understand that it all stemmed from Gary's treatment of me.

Hard as it was, I tried to forget about Teddy but, whenever

Gary and I went into a pub, blokes would start chanting 'Teddy, Teddy, Teddy!' It wasn't funny. And of course every time we watched football together, even if Teddy wasn't playing, I knew we would both be thinking about what had happened. The difference was that I was thinking about what might have been.

It was only later on that I realised Jenny must have stitched me up. No one else had known all the intimate details about my night with Teddy. No wonder she was so keen to hear all the juicy details. But when I confronted her she denied it, saying it was my best friend who was the source. Rubbish. It was her – I just couldn't prove it. I had learned the hard way that trust is the first casualty of being a celebrity.

But Jenny hadn't just stitched me up in the press and ruined my chances with Teddy; she went on to rip me off as well. I had left Sam Bond's agency and gone to her when she told me she could get me a lucrative one-year *Sun* contract. It seemed too good an opportunity to miss and so I joined her. But she didn't have my interests at heart at all. She was just out to make as much money as possible from me. Jenny must have thought she had struck gold. There I was, totally naïve about the business, letting her make the decisions and take most of the money.

She told me I would get £25,000 in monthly instalments for the *Sun* deal. But, when I asked to see the contract, she refused to show it to me. Eventually, after a lot of pestering, I managed to get it out of her – I urgently needed it because I was buying a house and needed proof of my earnings for the mortgage company. It made interesting reading. She was going to make a whopping £52,000 on the contract, over double what I would make, and I would have to pay her twenty per cent of my earnings. I didn't need to be a maths genius to realise that I was getting a raw deal. I went on to do a calendar for the *Sun* and she kept all the royalties for that. My solicitors tried to get my money back from her but, before they were able to, she went bankrupt. To this day I have not had a penny of what she owes me, and I'm not the only one – there were several other models she did the same thing to.

I rejoined Sam Bond's agency. I totally trusted her, and in this business that's a rare thing.

CHAPTER EIGHT

MY GORGEOUS GLADIATOR

For some mad reason I agreed to appear in panto over Christmas 1997 in Worthing, a seaside town just along the coast from Brighton. I played a princess in *Robinson Crusoe*. I had to wear a tight, red, cropped top showing plenty of cleavage and naval, a pair of flared see-through red trousers and a little crown. My job was to come on, look good, bat my eyelashes and stick out my chest. I didn't have a great deal to say, but I don't think I was booked for my acting ability. Apparently my nan cried when she saw me, but I don't think anyone else had that reaction. To be honest, I found having to go on and do the same thing every day – sometimes twice a day – a bit boring after a while. Acting definitely isn't for me. But then I met Ace, and suddenly panto seemed very exciting.

I was working with Mark Smith, aka Rhino from *Gladiators*. This was the ITV show presented by Ulrika

Jonsson where incredibly fit and muscly men and women would take on members of the public in a series of games in front of a live studio audience. One night Mark suggested we go along and watch another panto that some of his mates were in. Going to see *Peter Pan* wasn't exactly my idea of a wild night out, but I decided to tag along anyway. The show didn't make much of an impression on me, but the interval certainly did. Mark took me backstage to meet some of the cast, and it was there that I saw Ace close up for the first time. He hadn't been in the pantomime, but he seemed to know everyone there. I wanted to know all about him. I nudged Mark in the ribs and whispered, 'Who's that? He's gorgeous.' He told me he was Warren Furman, a good friend of his and one of his co-stars on *Gladiators.*

I never thought I would fall for a man who wore a Lycra leotard for a living – but, hey, at least you can see what you're getting. And whatever Ace had, I wanted. He was gorgeous, good looking with a fantastic body and what got me even more interested was the fact that he didn't really look at me or pay me any attention. In fact, he seemed to be with another woman, who I thought must be his girlfriend. As girls do, I cheekily thought, Oh, I'm better looking than her! The whole combination was like a red rag to a bull. I *really* wanted this man to notice me.

Over the next few days I kept going on to Mark about how much I fancied Warren. I discovered that actually he didn't have a girlfriend, and that made me even more determined to meet this gorgeous gladiator. Eventually Mark had enough of hearing this, so right in front of me he phoned Warren up and told him all about me. Then, to my surprise, he handed me his mobile and said, 'Right, he wants to talk to you.'

I was shaking my head and mouthing, 'No way!' At first I felt so shy I could barely get a sentence out, but Warren sounded very pleasant on the phone and I soon relaxed.

We arranged that I would go and watch him in his panto – *Snow White* – and we'd meet up afterwards. God, how many more pantos was I going to have to sit through? This had better be worth it. When the night came for our date, I drove to Hastings feeling pretty nervous. I had told Gary I was just on a girls' night out. I didn't feel bad about it, given the number of times I suspected he had lied to me, but all the same I couldn't quite believe that I was going on my own to meet a man I barely knew. I'd never do anything like that now – I'd always take a mate along with me – but there I was dressed to kill in my all-in-one skintight black catsuit, thigh-length leopard-skin boots, with a black jacket and a fur collar, all made up and waiting to meet my gladiator.

I arrived late at the theatre and the show had already started, so instead of slipping in unnoticed I had to make an entire row stand up to let me get to my seat. I had hoped that no one would recognise me, but there was no chance of that now, especially in that outfit. When Warren appeared on stage as the huntsman, the kids went wild screaming and whistling. I felt like cheering too, because he looked very tasty indeed. He wasn't wearing many clothes – just a tight leather waistcoat, so his muscular chest and arms were in full view, and tight trousers. I took a good long look at his body. Pretty much ten out of ten, I thought. He knew which row I was sitting in and it seemed to me that he looked straight at me. I felt a shiver of excitement. I couldn't wait to meet him.

We had arranged to meet in the canteen after the show – hardly the most romantic location. I felt quite embarrassed sitting on my own waiting for him because all the other actors had recognised me and were staring at me. Finally Warren appeared and I breathed a huge sigh of relief.

Relieved I may have been, but I was still shy of him at first. The plan was to go to a club with a group of his friends. First, though, Warren said we could leave our cars where he was staying. I imagined they would be in a hotel, but actually the entire cast was staying at a caravan park. How classy! As I followed Warren in my bright purple convertible Rover, I wondered what the night would have in store. Warren was driving a white Porsche, which was definitely an improvement on Gary's van.

Once we got to the club and I'd had a couple of drinks, I started to relax. I began to enjoy myself flirting with Warren. The only down side was when I went to the loo and I heard some girls talking about how fit Warren was and what a slapper Jordan was. Should I say something, I wondered. No, leave it, they're just jealous. All the same, they looked pretty shocked when I came out of the cubicle.

At the end of the night Warren invited me back to stay at his caravan. It was late and I had drunk too much to drive home. I half thought about phoning Gary and letting him know that I wasn't going to be back that night. Then I thought, Why bother? I'll deal with it in the morning. He never phoned me when he was going to be out late.

I asked Warren if I could borrow a T-shirt and boxers to

wear in bed. I definitely didn't want to spend the night in my catsuit, nor did I want to be naked. Then I took off all my make-up. I'm always a bit apprehensive when I do this with a bloke for the first time: part of me wonders whether they'll still fancy me, and the other half thinks, Stuff it, they better had! When I turned round to face Warren, he said, 'Don't you look different?' I wondered if he meant it as a criticism, but he explained, 'You look even better without your make-up on.'

Then there was the matter of the sleeping arrangements. Warren's caravan had a double bed in the back bedroom, but he didn't automatically assume that I would share it with him. He converted the sofa in the lounge into a bed for me. I was relieved that he wasn't going to try anything on, but at the same time I felt a bit disappointed. But then he pulled the mattress out of his bedroom and asked me if I wanted to share it with him, as it was a lot more comfortable and warmer. What a good idea, I thought.

That night as we lay next to each other we kissed and cuddled for hours, but he didn't try anything more – not that I would have let him, of course, because, however tempted I am, I never have sex straight away. The tabloids have always made me out to be a sex-crazed slapper who will jump into bed with a man at the drop of a hat. But I always make men wait at least a month, just to prove that they're interested in me for myself and not just looking to notch up a glamour model on the bedpost.

I was so happy lying next to Warren, feeling his touch, caressing his body. He was just wearing boxers and I thought, That is one fit body! Finally we both fell asleep; he

77

had his arm round me and I was lying with my head on his very manly chest.

In the morning I woke up with an incredibly stiff neck from falling asleep in that position. But I also felt completely relaxed, which I thought was a good sign. I didn't feel as if I had done the wrong thing spending the night with him. It felt like the beginning of something good. I kissed him goodbye and said, 'Call me.'

On my way home, I played Janet Jackson's *Velvet Rope* at full blast and had the roof down on my car even though it was winter and freezing cold. I had a really good feeling about Warren, which was making me feel all warm inside. I phoned Mark and told him all about the night before, but he already knew because Warren had called him. So he was keen too. Now I'd wait for him to ring me: as far as I was concerned I'd done my bit by going to see him; the next move was his. I didn't have long to wait – he rang me that day. But, before I took things further with Warren, I had to sort out Gary.

Gary believed my story that I'd been out clubbing with my girlfriends, but meeting Warren confirmed what I had known for a long time: Gary had to go. I had suspected for some time that he had been seeing another girl and one day the following week, when he didn't come back from football, I snapped. I phoned him up and told him he had to come and get his stuff out of the flat otherwise I was going to dump it on his mum's doorstep. I told him that I knew he was seeing someone else and that it was over between us. Even after all he had put me through I found it hard to end it. I suppose I had got so used to the rows and the lies. I had forgotten what a relationship should be like. He tried half-

Becoming Jordan – one
of my first topless shots.
©www.celebritymediagroup.com

With Gary Bolingbroke, my second serious boyfriend.

Starting to make a name for myself in the world of modelling.

©www.celebritymediagroup.com

Pit-stop pin-up. *Above*: With the Jordan F1 team.

Below left: Ralf and I, flirting in the pits. ©Sutton Photographic

Below right: With other Jordan pit girls, Melinda Messenger and Emma Noble.

©Rex Features

With Gladiator Ace – aka Warren Furman. When these pictures were taken, we were happily engaged, but the fairy-tale didn't last. ©Scope Features

Ever since I was a teenager, I have been mad about horses. This is me with my beautiful horse, Star. *Inset*: My dog Smurf.

A happy night out with Dane, before things turned sour between us.

©Rex Features

Ordinary girl Katie Price down at the stables with Dane, Sally and my sister Sophie.

heartedly to argue that he loved me, but I didn't believe him, and having met Warren I realised that I didn't need to be stuck in this relationship and get treated like dirt.

Some time after we split, Gary showed his true colours when he sold a kiss-and-tell story to a tabloid about our relationship. I remember reading it with disbelief: it was nearly all lies. Even so, I felt betrayed and hurt. Our relationship was supposed to be a private affair and yet there he was parading it for all the world to see, just to make a quick buck for himself. And I hated the fact that my family were so upset by what he had written. How would you like it if your mum and dad had to read about your sex life, even if most of it was a pack of lies? I discovered that he had used the proceeds to buy a new electrician's van. So that's what our relationship meant to him. My mum saw him out in Brighton and he tried to laugh it all off by saying, 'No hard feelings.' But he'd picked the wrong person. She told him she thought he was dirt and that he made her feel sick. It had no effect on Gary: some time after that he sold another kiss and tell.

Incredibly after what he had done he still thought there might be a chance I'd get back with him, and when I bumped into him in a club one night in Brighton he had the cheek to suggest it. He even tried to impress me by saying that he had his own business. He was pathetic. I said to him, 'I expect I paid to get that started, as well.' I looked at him and felt nothing. I had well and truly moved on.

Being with Jeff and Gary could have put me off men for life, or at least made me more careful who I had a relationship with, and to some extent it had. I was determined that no man was ever going to bully or hurt me again. But I'm a terrible romantic: I love being in love and I was in the mood for someone new. Warren seemed to fit the bill perfectly.

For our first date by ourselves we went to see the romantic comedy *Picture Perfect*, starring Jennifer Aniston. Right from the start, Warren treated me with respect and I felt safe with him. Our next date was at Browns in London, and pictures of us out together appeared in the press the next day. When I saw them I had that familiar sick feeling in my stomach. I remember thinking, Oh no, I hope this doesn't ruin things and put him off me. Straight away I remembered how the press had destroyed my chances with Teddy, and I couldn't bear it if it happened again. But Warren was great about it. He didn't seem bothered by the attention.

We started seeing each other all the time. I didn't try and hold back my feelings for him: I was falling in love. I let him into my heart and my life; we quickly became inseparable and did everything together. He would come on shoots with me and wait patiently for hours; I'd go to the gym with him and watch him work out. I loved being with him, he was so gentle and easy-going. It was a relief to be with such a nice bloke after my other bad experiences. He got on with everyone, and my family thought he was great too.

After we had been going out for a month, we finally slept together. I fancied him so much and he had such a great body that I was really looking forward to making love with him. But it wasn't quite the passionate experience I had been anticipating. He couldn't get a hard-on. I remember looking down and thinking, What am I supposed to do with this?

I pretended it was OK, even though I was very disappointed and frustrated. Then I tried to get him going by kissing and caressing him all over and pressing my body against his. I tried every trick in the book – and some of my own invention – but nothing would get him hard. When I finally gave up on getting him up, he told me it wasn't the first time this had happened to him. I don't know if that was supposed to make me feel better, but it didn't! This had never happened to me before and I was shocked. We girls might say it doesn't matter, but it bloody well does – you can't help wondering if it's something to do with you. The next couple of times we tried, the same thing happened. But we persisted, and eventually he got a hard-on. We made love at last.

Warren wasn't as adventurous as me in bed. Maybe the fact that I was more confident threatened him. Also, to try and get him going I did talk dirty to him – perhaps I had intimidated him. Fortunately it was good sex when he finally got going. I liked the fact that he was so manly and strong and had all that power behind him. Ask any woman: they don't want to have sex with a wimp. But he was quite shy in bed – it was me who made us experiment with sexy underwear and sex toys – and, even though he was a big guy, I definitely called the shots in that department.

Warren was very reliable and always phoned when he said he would, was there when he said he would be. He seemed so devoted to me. In spite of our rocky start in the bedroom, I couldn't imagine that our relationship would ever end.

I got that wrong.

CHAPTER NINE

PIT-STOP PIN-UP

While Warren concentrated on keeping his body in top condition, doing the odd personal appearance at clubs and filming *Gladiators*, my career was really kicking off. I was starting to earn serious money. It was such a liberating feeling, being able to buy what I wanted, within reason ... but I was careful too. I didn't want to blow it all. One part of me wondered how long this run of success would last. I was determined to make the most of it. I bought a house in Brighton, around the corner from my mum and I bought a beautiful horse called DJ. I had to hire someone to look after him, as my hectic work schedule meant I wouldn't have time to do all the mucking out.

As well as appearing as a Page 3 girl in the *Sun* and modelling for other tabloids such as the *Star*, I was getting offers to do shoots for all the leading lads' mags like *Esquire*, *Maxim*, *Loaded* and *FHM*. It was fantastic being so in-demand, and I loved appearing in these glossy magazines. It felt like I was really making a name for myself. I got whisked here, there and everywhere for exotic, big-budget shoots.

Most excitingly of all, I was asked to be a Formula 1 girl for Eddie Jordan's team. It was a huge ego boost and I was really flattered: Formula 1 only ever employ top models as their pit girls, and it proved that I was there with the best of them. I was definitely on my way up.

The race season lasts from March to November and I would go with the team to the different Grand Prix races all over the place. One week I'd be in Malaysia, a couple of weeks later it would be Spain, then Germany, then back to good old Silverstone. My job was to look as gorgeous and sexy as possible, along with the other models like Melinda Messenger and Emma Noble. We would all be dressed in skimpy little outfits – cropped tops, micro-minis and thigh-length boots in the team colours of bright yellow and black. The work involved posing next to the car and the drivers for the press call before the race. It lasted all of five minutes, then the rest of the time would be spent chatting, drinking and generally having a laugh. And I was being paid very good money. It doesn't get much better than this, I thought. It was such a brilliant job that frankly I'd have done it for nothing – though I'd never admit that to Eddie Jordan!

I really felt I was living the high life. There would always be fantastic buffets laid on with the best caviar and champagne, and a great party atmosphere. Eddie Jordan and the rest of his team were a real laugh. They all thought that I was a total wild child because, once I've had a drink, that's it: I have no inhibitions and the entertainer comes out. I was in my element, surrounded by fast cars, mega-rich famous drivers and exotic locations. And I loved watching the races. When I used to see the Grand Prix on television, I thought it was dead boring, but when you're actually there it's incredibly exciting: the noise, the speed of the cars, the thrill when your team wins – not that our team won much! I got a real buzz from it.

I was loving my life, and to cap it all my relationship with Warren was going well. It was everything I wanted: intense, passionate and loving. It was wonderful being with a man who wasn't afraid to show his feelings, and who I knew I could trust. He made me feel safe. But I did scare the pants off him on our first Valentine's Day. Because we'd only been together a few months, I thought I'd treat the whole thing as a bit of a laugh, so I nipped into Ann Summers and splashed out on a selection of very naughty goodies. I bought massage oil, body paint, a couple of vibrators, love balls and a set of handcuffs. When Warren opened the bag, he looked completely shocked. I have to admit I did laugh seeing a big bloke like him so terrified by a pair of furry handcuffs. I thought he'd love the surprise. He just went very quiet and handed me my presents: some gorgeous silk French knickers and a Gucci watch. He wasn't at all keen on using the gifts I had bought, but I made sure we did.

I definitely wore the trousers in our relationship, both inside and outside the bedroom. Thinking about it, maybe that was wrong; you need to have more of a balance in a relationship. Friends used to say that I treated him badly and that I was too bossy, always telling him what to do, but he never seemed to mind. I'd be the one who would decide what we were doing, where we were going and who we were seeing. I'm terrible: once someone lets me have my own way, that's it, there's no going back. One time I nearly drowned him when my little Sherpa puppy, Storm, jumped into a river. Even though I'm a very strong swimmer, I have suffered from panic attacks in the past when I get out of my depth; so I made Warren go in after him. He can't swim very well at all, but he did it for me –winter clothes and all – and rescued Storm.

We quickly moved in together. At first we lived in his house in Essex. Initially I must admit I was a little surprised when I saw it. From the way he talked about it I had imagined it would be very luxurious, but actually it was just a normal house, nothing special. It bugged me a bit that he'd made out that he was a lot more successful than he really was, but because I was so into him I quickly forgave him. I loved him, so I wouldn't have minded what he did; I just didn't like the fact that he'd sort of fiddled the truth. I wanted to believe everything was perfect, and I shut my eyes to anything that wasn't.

Then we rented a flat in Lawrence Moorings, down the road from where Posh and Becks were living. The one thing I couldn't get him to do was to live with me in Brighton. I was having to rent out the house that I owned there, and I really missed my family and friends. I would often spend weekends away from Warren, which he didn't like, but I wasn't prepared to give up everything for him. I had done that before with Jeff, and I had promised myself it wouldn't happen again.

But, living arrangements aside, at the beginning our

relationship seemed almost too good to be true. Warren was really laid-back about my work, one of the few boyfriends who have been. He totally accepted the fact that glamour modelling was my job and that just because I made a living out of looking sexy didn't mean I was going to be unfaithful to him. After all, he could hardly complain, as he made his living by running around showing off his assets in a skintight leotard. He was always paying me compliments about how I looked, which was so reassuring after Gary's put-downs, and he took me seriously when I talked about my ambitions. As well as being my lover, I also saw him as a great friend. I allowed myself to imagine that I might have a future with this man.

He got on brilliantly with all my family, and we even went on holiday together. Paul is really into sport, and he and Warren spent hours working out and playing tennis. My family are so important to me, and I loved the fact that Warren fitted in with them so well. The only slight downside was his family: his mum hated me. His mum was very unpredictable: sometimes she'd be as nice as pie, at other times, she wouldn't even speak to me. I think she had a problem with her son going out with a Page 3 girl. It pissed me off. Just because I was a topless model, it didn't mean I was a bad person. In the end, things between us got so tense, that, whenever Warren went round to see her, I would have to wait outside in the car. At times I also found his three brothers a bit too much to take – sometimes it felt like Warren and I could never be alone together. But these seemed like minor problems. Overall, I was very happy.

After a few months we went on a romantic holiday

together to Torremolinos – not the most exotic destination! Things were going so well between us that I couldn't imagine they could get any better. Then he bought me a beautiful Chopard heart ring with a happy diamond in it. He said it could be a first engagement ring and that he would buy me a proper one when we got back home. I was thrilled. I had always dreamed of a fairy-tale wedding: a white dress, a church, bridesmaids, a horse-drawn carriage. Perhaps Warren was the one to make my dreams come true.

When we returned home he was true to his word and bought me another ring with an even bigger diamond. We were officially engaged and I was on cloud nine. Then one night one of his brothers said something which nearly shattered my dreams. When we showed him the ring, he said, 'Does it matter what ring you've got? You're only doing it for the publicity.' I couldn't believe what I was hearing. I knew my career was going really well and, even though Warren didn't seem to have quite so many options open to him, I refused to believe that this gentle giant would do something so cynical. I decided to ignore what his brother had said, and put it down to jealousy. I loved Warren. Surely he would never hurt me.

CHAPTER TEN

I DID IT MY WAY: THE STORY OF MY SURGERY

Everyone said don't do it. Everyone: Warren, my mum, my stepdad Paul, my friends, my agent. I had photographers who had worked with me phoning up and begging me not to do it and saying that I didn't need to have it done, that I looked great just the way I was, that I was mad. But, even when the *Sun* ran a poll asking the readers what they thought and eighty per cent of them said don't do it, me being me, I still went ahead with it. Yes, it's time to talk about my biggest assets, the ones that have put me in the papers more than anything else: my boobs.

I swear I don't know what all the fuss is about. I wanted bigger breasts, now I've got them. I'm no different from the millions of women who have had surgery; but for some reason when I have it done I'm called a freak, unbalanced and disturbed. I'm told that I must hate my body, that I'm addicted to plastic surgery. What rubbish. I've even been compared to the porn star Lolo Ferrari, who died a couple of years ago. She had practically every part of her body altered by surgery and made the *Guinness Book of Records* by having breast implants taking her to a 54J. I even heard that airlines refused to let her fly in case her implants exploded. She had to sleep sitting up. Now *that's* what I call weird.

I have always been honest about my surgery. I'm not ashamed of it, and I've never tried to hide it – mind you, it would be quite hard to deny that I've had my boobs done! But look at Victoria Beckham: she has never admitted to having surgery, but I promise you she's had a boob job. How do I know? Because one night I was out for dinner with her, David and Dane Bowers at around the time she and Dane were working on their single together, and we had an interesting moment in the ladies' loos. Somehow the conversation got round to boobs. I showed her mine, she showed me hers. She knows that I know that she's had it done, so I don't know why she denies it. In fact, she told me how much she admired mine – and how much David likes big breasts. Well, show me a man who doesn't! You only have to look at her – skinny all over except her boobs. I know that she's faking it. I cannot believe she achieves that big-cleavage, boobs-standing-to-attention look with tit tape alone: it's good, but it's not *that* good. I can spot a boob job a mile off, not because I spend all my time staring at other women's breasts (whatever people would have you believe about my lesbian tendencies ...) but because in my line of work you get to see a lot of them.

What's the big deal about having surgery? The services are out there, and it's safer than it's ever been – clinics wouldn't be allowed to practise if it was dangerous. I don't think plastic surgery is any different from people having tattoos done or getting their bits and pieces pierced. You probably know about my two tattoos – the bow just above my bum and my pink heart that's in another very cheeky place! I draw the line at piercings though.

I knew I would look sexier with bigger boobs, and I was right. My one regret is that I didn't just have one operation taking me to the size I am now, which for the record is a 32DD and not a 34FF. I think that having three separate operations made the media more obsessed with the whole thing, and more determined to make out that there was something wrong with me.

The fact is that I had always wanted bigger boobs, even when I was at school. When I first started modelling, I felt quite self-conscious about their size. I thought that I looked flat-chested and not as sexy as the other girls on the glamour circuit. I was naturally a 32B/C, which is probably OK for most women, but I was making my living as a glamour model and I just didn't think they were big enough. I believe bigger breasts are sexier, more womanly and I think I suit them. I've never been one for the 'natural look'. I like the 'fake' look: big hair, big make-up, big boobs. Pamela Anderson has the perfect figure as far as I'm concerned.

I was only sixteen when I first thought about having the operation, and I admit that that is too young. I went to a clinic called Transform but they told me that I needed my parents' consent. Of course, my mum wouldn't give it. In fact, she went ballistic! That was around the time that I was being a right handful as a teenager, so I bet she thought, Oh God, there she goes again.

I had been on Page 3 for over a year when I decided to go for surgery, and I knew that if I had the operation it would dramatically change my career. For a start the *Sun* said that if I went ahead with the implants I wouldn't be able to be a Page 3 girl for them. They wanted strictly natural boobs on that page, although, if you ask me, quite a few models have appeared on it who have had a bit of help in that department. But that was OK: I wanted new modelling challenges.

Surgery wasn't something I rushed into. I was actually booked in three times for the first operation, but then chickened out at the last minute. My mum even called the clinic and cancelled one of the appointments as she was so determined to stop me. Then something just clicked inside me and I thought, Yes, this is the time to go for it. It didn't matter what the people close to me thought; I had my own ideas. Even Warren eventually came round to my way of thinking. I think secretly he was quite intrigued by the whole thing – what did I tell you about men and big tits?

My surgeon was going to be Dr Jeya Prakash. He had been recommended to me by Jeany Savage and had a great reputation as a plastic surgeon. He was one of the best in the business, so I knew he would do a good job and I trusted him. Mind you, he was strict with me and gave me quite a hard time about having the operation in the first place. It was September 1998 and I was twenty. He spent a lot of time going through my reasons, and eventually I managed to convince him that I wasn't doing it for anyone other than myself. I wasn't trying to impress my fans, or a man: it was just for me. Some people think you can just go and have the surgery there and then, with no more thought than having a bikini wax. It is not like that at all.

He advised me to go for silicone implants, simply because more is known about them. Dr Prakash demonstrated how tough they are by making me give the sacks a good old punch. I think I even stuck pins into them, but nothing leaked out. The implants come in all different shapes and sizes. I had to try them out in my bra under a T-shirt, which, to be honest, doesn't really give you a clue what your new boobs will look like.

On the actual day of the operation I felt sick with nerves; in fact, I totally freaked out. By the time Warren and I arrived at the private hospital I was seriously having second thoughts, especially when Dr Prakash came in and drew in felt pen on my boobs where he was going to make the incisions. I remember looking in the mirror at all these dotted lines on my breasts and thinking, Oh my God, what have I got myself into this time?

Then a nurse came into the room and told me to put on a gown and take off my nail varnish. It was weird sitting in a wheelchair and being taken down to theatre as if I was suddenly helpless. Everything seemed strange and muffled. There was hardly any noise, just doctors padding by in their gowns; and everywhere had that clinical, antiseptic smell that all hospitals have. This was serious stuff.

Now I was there I was desperate to get it over and done with, but I had to wait outside theatre while the nurse ran through her checklist. Was I allergic to this or that? Did I have any crowns? All the time my heart was pounding. I kept thinking, This is the last time I'm going to be seeing my boobs in their natural state. Do I really want to go through with this? I thought of all the arguments I'd had with Mum about it, and about all the people who thought I was crazy to be doing it. Were they right?

When the nurse finished her list she just made small talk and I thought to myself, Don't try and sweeten me up, I know that you're going to be sticking a needle into me any minute now. I have such a phobia about needles. Then the anaesthetist turned up and explained what was going to happen, that I would just feel a little prick in my hand (I resisted the temptation to make a cheeky remark) as the needle went in, and a cold sensation creeping up my arm as the anaesthetic entered my bloodstream.

I was so convinced that the anaesthetic wouldn't work and I'd feel everything, I swear I almost broke the nurse's fingers because I was squeezing her hand so hard. I had to look away when the anaesthetist put the needle in, and then he told me to count down from ten. One second I was staring up at him, the next I was out of it. It is such a strange sensation because you almost think that you can fight the anaesthetic and stay awake, but of course you can't. It might sound weird, but I actually like the feeling of going under.

When I came round two hours later I felt sick and was in total agony. It was by far the worst pain I had ever experienced – this was before I gave birth. I looked down expecting to see my breasts looking bigger, but I couldn't see anything through the bandages. I had to stay in hospital overnight and I felt pretty sorry for myself. I couldn't lift my arms and my boobs were throbbing. I was a complete wreck. Warren was very sweet to me though. He drove me home the next day, me screaming in pain whenever we went over a bump. He tucked me up in bed, but I just couldn't get comfortable. I couldn't sleep on my side and every time I moved pain shot through me. In the end we had to phone up the doctor and ask for more painkillers.

The next day I had a bath and took the bandages off. When I saw the stitches I felt even worse. I am quite squeamish. I remember looking at my boobs and wondering if I even liked them after all that. I couldn't see that they looked any bigger. The operation was supposed to have taken me to a full 32C, my natural size being 32B/C. I was dying to try on some of my tight little vest tops to see what kind of cleavage I had now, but I was much too sore.

For three weeks I had to wear a sports bra, hardly the sexiest piece of lingerie. I felt like a right old granny, and I even had to stuff it with cotton wool to stop it from rubbing the scars. I didn't feel like Britain's most famous pin-up at that moment. I felt like shit.

But the ordeal wasn't over. I nearly fainted when I returned to the doctors to have the stitches removed. When I saw him coming towards me with the tweezers, I said, 'Aren't you going to give me something so I don't feel anything?' But he just told me to look away and keep talking while he pulled them out. Ouch!

Once the scars had healed I was pleased with the results. My boobs looked fuller and I definitely felt sexier. I think Warren found them a real turn-on too. My family had been furious that I'd gone ahead and had the surgery, especially my mum. But I even managed to convert her. She was so impressed by my surgeon that she ended up having a face lift. But something was bugging me: already I wished they were bigger.

I swore I would never do anything like this again. But then you should never say never, should you? A year later I was back having another operation to take me to a 32D.

The second time, probably because I knew what to expect, it didn't seem to hurt as much. I liked the new look, but I wanted to change the shape. You know what they say: third time lucky, and a year later I was booked in to have my breasts done again. I had just split up with Dane Bowers. He had said that there was no way I was having another boob job and that if I did he'd leave me. So when we did break up I thought, Right then, there's no one to stop me now.

Dr Prakash refused to do the third op. He prefers to make boob jobs look as natural as possible and he said having another operation wouldn't suit my body. I told him I just wanted a different shape but he wouldn't budge, so in the end I went to Transform. This time I ended up a 32DD, but the operation was more about getting my boobs reshaped and uplifted, not the size. It took me even less time to recover. In fact, just two days later I was out again at Britney Spears's birthday party.

People always ask me what my boobs feel like now, and I can honestly say it hasn't made a difference: they are just as sensitive, if not more sensitive than they were before. I think I've been lucky because they still look natural. When I lie down they naturally fall to the side, they're not all rock hard and rigid. And I've never had any complaints from the men I've been out with. Far from it: bigger is definitely better when it comes to breasts.

Another thing people think is that I have to have my bras specially made for me, but I can get them anywhere. My favourite shops are Debenhams, La Senza, Marks & Spencer, and even Asda do some good ones!

Three operations later, do you know how I feel? Great. I don't have a single regret about the breast surgery. It made me even more famous and brought me even more work. The silicone-enhanced Jordan has been in constant demand. And by the time you read this, who knows? I might even have gone for op number four.

CHAPTER ELEVEN

FORMULA 1 LOVE

My new boobs changed Page 3 forever. After I had them done, the paper brought in a strict no-silicone rule, so I couldn't model for that page any more. But that didn't bother me in the least. I had loads of other work on, and I decided to be a right little tease and keep my assets under wraps for a while.

In fact, it seemed as if I was more in demand than ever. I had all kinds of offers, not just to do with modelling. I went out on morale-boasting trips to see the troops in Kosovo; I was invited to do personal appearances in clubs; I appeared on television; and I carried on working as a Formula 1 girl.

But I didn't let all this attention go to my head. I've never been one for loads of diva-style demands, and I always laugh when I read about celebs ordering this and that for their dressing rooms – the scented candles, the fresh-fruit platter, the white sofas, the mineral water. My demands are

99

much more down to earth, usually a cup of tea and a McDonald's or a baked potato. And I'm lucky if I get a dressing room. As far as I'm concerned I'm there to do a job and to get on with it. The only times I do get annoyed are when I feel that there are too many blokes standing around leering at me. I know they're going to be looking at pictures of me half-naked, but I don't particularly want to see all those faces when I take my top off. I can feel vulnerable when I'm posing.

While I was pleased with my new boobs and my career, my relationship with Warren was looking decidedly droopy. We were booked to do a photo shoot with *Hello!* to talk about our engagement and our wedding plans, but, as we posed together and smiled for the cameras, I just couldn't get his brother's words out of my head. Was Warren only marrying me for the publicity? My heart wanted to scream 'No!' but my head wasn't sure. I began to see cracks in our relationship that hadn't been there before ...

It got worse. My gentle giant was beginning to show a nasty streak. Suddenly he was becoming jealous and possessive. Why did this keep happening to me? In particular, he started to get funny about my good friend Neil. Because Neil is such a great-looking bloke, Warren just could not believe that there was nothing going on between us. I couldn't convince him; he would even phone Neil and demand to know the truth about our relationship. It was all rubbish of course. I've known Neil for ages, and when I was younger I did fancy him, but now I definitely saw him as a friend. I know much too much about him and what he gets up to with other women to ever want a relationship with him. It made me so angry when Warren made these accusations. Why had he stopped trusting me?

If I went out clubbing without him, when I got home he'd start saying things like, 'I know what you've been up to. I've been told you've been chatting up some blokes. Don't deny it, because you've been seen.' It was just him playing mind games, trying to make out that I was being watched, trying to make me paranoid. But I had nothing to hide, I really wasn't doing anything. I admit that when I've had a drink I might look like a flirt, but I would never go further than that.

I hated the way Warren was becoming jealous for no reason. I felt suffocated and unhappy. I stopped wanting to spend all of my time with him. I looked forward to going to work so that I could be free of him. I especially looked forward to my Formula 1 engagements – where a certain German driver caught my attention.

I first met Ralf Schumacher when we were both doing a shoot for *Esquire*. He was very good-looking and charming, but I was slightly put off by the way everyone was rushing around after him as if he was royalty. I bet he's really arrogant, I thought to myself.

He came and introduced himself to me while I was having my hair done. I asked him whether my hair had looked better before or after I'd had it styled, and he said before, cheeky sod! So I thought, Right, I'm going to be lippy back to you. I can give as good as I get. He seemed to like the fact that I was so outspoken, and before I knew it we were flirting together.

That was obviously my day for meeting men because Robbie Williams was doing a shoot at the same studio and, after trying unsuccessfully to get my number from my stylist, he came up to me and asked me out that night. Unfortunately I was with Warren so I had to say no, but it wasn't easy. I went home thinking, Blimey, two really eligible men are interested in me.

When Warren started having a go at me about flirting with other men, I started thinking, There are other men out there who won't treat you like this. There was definitely a spark between Ralf and me. My heart used to beat faster every time I saw him, and I'd often catch him staring at me after the races. The feeling was mutual. It all seemed very romantic: there we were, irresistibly attracted to each other, willing everyone to go away and leave us alone together. My friends were always telling me to go and talk to him, as it was so obvious that we wanted to be together. Sometimes I would find myself gazing at him and wondering where this flirtation might lead. But I would have to pull myself together. You're with Warren, I told myself. Don't go there. But I couldn't stop myself.

Everyone said he was different when he was with me, more relaxed and open, less arrogant. As we saw more of each other at Grand Prix races, so our flirtatious friendship started to grow. I sat next to him whenever I could. I would even pop into his caravan and talk to him while he was having a massage. There's a picture of us together, both of us dressed in the Jordan racing colours of yellow and black, me in a tiny pair of shorts, a cropped top and black leather boots, him in his racing suit; he's lifting me up and both of us are grinning away at the camera. This kind of cheeky behaviour was unheard of for Ralf as he usually never smiled and never wanted his picture taken with any of the other pit girls. He seemed interested, and so was I. He seemed to have everything: he was an international sports star, a multimillionaire, he was charming and witty – *and* he was good looking.

Once I met Ralf, my relationship with Warren went into terminal decline. He was no longer the warm, loving man I had met. I hated his jealousy and possessiveness; it made me feel so claustrophobic and I wanted to be free of him. Suddenly he was the last man I wanted to marry. I decided I would move back to Brighton into my house. I missed my family and friends. I gave Warren the chance to move back with me, but he claimed there was nothing there for him. We both knew in our heart of hearts that it was over between us. We didn't say anything. We didn't need to: it was obvious. What had started out so sweetly was turning nasty and bitter.

It was such a relief to be back home and away from Warren. Now I was free to think about my sexy racing driver. When Ralf called and asked me if I wanted to visit him in Monaco, I didn't hesitate.

Even though to all intents and purposes we had split up, Warren called me all the time. During one of our phone conversations I told him I was going away. Immediately he started questioning me about who I was going with, but I wouldn't tell him anything. I told him it was a work engagement, but he didn't believe me and got very aggressive. The next day I was due to fly out and meet Ralf and all I wanted to do was pack and get ready. I didn't want to deal with Warren's jealousy any more. But he wasn't going to disappear from my life so easily.

That night I was woken up at two o'clock in the morning by a phone call. It was Warren and he told me he was outside my house and desperate to see me. He was the last person I wanted to see, but very reluctantly I let him in. Straight away he started having a go at me, wanting to know where I was going, and who I was going with. I told him yet again that it was over between us and that he should leave. He got more and more angry and started shouting at me, 'I know you're up to something.' He was beginning to scare me as he was getting so wound up and I had never seen him like this before. He is a big bloke, and I didn't know what he was capable of. I kept telling him to get out and leave me alone, but he wouldn't. Suddenly he grabbed my shoulders and pushed me to the ground. I was terrified. I couldn't move as he had me pinned down. Then he seized my hand and pulled off the rings he had given me. I was shaken and upset. It was such a brutal thing to do. I hated him then; I really hated him.

'What are you doing?' I screamed. But he didn't reply, just looked at me coldly, got up and stormed out of the house. I was so relieved that he had left so easily, because I was dreading that I'd never get rid of him. After he had slammed the door shut, I went downstairs to check the lock and that's when I saw that he had taken my bag which I had left in the lounge. He had also gone off with my passport and my car keys. How the hell was I going to see Ralf now?

I phoned Warren's mobile, but he didn't answer. Frantically I called my mum and told her what had happened. She tried to get me to calm down and told me she would drive me to Warren's the following day and that we would sort everything out. Early the next morning, after a totally sleepless night, my mum came and picked me up. We kept calling Warren and his brothers but they wouldn't answer their phones. I was beginning to despair, but finally we managed to speak to them and they promised to hand my things back. I was feeling desperate: Ralf was expecting me to be on a flight that afternoon and I couldn't see how I would make it.

When we arrived at Warren's house there was no one there. We tried calling his mobile, but he'd switched it off. We waited a while, and then my mum said, 'That's it, we're going to the police. He can't just take your passport and expect us to do nothing.'

We spent four hours at the police station. We spoke to Warren and told him we were reporting him for theft, but he wasn't even bothered. There was nothing more we could do. Mum drove us home as she had to prepare for a murder-mystery dinner party at her house that night. I had to speak to Ralf. I couldn't tell him the truth – it sounded so tacky – so I just said that something had come up but I'd definitely be on a flight the next day. I prayed I could be. I couldn't bear it if Warren messed things up for me.

The following day Warren turned up again outside my house. This time he'd brought two friends and a truck. He wanted his bed back. If I hadn't been so desperate to see Ralf I would have been laughing: this was turning into a complete farce. I opened the window and called out, 'If you let me have my passport, you can have your bed.'

He was waving the passport in my face. I tried to grab it, but couldn't. 'If you let me in, you can have it,' he taunted.

I opened the door and he rushed inside. Before I had the chance to say anything, he pushed me over and pinned me to the floor, completely winding me. I felt as if I couldn't breathe, but this time instead of being scared I was angry. He started shouting at me again: where was I going, who was I going with? I was screaming at him to get off. His friends tried to calm him down, and by now I was crying tears of rage and frustration. But, just as I thought I was never going to get out of this situation, I caught sight of my passport in his pocket and grabbed it without him seeing. At that moment one of his friends pulled him off me and I went mad shouting and screaming at him to get out of the house – hell hath no fury like a woman about to miss her flight. I managed to get them all outside, then slammed the door shut and locked it. Warren banged on the doors and windows, but I wasn't going to let him in again. I had my passport back; now I had a plane to catch.

While Warren raged outside like an angry bear, I rushed around throwing clothes into a suitcase. There was no time to lose, as my flight was in a couple of hours. I didn't even have time to get changed or do my make-up. I had to leave in the clothes I was in – grey tracksuit bottoms, a black hooded jumper and trainers. It was hardly the look of a glamour model, and hardly what Ralf would be expecting – usually he saw me looking polished and sexy. I looked like I should be slobbing in front of the television, not meeting the man of my dreams. But there was nothing for it. I was dreading that Warren would still be outside, but he had given up. My mum and Paul arrived to take me to the airport, but I insisted on driving as there was no way I could sit back in the passenger seat. The traffic was terrible and I ended up driving on the hard shoulder. At the airport I didn't even have time to get any cash out of the machine, and I was so late I had to get a buggy to the plane.

I sat back in my seat, took out my mirror and examined my face. I looked terrible: my eyes were so swollen and puffy from crying, it looked like someone had punched me. I got out my make-up, knowing that somehow I had to transform myself into the girl Ralf knew. But it wasn't going to be easy – in those days, I wasn't very good at doing my make-up. I plastered on the mascara and put on a bit of lipstick; that would have to do.

As I sipped my drink, I tried to calm down, but I felt so stressed. I had no money with me, and I hate not being able to pay my own way; I'd only managed to grab one outfit for going out in – some smart black trousers, a Karen Millen top and some heels. It wasn't going to be enough, and the last thing I wanted was for Ralf to buy me clothes. It would look like I was sponging off him, and I'm not that kind of girl. I had wanted everything to be perfect when I met Ralf; I was bitterly disappointed that it wasn't.

I cheered up when I saw him waiting for me at the airport. He was charming and looked gorgeous. I felt that butterfly feeling inside, and there was no denying how attracted I was to him. I just wanted to go back to his house, but Ralf said we were going to meet some friends for dinner. Immediately I started to feel nervous and self-conscious. I felt totally out of place in my casual clothes in the very posh restaurant. I barely ate, and I didn't talk much either. Ralf must have wondered what had happened to the sparkly, flirtatious girl he knew.

Back at his luxurious apartment, I started to unwind. But I couldn't help wondering what Ralf had in mind for later. Where was I going to be sleeping that night? Ralf must have been reading my mind because, as he showed me round his apartment, he directed me to his bedroom. I was half-excited, half-nervous. Much as I fancied him, I had no intention of having sex with him so quickly, and I hoped he would understand that.

As it turned out, I needn't have worried about Ralf coming on too strong. When I slipped into bed next to him wearing boxers and a T-shirt, he just gave me a kiss on the cheek, then turned over to go to sleep. After the nightmare few days with Warren, I was desperate for some reassurance from Ralf. I longed to feel his arms around me, to feel safe and wanted. I must admit I was a bit surprised when he didn't even try to cuddle me. I was expecting a little more passion from him. I'm not used to getting into bed with a man who doesn't at least try and kiss and cuddle me. Instead of thinking that it showed Ralf respected me, it made me feel paranoid; I tormented myself by thinking that maybe he didn't like me.

The next morning I woke up to an empty bed. Ralf was already up and dressed. Again I felt anxious: why was he so keen to leave me? I got up and found him in the elegant living room. I asked him if I could make him some tea, but he said, 'Let my housekeeper do it.' I was feeling more out of place than ever.

Later that day he took me to see the boat he was having built. I was impressed – here was a man who could have anything he wanted. Everywhere we were surrounded by luxury and wealth. It was a million miles away from my life with Warren. But it wasn't just about his success. I was fascinated by the man himself, and I wanted to know more about him: what inspired him, what made him tick. Above all I wanted to know what he thought of me.

I kept expecting Ralf to reveal his feelings for me. I knew he must be attracted to me after all our flirting at the Grand Prix, so I kept waiting for him to make a move on me. He didn't. One night we went out with another couple; we all had a few drinks and ended up back at Ralf's for some more. Ralf was more relaxed than I had ever seen him. He even got his karaoke machine out and serenaded us with 'I Swear' by All-4-One – not a bad performance at all. I thought the drinks might loosen him up in bed and that he would start to give me the attention I longed for. But no: yet again we slept together and nothing happened.

I ended up staying three nights with Ralf, but he didn't lay a finger on me; we didn't even kiss properly. I even started to wonder if he was gay. But, when I told him I had to return to England for a modelling job, he told me that he didn't want me to go, and really wished I could stay longer. I was totally confused. As we said goodbye he said that I must come and visit him soon at his home in Germany. I promised I would. I longed to break through his reserve and get closer to him. Ralf Schumacher was frustrating me, and I wasn't used to that feeling at all!

Back home it was strange not seeing Warren. My relationship with him had been on the whole a good one, which made it all the sadder that we had split up on such bad terms. I found out that he had my rings melted down and made into a single ring for himself, which seemed such a cheap thing to do. He was full of bitterness, not the man I had been in love with. He even took a load of my photographs and letters. These weren't modelling pictures which I could easily get copies of, but personal ones of me as a child and a teenager. To this day I've not been able to get them back, nor have I been able to get copies of them.

When we split, Warren's career was not going well. *Gladiators* had finished on television, and he didn't really have any other work lined up so he was probably short of cash. But that was no excuse for what he went on to do: two kiss and tells revealing intimate details of our sex life. I might have expected it of someone like Gary, but I couldn't believe that Warren would sink so low. I was devastated. The headline in the tabloid screamed JORDAN: WILD AND OBSESSED. TRAGIC WORLD OF PORN, BONDAGE AND WEIRD SEX THAT KILLED OUR LOVE. It was mainly rubbish of course, and what was true was sensationalised out of all proportion. Apparently I had an 'endless need for bizarre and warped sex' which destroyed our relationship. I had 'no idea of what normal love-making was all about'. I had 'dressed in PVC bondage gear and produced a huge bullwhip on our first night of sex'. I mean, please! Bondage does nothing for me – OK, I like a bit of tying up to the bedpost, but who hasn't done that in their time? He claimed that I watched porn films every day. I'm a busy working girl – I don't have time for that kind of thing, even if I wanted to! Warren even said that we'd had sex in the toilet on a plane once. How likely was that? The man weighed seventeen stone – I doubt we would even have fitted in there, let alone got up to anything.

Looking back at that time I can almost laugh it off. They're not going to sell papers with the story that I only like having sex in the missionary position once a month with the lights off, are they? But at the time I was bitterly hurt by the fact that Warren had betrayed my trust and gone ahead and said all these things just to make money out of me. Even if I knew the stories to be untrue, other people would read and believe them. They would think that I was some kind of disturbed, sex-mad freak, when the truth is nothing more exciting than the fact that I'm a girl with a healthy appetite for sex who likes a bit of experimentation, and who gets bored of having sex in bed the whole time. And I'm not the only one. Look at how successful Ann Summers has become, look at how popular television shows like *Sex and the City* are. I'm no prude when it comes to sex, but I don't think that's anything to be ashamed of, do you?

We split up years ago, but even today I'll see Warren every now and then on television talking about our sex life – or rather about our imagined sex life. It's sad really. We could perhaps have stayed friends, but he destroyed any chance of that.

When we broke up back in 1999 I even thought about seeing my lawyer to find out if I could get any future boyfriends to sign a legal contract that would stop them from doing kiss and tells. I couldn't bear for anyone else to betray me. My trust in men, which was already quite shaky, was becoming even more fragile.

CHAPTER TWELVE

NIGHTMARE IN GERMANY

But there was one man who I was sure I could trust. A man in a different league to my previous boyfriends. A man who excited and intrigued me. I felt frustrated by my trip to Monaco because things hadn't moved on between us, but then Ralf called and asked me to visit him at his home in Germany. I jumped at the chance. The plan was for me to stay at least a week. At last, I thought, we can really get to know each other. I'll be able to find out for sure what my feelings for him are, and what his are for me. The fact that he wanted to see me again seemed very promising.

The visit got off to a great start. This time I was prepared and I had an outfit for every possible occasion – although I still had to phone my mum constantly to check with her what I should wear. I was so keen to make a good impression. Ralf was obviously pleased to see me, and I was thrilled when he introduced me to his mum and close friends as his girlfriend. This was definitely progress. I really started to feel that he was letting me into his life. We had barbecues with his family and friends; he took me shopping; we played badminton together and went to the gym; I even became a domestic goddess for a morning when he went out with a friend and I stayed with his mum preparing lunch. I was delighted with the way things were developing.

The only trouble was, nothing happened in bed. Ralf didn't lay a finger on me. Didn't he realise how frustrated I was? Wasn't he frustrated too? It didn't seem like we'd be rushing into anything, so it was the perfect time to take our relationship one stage further. I wanted him. I lay next to him, burning with desire, but I didn't feel able to initiate things myself. I needed to know that he wanted me too. There was a minor breakthrough one night when we came back from clubbing: he pulled me on to his lap as we sat in the lounge, and he kissed me. I was convinced that this was the beginning of his seduction, but when we went to bed – nothing.

Relax, I tried to tell myself, there's plenty of time. But my hopes were shattered the next morning as we were getting ready to go riding. The phone went and Ralf answered it. I couldn't understand what he was saying, but I could tell something was very wrong. He looked furious. He ended the call, stared accusingly at me and said, 'Have you been talking to the press about us?'

I went cold all over. 'Of course not. I would never do that,' I said. 'Why, what's happened?'

But Ralf refused to open up. He just said icily, 'I would like you to pack your bags, please, and my driver will take you to the airport. You are leaving now. Your flight has been booked and you must go this minute.'

It was like a bad dream. I tried reasoning with him, telling him over and over again that I would never talk about him to the press, but he wouldn't listen and he refused to say another word to me. In the end I gave up. I just couldn't get through to him. Feeling totally shaken, I went upstairs and started packing, my mind in turmoil. I felt shocked and humiliated to be leaving like this in front of all his family. It made me look as if I was guilty. But I hadn't said anything to the press. Why wouldn't he believe me?

In desperation I phoned my friend and stylist Sam Howard, who was one of the few people who knew about me staying with Ralf. I was stunned when she informed me that I was plastered on the front page, and there was a double-page spread in the *News of the World* all about my trip to Monaco with Ralf. The headline said JORDAN GOT SCHUMACHER IN POLE POSITION, BUT HE KEPT PASSION IDLE. I wanted her to read out the whole article to me, but before she could my phone battery went dead. I felt sick. It was obvious someone had stitched me up, but who? The only people who knew all the details of my trip and what had happened – or rather what hadn't happened – between me and Ralf were Sam and my hairdresser, Jodie. They were supposed to be my friends, and friends aren't supposed to betray you like this. Sam had sounded really excited about the story, so maybe it was her. Why had I said anything to them? It was obvious that no one could be trusted.

Miserably I finished packing and went downstairs. Ralf didn't even say goodbye to me. I got into the chauffeur-driven car, trying to hide my tears behind my dark glasses. All I wanted to do was convince Ralf that I was telling the truth, that I had been betrayed, that I wouldn't sell a story about our relationship. But it was like the Teddy Sheringham incident all over again: I was being blamed for something I didn't do.

At the airport I tried to check in but discovered that I wasn't booked on any flight after all. The next plane to England wasn't until six that evening. I had hours to go, as it was only ten in the morning. I went to try and buy a paper and read the story for myself, but they wouldn't accept my English money and there wasn't anywhere to change it. I didn't have any German currency with me, or any credit cards. I was trapped at the airport and I couldn't even phone my mum because the operator wouldn't accept a reverse-charge call. All I wanted to do was get hold of the paper and find out what had been written. I could see a copy of the *News of the World* on the shelf behind the till at the newsagent, but I couldn't read it without buying it. How ironic: there I was on the front cover, and I couldn't even find out what had been said about me. It was an absolute nightmare.

It was such a relief to get home, but when I finally read the story I felt even worse. My picture was plastered all over the page, so people were bound to think that the story had come from me; and yet what was written was largely untrue. The article made Ralf out to be frigid and passionless, more interested in falling asleep than getting close to me. No wonder he had been so angry.

Straight away I phoned Sam and accused her of selling the story, but she promised me she hadn't said anything.

That's it, I thought. It has to be Jodie. I was so angry that I actually went storming round to where she worked and confronted her there and then. Of course she swore she hadn't said anything, but looking back, who else could it have been? The article had mentioned the one outfit I'd taken to Monaco. She was the only one who knew that I'd bought it from Karen Millen – I'd shown it to her when she had been doing my hair.

I was devastated. I tried calling Ralf and left messages, but he never returned my calls. I really thought this had destroyed any chance I had with him. It seemed so unfair: yet again, the press had brought me grief. I tried to push Ralf to the back of my mind and forget about him, but I couldn't help thinking about the handsome driver and wondering what might have been. Although I got on with my life, Ralf Schumacher was never far from my dreams.

CHAPTER THIRTEEN

POPTASTIC

After my traumatic break-up with Warren, and with the chance of getting together with Ralf in ruins, the only constant things in my life seemed to be my family and my horse. At least they weren't going to rush off and sell a made-up story to the papers about me. I had this horrible feeling that I couldn't trust anyone any more. I am naturally a very open person, but I've had to learn to hold back. I find it hard to trust people now. I have a tight circle of friends, including some girls who I grew up with, and Sally, my make-up artist, who I trust completely. But I don't make friends so easily any more, mainly because there have been too many times in the past when people have let things slip to the press.

Right from the beginning of my career the press have been obsessed with me. Of course, I realise I wouldn't have made it without them, and I've got a lot to be grateful for, but

I wish they weren't so quick to shoot me down. The thing they love to go on about the most is that I'm like two people – sweet Katie Price and sex-mad Jordan, how Jordan has taken over Katie and ruined her. Well, it makes good newspaper copy, doesn't it? I do put on an act for the cameras – but I know I'm doing it. I haven't got a split personality. Jordan is who I am when I'm working. Everyone is different at work from how they are at home: in my case, it's just probably more noticeable. I've got a sexy and outspoken reputation to live up to, and I'm not stupid – I know what will make people interested in me. I'm not going to be put on the cover of men's magazines by talking about how I like curling up on the sofa with a cup of hot chocolate and watching *EastEnders* in my pyjamas!

For a while I enjoyed being a single girl, going out and having the odd flirtation, nothing serious. I met up again with the footballer John Scales, who I'd first encountered at the time I was introduced to Teddy. We went on a couple of dates and I really liked his company. He was funny and charming, not just a typical man wanting to get me into bed. Thinking about it, he has the best personality of any of the men I've met. I have a lot of respect for him.

At first I felt self-conscious around him, but as I got to know him I relaxed. I stayed at his apartment a few times, but, in case you're wondering, no, we didn't have sex. I was definitely attracted to him, but he was cagey about revealing what he thought of me and I never quite knew where I stood. Rightly or wrongly, I'm definitely someone who wants relationships to be full on from the first meeting. But John wasn't like that, which probably explains why we never got beyond the flirting stage and why I was free to fall suddenly and passionately in love with someone else in August 1999.

I definitely wasn't looking for love, but that's when you're most likely to find it, in my experience. In this instance I was totally swept off my feet. Within weeks of meeting him, I was seriously thinking that at last I had found the man of my dreams, the man I wanted to marry. I believed that I had found my soul mate, someone I could totally trust to love me for myself. That someone was Dane Bowers, the nineteen-year-old pop star from the boy band Another Level.

I only met him by chance. It was a hot August evening in London and I was driving home from a quiz show I had just recorded at the BBC. I was sitting in the traffic listening to music when I got a call inviting me to a party following the film premiere of *Wild Wild West*. I was all set to go back home to Brighton and couldn't decide what to do, so I kept driving round and round this roundabout trying to make up my mind – typical me! In the end, I decided I'd go to the party. Luckily I always keep a spare set of clothes in the car, so that wasn't a problem.

I drove back into central London, parked the car and squeezed myself into my party outfit. Thanks to my blacked-out windows there was no chance of anyone leering in. I went for the full-on, glammed-up look: a fitted black jacket with nothing on underneath except a wonderbra, which of course gave me the most sensational cleavage, tight black trousers and heels. Then I put my hair into pigtails, and touched up my make-up. I was ready for some serious partying.

When I got to the venue it was packed, and I spent a few

anxious minutes looking around for familiar faces. I never like arriving at places on my own; it makes me feel insecure. But before long I managed to locate a group of girls I knew and we were soon joined by Bobak from Another Level, who I'd been to school with. We were all drinking and chatting away when my attention was caught by a handsome, dark-haired man in a well-cut cream suit. He walked past our group looking straight at me. I felt a jolt of excitement. He was gorgeous and I recognised him. It was Dane Bowers. I stared back at him. Suddenly I didn't want to be part of a group, I wanted to talk to this man one to one. The night had taken on a whole new meaning for me. I willed him to come over and start talking to me, and when he didn't I put my own plan into action. One of the girls I was with needed a light, which gave me the perfect excuse to go over and ask Dane for one. I walked over to where he was standing, confident that I was wearing something which made the most of my figure. I could tell by the look on his face that I was making an impression on him. So far so good. He said he didn't smoke, but immediately we got talking. My cunning plan had worked. He told me I looked great when I was modelling in magazines and papers. I returned the compliment by telling him what a big fan of his music I was.

We were flirting together nicely when suddenly I remembered that, earlier in the evening, I'd arranged to meet John Scales at the Met Bar. Typical! Any other time I'd have jumped at the chance of spending time with John; now all I wanted to do was to get close to this sexy young singer. But there was nothing for it. The only consolation was that Dane seemed genuinely disappointed that I was leaving, and asked me if I really had to go. I told him I did, and he asked for my number.

I left the party praying he would call me. I really fancied him and wanted to see him again. So I was over the moon when I got to the Met Bar and checked my messages. I'd only said goodbye to him an hour ago, and already I had three voicemails from him and a text saying he'd love to meet up with me. It put a big smile on my face: it's always nice to know when a guy is keen. Where could this lead, I wondered.

I didn't call him straight back. I left it to the next day – well, there's nothing wrong with keeping a man waiting, is there? He wasted no time in asking me out. I liked him all the more when he said it was simply to come and meet him and some of his friends in Croydon where he lived. It made him seem more down to earth.

As usual for a first date, I spent ages wondering what to wear. In the end I went for my combats, a tight T-shirt and funky trainers. I wanted him to see me as Katie, not Jordan. He had met me in my full-on party kit; now he could see a different side to me.

We arranged to meet at a club in Croydon, and I had brought my friend JoJo with me. We had terrible trouble finding the place. It was dark and pouring with rain, and I have an awful sense of direction. As it got later and later, I started agonising. 'Oh, God,' I said to JoJo, 'will he still be there?' Eventually, and after a lot of frantic mobile phone calls to Dane, I found the club. He was waiting outside in the rain, soaking wet, looking out for me. I remember thinking, How romantic, what a gentleman.

We had a quick kiss in the rain. Then we went inside and

had a drink with his friends. I couldn't really relax because I knew I was driving and I didn't want to drink and drive. Dane offered to drive back to his mum's with me so that I could park my car there for the night and not worry about it. As he got in the car next to me I showed him the cover of his album which I had with me. 'You'll probably think I'm really sad because of this,' I said, 'but I love your song "From the Heart". I play it all the time.' It was an odd but magical feeling driving along with him beside me, playing his music. It even made Croydon look special.

Once I'd parked my car at his parents', we had some time to kill before the cab arrived to take us back to the club. Dane went to put on some dry clothes and I sat in the lounge. Suddenly I noticed a photograph of Dane, a woman and a baby on the television. Oh no, I thought, he's with someone. Immediately something inside of me crumbled. When Dane came back into the room he saw where I was looking and told me that was his son. I was desperate to ask if he was still with the girl, but he didn't say anything and I didn't think it was my place to ask. I felt very disappointed, though: did I really want to get involved with someone who had a child? It was bound to make things complicated. But, in a funny way, it made him more attractive to me. I knew that, if I did get involved, there was a hell of a lot at stake.

But I pushed these thoughts to the back of my mind and we went to the club and got down to some serious flirting. I had a few drinks, but I was only merry, and I knew exactly what I would and wouldn't do. Then Dane had to go off and do a DJ set. Afterwards he found me and asked for a kiss. I said no, but he was quite persistent and inside I was thinking, He *is* nice. At the same time, though, I couldn't help remembering the picture of his son, and I wondered exactly what Dane's situation was.

After the club we went back to his mum and dad's and hung out in the bar room. My friend JoJo had hit it off with one of Dane's friends and they were busy getting closer on the sofa bed. Dane and I were lying on the floor cuddling, fully clothed. The film *Scream* was on in the background. I can't say I was paying much attention to it because Dane and I finally had our first kiss, and I thought, Wow, that was one great kiss.

And that was all it took. If I'm attracted to a man, then I fall for him quickly. Even though I've been hurt in the past, and it frightens me when I feel like this, I hate playing games. I believe in showing my feelings, and I didn't want to hide what I felt from Dane.

As I drove back to Brighton with JoJo the next day, I couldn't stop talking about him and wondering when I would see him again. I knew he was going to America soon with the band, and I was desperate to find out what he thought of me. Dane obviously wasn't one for playing games either, because he texted me straight away saying how much he had enjoyed our evening and that he couldn't wait to see me again. Result!

In the few weeks before he went away, I spent as many hours with him as I could. He was working with the band so it was hard finding time to be together, but I would drive up from Brighton, get to his house around midnight and spend the night with him. We were at that stage when you can't bear to be apart. All day I would be longing to see him and feel his arms around me, to kiss him, hold him and touch him. I thought about him constantly.

I have to admit it was a little bit strange staying with him at his parents' house. I would always feel awkward in the morning when I heard his mum in the kitchen and I didn't want just to look like some old trollop who was sleeping with her son. The truth is, though, that at this stage we hadn't had sex. I would make myself go downstairs and talk to her and, though we were both embarrassed at first, we soon got on fine. In fact, I got on very well with all of Dane's family right from the start, which was very important to me.

Dane also cleared up the situation between him and the girl in the photo. To my huge relief I found out that they weren't together any more. She had been his girlfriend at school when he was seventeen. When he tried to finish with her, she told him she was pregnant and that she wanted to keep the baby. Dane told me how upset he had been when she told him, and how he tried to stay with her for the child's sake. But it didn't work. He felt too young for the responsibility, and they split up. I was relieved that Dane was free to be with me, but deep inside I wished he didn't have a child. I knew it would complicate things. Even though the relationship was finished, I felt jealous of Dane's past – the fact that he had a child seemed like a threat to me.

Throughout his American trip Dane called and texted me all the time, which was so reassuring. I wasn't just imagining it: there was something strong between us. While he was out there a tabloid reported that I had fallen in love with him and that I was desperate for him to propose to me. I was a bit unsure about what Dane would make of this, but deep down

I didn't care. I *had* fallen in love with him. True, I'd only known him for a few weeks, but I was convinced he was the one for me and I knew he felt the same.

I couldn't wait for him to get back. When he finally did it was wonderful. We were just like teenagers in love. He had bought me a really cute Mickey Mouse T-shirt and a bottle of Jean Paul Gaultier perfume. He had remembered my passion for perfumes, and I was touched.

We saw each other whenever we could, but I never felt it was like my relationship with Warren where he had always tagged along after me and I had called the shots. Dane was very much his own man, with his own career and ambitions. I admired him for that as much as for his singing and songwriting talent. For the first time, I had met a man who was my equal, someone with whom I could at last be myself.

Both his looks and personality drew me to him. He was a bit like me in some ways: like me he was very upfront and said what he thought about his feelings; like me he didn't keep anything back, and he refused to play games. He was a strong character who knew his own mind. He also wanted to know the truth about everything. I couldn't keep anything from him. He could also make me laugh, and there's nothing more sexy than a man who can do that. It was so refreshing being with him.

Even though we were wildly attracted to each other, it was over a month before we finally made love. Dane was desperate to get me into bed. He would say, 'How much longer do you expect me to wait?' But I resisted. I wanted to make him wait because of my job and my image. I didn't want to think that Dane just wanted to shag Jordan. I had to believe that he wanted me, Katie. If he really likes me, I thought, then he'll wait, and if he doesn't then he isn't worth having.

I'm sure he would agree, even after all that has happened between us, that it was worth waiting for. Out of all the lovers I've had, I had some of the most adventurous sex with Dane. True, he had the smallest willy, and his body could have done with some serious toning, but I loved him, and when you love someone you don't expect their body to be perfect. I admit it was strange having sex with him after Warren, who definitely had the best physique of any lover I've had, and at first I did miss his powerful and muscular body (and, if I'm honest, his bigger willy), but Dane was definitely a better lover in terms of trying new things, and he was much better with his hands.

At the start of our romance, the only downside was his past relationship. This is going to sound awful, but the honest truth is that I didn't like him seeing his son. I was paranoid that, when Dane went to visit him, his ex would try and get back with him. I felt she really wanted to. She was forever telling Dane she didn't want her son being involved with someone like me. It was pretty rich given that she didn't even know me, and I retaliated by slagging her off to Dane. I know it really upset him. He ended up feeling like piggy in the middle because he wanted me to get on with his son.

The whole situation made me feel jealous and insecure. I wouldn't be like that now, of course, but then I felt threatened by anyone who had a hold on Dane. I shouldn't have been so selfish, and I regret being like that. Looking back, I think Dane put me before his son, which was wrong.

He used to say that he wouldn't see his son because he knew that I didn't like it. A child should always come first.

Apart from that, ours seemed like a perfect relationship. We were so well-matched: we had the same taste in music, and in clothes; we liked going out to the same places; we got on with each other's family. As well as having a great physical relationship, we were emotionally close and could talk for hours. Above all, I knew I didn't have to put on an act for him. I didn't have to be a full-on glamour model the whole time. He actually preferred me with no make-up on, and liked it when I dressed as casually as possible.

After a few months we moved in together. I was renting a flat with Sally Cairns, my friend and make-up artist, and knew she couldn't afford it if I moved out, so the perfect solution was for Dane to move in. We were both very excited to be living together, as we hated being apart.

I felt so comfortable with him, knowing that however I looked he would still love me. He was also very demonstrative, always giving me cuddles in front of other people. Whenever he had a DJ set, he would make sure that his mates watched out for me; at home he would cook fantastic meals. I felt completely loved.

CHAPTER FOURTEEN

TORN BETWEEN TWO LOVERS...

Dane seemed perfect, but something – or rather someone – was still nagging at the back of my mind: the multimillionaire Formula 1 driver Ralf Schumacher. After our disastrous time together in Germany when he had practically frogmarched me out of his house, we did see each other again at Grand Prix races and gradually he stopped ignoring me. Our old flirtation sparked up and I was left wondering what this handsome sportsman really thought of me. Then one day, out of the blue, he phoned to invite me to stay with him in America. I didn't know what to do. I was with Dane, and even though the relationship was in its early stages, I really did love him to bits. But doubts started to eat away at me. What if I was meant to be with Ralf? There was a definite chemistry between us, and I was impressed that he still wanted to know me after all the rubbish in the papers. I believed that, if I was going to settle down with Dane, then I had to know where I stood with Ralf once and for all.

After agonising for a few days, I decided that I would fly out and see him. I couldn't tell Dane the truth but I didn't want to lie to his face, so I decided I would just leave and then make up some excuse when I was in the States. The night before I left I felt awful getting into bed with Dane knowing that I was going to see Ralf. As we made love, I felt like a traitor. I was struck again by how much I felt for Dane, and I nearly blurted out my plans. But something stopped me.

The next day as I drove away from the flat my head was pounding and I felt dizzy. I couldn't believe that I was betraying Dane like this. God knows how he would react when he found out I had gone away. On the way to the airport I texted him, telling him I was going away for a week because I had a lot on my mind and needed space to think. He was obviously shocked and kept trying to ring me to find out what was going on. But I kept cutting him off, saying I couldn't talk but that I'd be back soon. I knew that if I spoke to him directly I would never get on that plane. I felt terrible because he sounded desperate. Suddenly flying out to see Ralf seemed like a really bad idea. What if there was nothing between me and him? What if I was throwing away my relationship with Dane?

On the plane I sent my final text to Dane before take-off. What the hell am I doing? I thought. I love this man, why am I hurting him like this? I'm being a complete bitch, lying to him and going away. I knew that if he found out I was seeing another man it would absolutely break his heart. The cabin crew hadn't shut the doors yet, and I kept thinking, Shall I get off now, go back home and pretend none of this ever happened? But I didn't move. I just sat there tormenting myself by going over everything.

As soon as the plane took off I suddenly thought, Oh my God, it is Dane I want. My eyes filled with tears as I listened to his album through my headphones. I couldn't believe I was doing this. Then I tried to tell myself that I had to see how it went with Ralf, that there must be something there. It was as if there were two people fighting inside me – typical Gemini! One was saying, 'Just go, think of the lifestyle you'll have if you get together with Ralf.' The other didn't agree. 'Forget the lifestyle,' it said. 'Follow your heart, it's Dane you really want.'

When I landed at Miami airport I felt emotionally drained. I just wanted to see Ralf and know that I had made the right decision. But typically for me I got lost. In the end I had to phone up my mum and ask her to call Ralf on his mobile and tell him where I was because my phone didn't work in the States. It was like a farce. In the end it took about an hour to meet up with him, and by then I was feeling more and more like I shouldn't have abandoned Dane.

As soon as I saw Ralf waiting for me, looking so handsome with his gorgeous blue eyes, I felt torn by my desire for him and guilt for what I was doing to Dane. He kissed me on the cheek and said he was going to fly us back to the hotel in his helicopter. 'Sure,' I said, trying to sound as if I always went by helicopter! As we flew to the hotel, I could have wept. I just wanted to fly back to Dane, tell him I loved him and never let him go.

We were staying at the Ritz in Miami, and Ralf had an

entire floor to himself. It was incredibly luxurious with gorgeous furniture and panoramic views of the coast. Ralf made it clear that I could have absolutely anything I wanted – any food, any drink, any kind of beauty treatment. It was a bit like being Julia Roberts in *Pretty Woman*. As I took in my glamorous surroundings, I began to wonder what would happen that night. Would I be sleeping in the same bed as Ralf? And, if I did, would he try and make love to me? If our previous encounters were anything to go by then probably not. I half-wanted something to happen, and half-not; I found him so attractive and I wanted to know that he felt the same way about me, but I couldn't bear the thought of being unfaithful to Dane. The trouble was, I wanted both men.

I tried to relax by taking a long bath in the beautiful marble bathroom, but when I started to reapply my make-up in the mirror I could hardly bear to look at myself. What kind of person was I who could do this to the man she loved? I started crying and my mascara ran down my face, so I had to put it on all over again. I had to pull myself together. I quickly got dressed in a tight T-shirt, tight jeans and heels and walked into the lounge. Ralf told me I looked gorgeous. I smiled and tried to make a comment about how good he looked, but could hardly get the words out. I blamed it on the jet lag and asked him to fix me a drink – anything to get me through the night.

He asked me if I was hungry, and I pretended I was. The food was exquisite, and he ordered the best-quality champagne, but I couldn't eat. Ralf was flirtatious and attentive, but I couldn't respond, my heart felt so heavy. I felt sick with anxiety about what Dane would be thinking, wishing that I was back in our flat. The wonderful hotel meant absolutely nothing to me. I was starting to feel out of place and self-conscious. Suddenly I thought that I was wearing the wrong clothes, I should have dressed up more. Instead of being able to flirt and chat with Ralf like I usually did, I clammed up. I didn't want to say anything stupid. I kept waiting for Ralf to make a move on me but he didn't. I couldn't understand him. Surely he fancied me, otherwise why was I here?

That night I spent ages in the bathroom, taking off my make-up and wondering what the night had in store. Half of me hoped that Ralf would be asleep when I got into bed and that way I could avoid any physical contact with him; the other half hoped that he might finally demonstrate his passion for me.

I came out of the bathroom wearing nothing but my black lacy underwear: if this didn't have some effect on him, then I didn't know what would. Ralf was already in bed. He wasn't asleep. I pulled back the sheet and got in next to him. I was a bit shocked when I saw what he was wearing – a pair of the tightest Lycra boxers I have ever seen. I'll just say they left nothing to the imagination! I made a big deal about how exhausted I was. He must have taken the hint because he simply leaned over, kissed me, said goodnight and switched off the light. As I lay back under the expensive linen sheets, I felt a mixture of disappointment and relief.

In the morning Ralf got up before me to go to his flying lesson. He told me one of his friends would take me shopping and that I could get anything I wanted. As soon as he left I leaped out of bed and rang my mum. She told me Dane had been ringing her non-stop to find out where I was. I told her to phone him and tell him that I was coming home soon. She tried to get me to calm down, told me to stay and enjoy myself, but I said it was impossible. Then I called Sam Bond my agent to tell her I'd be away for a couple of days, but would be back soon. Dane had even been ringing her in his desperation to find out where I was. What was I doing to him? It was torture to be so far away. I put the phone down and lay on the bed crying.

I tried to snap out of it: I couldn't let Ralf see me like this. I got dressed, disguised my reddened eyes with make-up and put on my shades. Then I went out shopping with his friend. I wasn't interested in any of the designer clothes or jewellery, I just wanted to buy a mobile phone so I could text Dane. I bought the first one I saw, and £200 worth of credit. I was desperate to let him know that I still loved him and that I'd be back soon. But to my horror the line was down and the phone didn't work. It was like a bad dream. I just knew that if only I could text Dane then I could concentrate on what I really felt for Ralf. The fact that I couldn't get hold of him was making it impossible for me to relax and enjoy myself.

When Ralf returned to the hotel, he told me he was taking me out to dinner to one of the most exclusive restaurants in Miami. Immediately I started to panic about what to wear. Usually I'm pretty confident about what clothes look good on me but now, because of my state of mind, I couldn't decide. In the end I went for a tight black top, short skirt and heels.

The restaurant was superb but yet again I could barely eat

a thing, which was completely out of character for me. I just picked at the food and knocked back the wine instead. Ralf must have thought I had undergone a complete personality transplant. Usually I'm outspoken and flirtatious; now I was like a shadow, going through the motions. Over dinner Ralf asked me if I would like to fly to a private island to have lunch the next day. 'That would be perfect,' I lied. I was starting to feel I would go mad if I didn't speak to Dane soon.

As I slid into bed later, I thought, If nothing happens tonight, I have to go back to Dane. I can't go on like this. Then Ralf started kissing me. At last, I thought, kissing him back. He started touching my body. I closed my eyes and lightly caressed his back. I wanted to lose myself in the moment, finally to get close to him, but it just wasn't working. He was touching me but it didn't feel like he really meant it. Finally he put his hand on my breast, but there was nothing sexual about it. It was like he put it there because he felt he should. He just didn't seem to know what to do with me. I would love to have shown him, but my feelings for Dane held me back.

After a while he kissed me again, said goodnight and turned over to go to sleep. I couldn't work out what was going on in Ralf's head. Why didn't he seem to want to make love to me? Usually the men I go out with can't wait to get me into bed. Maybe Ralf wanted to take things really slowly. But I couldn't wait any longer. As I lay next to him listening to him breathing, I thought, I have to go home. The plan was for me to stay at least a week, but I couldn't bear to stay any longer. I felt I would go insane if I had to spend another day in this luxurious hotel with a man who was treating me like a princess but not showing what he felt about me.

The next day Ralf had another flying lesson. Straight away I was on the phone to my mum. She told me that Dane had called her again and said that I had hurt him so much that he didn't know if he could carry on the relationship. I was distraught. 'Mum,' I cried. 'Please tell him I want him, that I'm coming back. I'm counting on you.'

As soon as I had put the phone down, I booked myself a flight home for later that day and frantically packed my suitcase. When Ralf returned to the hotel I pretended that I'd received an urgent call about an important job and that I had to go home immediately. He appeared shocked and asked me if I really had to do it. I replied that I did, but I promised to fly straight back out to him. And all the time I wanted to scream, 'Why won't you tell me what you think of me?'

As I said goodbye to Ralf, he was still saying, 'Do you really want to do this job?' Now I was starting to have second thoughts. If I went home now, what would I be throwing away? If only Ralf would make his feelings clear to me, then I would know what to do. But when he kissed me goodbye there was no real passion in his kiss. The man was a complete enigma.

Gentleman that he was, he arranged for a car to take me to the airport. As I drove off I felt like I was in a movie. I had just said goodbye to a guy who had everything and who could give me the most amazing lifestyle. I would never have to work again. I'd be able to do whatever I wanted, have whatever I wanted. I would be treated like a princess.

As soon as I'd checked in, I called my mum. I told her to ring Dane and tell him to meet me at Heathrow and that if he wasn't there I would know it was all over between us. But, as the plane took off, it wasn't Dane I was thinking about. I had been desperate to get back and see him, but now I realised I was making a mistake leaving Ralf. I should have stayed to find out what he thought of me. All the way over to the States I had thought about Dane; all the way back I thought about Ralf.

I knew I had to stop obsessing over Ralf because when I saw Dane again I couldn't reveal where I had been. But, after I walked through customs, I couldn't see him. I was surrounded by couples and families embracing, but there was no Dane. My heart sank. That's it, I thought. I've completely blown it with both men. Now Dane doesn't want to know me. I just wanted to collapse into a corner and cry, but by force of habit I wandered into a shop and picked up some papers. Then I heard a familiar voice. 'I've got the papers in the car.' I spun round; it was Dane. I ran into his arms and we kissed passionately.

Then Dane pulled away and said, 'So where were you then?' I told him I had been staying with my aunt in Miami, that work had really been getting on top of me and I needed a bit of space. Fortunately he believed me. I felt like a total bitch, but I was also relieved. I was back with the man I loved. We drove back to the flat, went straight to bed and made love for hours.

CHAPTER FIFTEEN

FROM THE HEART

So I had chosen Dane, but Ralf was still there in the back of my mind and every now and then I would wonder about him. It was like an itch that wouldn't quite go away. But my relationship with Dane was so full on and passionate that there wasn't really much time for brooding over anyone else.

Now I was with Dane, I could see how destructive and warped my early relationships had been. We were terrible romantics and were always leaving love letters for each other and buying little presents. I would always buy him candles so we could have baths by candlelight. He even bought a dog for me because he knew how much I loved animals and how I had been wanting one for ages. He was so thoughtful.

He was definitely the most romantic lover I've ever had. One time we were on holiday in Cancun, Mexico and we were window shopping. I saw this beautiful necklace – a heart with a diamond – and I tried it on, never dreaming that I would own it. Dane said it looked stunning, but I thought no more about it.

Then a few days later back in London it was Valentine's Day. Dane told me to be ready by eight and not to be late. I was getting dressed and there was a knock at the door. It was Dane's driver, but no Dane. He asked me to get in the car and inside on the back seat there was a big cuddly toy rabbit, a bunch of red roses, a card and a jewellery box. I opened it and inside was the necklace. I was so touched. But the surprises weren't over. We drove to the Bluebird restaurant on the Kings Road and there was Dane standing outside waiting for me. He gave me a kiss, and in the lift on the way up to the restaurant he put the necklace on me. It was a perfect moment.

We had a wonderful meal together and I thought the night would end there, but when we got in the car he said that we had one more stop – The Dorchester. He had booked a suite. He made me open the door first and I couldn't believe my eyes. The room was lit by lots of pink candles and filled with pink balloons that he had spent hours blowing up! He knew that I loved pink. And in the middle of the bed there was an even bigger cuddly rabbit holding a bottle of champagne with two glasses. It was so romantic.

The emotional bond between us was incredibly strong. Sexually, too, we were a perfect match. We knew exactly how to turn each other on. I'm not being big-headed, but I definitely think I fulfilled his sexual fantasies. I would regularly turn our lounge into a love pad: I would light candles everywhere, close the curtains and shut out the world so it was just me and my lover. I would go through my massive collection of sexy lingerie, choosing the outfit which I knew would have the most impact. Stockings, suspenders and lacy thongs usually did the trick, or if I was feeling particularly naughty I would take everything off and put on my long black leather boots. It was guaranteed to get Dane going. I loved planning a night of pleasure.

'Come on, I've got a surprise for you,' I would say to Dane. I'd put on a porno film, and gradually and seductively strip to reveal my sexy underwear. I would make him lie on the sofa next to me and as we watched the film we'd start caressing and teasing each other with our hands, mouths and with sex toys. Finally we'd get ourselves into such a frenzy of desire he'd take me from behind, him on top, me on top – you name the position, we tried it. It was mind-blowing. With him I could be totally uninhibited, I could lose myself in desire and tell him exactly what I wanted. I really let myself go.

I loved the fact that I could be so free with him and do the things that really turned me on without being judged. I've always liked sex toys, and with Dane I was able to use them as part of our love-making to add to our mutual pleasure. I regularly raided Ann Summers for new models, and eventually built up a collection of about fifteen!

I also let him fulfil the ultimate male fantasy. I had a threesome with him and another woman. Once I had got Dane going sexually, there was nothing stopping him. One night after we had made love, we were lying wrapped in each other's arms and he asked me if I would do something for him. When he whispered what it was I wasn't sure how to react. It might have been his ultimate fantasy, but it certainly wasn't mine. I agreed, hoping that he'd forget about it. But, of course, he didn't and one night he got his chance. By then we had our own flat together. It was late and we had just got back from a night out with a close friend of mine. We had all been drinking and back at the flat we carried on, becoming more and more outrageously drunk. Suddenly Dane leaned over to where I was sitting with my friend. He raised his eyebrows suggestively and said, 'How about having that threesome then?'

If I had been sober, my first reaction would have been, No way. But I was so drunk that I had lost all my inhibitions and I thought, Why not? You'll be disappointed to learn that I can't really remember very much about it – it was all in a drunken haze. I remember watching Dane kiss my friend and feeling a mixture of jealousy and excitement. At some point we must have taken off our clothes. Dane seemed to be getting the most pleasure of all of us, especially when my friend went down on him. Then came the bit he'd been waiting for. My friend and I started kissing and touching each other. I didn't let her get too intimate with me, but I caressed her breasts for a while and then got more adventurous and turned her on using one of the sex toys. I felt like I was putting on a show for him more than doing something for myself.

But what should have been the erotic highlight of Dane's life turned into a complete laugh, because one of us managed to spill red wine all over the new cream carpet. Instead of concentrating on the sex, we were more worried about clearing up the mess.

I only had that one threesome with Dane, and it was definitely something I did for him rather than myself. I'd never do girl-on-girl on my own. But that wasn't the only fantasy I fulfilled for him. The other thing he longed to do was film us having sex. Being a total exhibitionist, and being used to the camera, I was definitely more into this idea. So when Dane came home with a video camera and a big grin on his face, I knew instantly what he had in mind. But again it took a lot of alcohol to get me in the right mood. We were drinking with another good friend of mine and told her she had to be the camera woman. She took a lot of persuading because, although she is a model like me, she is also quite shy, and if she hadn't had a few drinks she would have been much too embarrassed. When Dane and I got down to it, he kept telling her what to film and when to zoom in. Poor girl, she was desperate for us to finish and kept saying 'Hurry up!', which didn't exactly create an erotic mood. I think Dane took it more seriously than me – because my friend was there I found it more of a laugh than a turn-on.

There is no doubt that in the beginning I was blissfully happy with Dane. Of course, we would argue – ours was a very passionate relationship and there were times when we would be at each other's throat. But it was never for very long. If we had a row, he would always go and sit in the car and text me to tell me to come out and talk. I would say to Sally, 'I'm just going out to the car for a while,' and we'd both try not to laugh. Another time, Sally and I had gone with him to a club where he was DJ'ing. We really didn't like the club because it was much too indie for our tastes, so we sat in the ladies' drinking champagne and getting pissed. The next thing we knew, the music had stopped and the cleaner had come into the toilets. Dane was looking everywhere for us and was convinced we'd gone off with some other blokes. When he finally tracked us down he had a massive go at me. He told his driver to take me straight home and I was drunkenly saying, 'No way, take me to the airport, I'm going to Tenerife to see my mate Neil, he doesn't treat me like this.' But, of course, I ended up going home with Dane, and we soon made up.

It wasn't long before Dane and I decided we wanted to have our own place – just the two of us. We gave Sally plenty of time to find her own flat and then Dane and I moved in together in Fulham.

I did hear from Ralf again, and terrible as this sounds I wanted to see him. Even though I had chosen to come back to Dane I thought I should take Sally to meet Ralf to see what she thought of him, just in case I was making a huge mistake. Also I felt that, if I was with Sally, I would be able to be more like myself, not so self-conscious. So we decided that we would tell Dane we were going away for a weekend shopping trip. Really we were going to see Ralf in Austria. I left it to Sally to book the tickets, as I didn't want Dane to find out. When I told Dane our plans, he really didn't want me to go. 'Don't be silly, babe,' I told him, 'we're only going shopping.'

I felt guilty, but also excited. But at the airport, when we tried to collect our tickets, we discovered that Sally's credit card had been over the limit and so had been declined. Originally the tickets were going to cost £150 each, but if we wanted to get them now they were going to be £700 each. I didn't have enough cash on me to cover them, and I didn't want to use my credit card in case Dane found out. I agonised over what to do, but in the end decided not to go. I called Ralf and left a message on his answerphone explaining what had happened and that we couldn't get on a flight. I don't think that went down very well because a few hours later he left a message which made it clear he didn't believe me and that I was messing him around. After that he didn't call, and when I saw him at Grand Prix races we barely spoke. If only I had gone to Austria, who knows what might have happened between us. Perhaps Ralf would have finally revealed his feelings for me. When I found out a few years later that he had got married and had a child, I was absolutely gutted: I knew that might have been me.

When I look back at this time, I can't help wishing things had worked out between me and Ralf, because what happened next with Dane probably counts as one of the worst experiences of my life. The more involved we became, the more my work caused conflict between us. I was mainly doing glamour shoots for glossy lads' mags like *Loaded* and *Maxim*, and was still working for papers like the *Star*. It was no different from the work I was doing before we were together, and Dane had even been out with glamour models before so he knew what to expect. But he grew to hate what I did. He hated me showing off my body and he hated the fact that other men would be looking at pictures of me. We started having terrible rows that tore us apart.

He would go mad and become aggressive. 'Why do you have to flaunt your boobs? You could do better than that. I don't want other men leering at you in your underwear.' Then he would lay it on really thick, asking me how I could bear to show off my body like I did knowing that men would

147

be masturbating with my pictures in front of them. He would go on and on about how he hated me being Jordan.

My heart would sink, and I would try to pacify him saying, 'It's just my job. You knew what I did when I met you. You're the only one who gets to see the real me, I promise.'

But increasingly he couldn't handle it. I started to dread new pictures of me being published. Dane would come storming home holding up the magazine or newspaper, furious and upset. He hated the pictures and he hated it if I did any interviews where I talked about sex. What was I supposed to be talking about in my line of work, the economy? I would try and reason with him, but it was pointless. Inside I started to burn with anger at the way he was treating me. At those times I thought I hated him and that I wanted to leave him. The pictures weren't even that revealing. I couldn't believe that Dane was behaving exactly like all my other boyfriends. It was such a predictable and depressing pattern.

My work caused such problems between us that at times I was tempted to give up my job for him; but I am so used to my independence and paying for myself that I couldn't imagine relying on anyone else, even if it was the man I loved. I've always had my own money, and no man has ever known how much I earn. I intend to keep it that way. Also, I loved my work. I didn't want to stay at home doing nothing, it's just not in my nature. But I did turn down jobs for him. There was a calendar I was supposed to do and Dane didn't want it released because I was going to look too sexy (which was the idea, after all). He ended up phoning my agent and the photographer and said he would pay them but he didn't want the calendar to be published. To keep him happy I went along with it. I was also asked to audition for American *Playboy* but I turned that down, even though it had been one of my long-held ambitions. I knew there was no way on this earth Dane would let me do it.

Dane kept saying he didn't mind supporting me, and he went on and on at me to give up my work. We just went round and round in circles arguing about it. I would say, 'So you're trying to make me choose between you and my modelling?'

'Yes.' He wouldn't listen when I said to him that I would never ask him to give up his job. I told him that when he was in the band lots of women fancied and fantasised about him. And when he was DJ'ing he would have loads of girls crowding round the box trying to get off with him. He said that it was totally different because he kept his clothes on. He wouldn't have it when I pointed out that it wasn't *that* different from my work because of the sexy dance routines the band did with the scantily clad dancers. It was an argument that just wouldn't go away. Even his mum took my side, saying that I shouldn't put up with him telling me what to do and if it carried on I should leave him.

Eventually I said that, if he showed me more commitment, I would consider giving up work. But he replied that he wouldn't marry me unless I gave up my job. I couldn't accept this ultimatum: at the very least we would need to get engaged. I wasn't going to give up my job and then wait for him to marry me, without any guarantee that he actually would. I had worked hard to achieve my success, and I knew that if I did leave modelling it would be hard to get back into it.

But it wasn't just my work. He was becoming more and

more possessive over me. He hated me going out with my friends because he was paranoid about me flirting with any other men. He would phone or text me every five minutes to find out what I was up to; even when I was working he'd be checking up on me all the time. When we went out together I couldn't leave his side for a second – he would even follow me to the loo to make sure I wasn't meeting another bloke. If I so much as looked at another man, he'd have a go, saying, 'What are you staring at him for?' And he got really angry if I wore anything too revealing, especially if I was going out without him. He tried to stop me wearing any cleavage-showing tops or miniskirts, but he was certainly fighting a losing battle with me when it came to clothes! I can laugh about it now, but at the time it was stressful.

Usually Dane's outbursts were verbal, but once he did lose it so badly with me that he unintentionally knocked me unconscious. After a night out we were driving back to our flat and I wanted to go on to a party to meet some friends of mine. He didn't want me to, and was getting more and more wound up about it. When we got out of the car he grabbed me and pushed me violently against the door to the flat, slamming my head against it. The next thing I knew I was lying on the floor looking up at everyone, totally dazed. The people with us were asking me if I was alright, and I remember thinking that I couldn't get up and I couldn't speak. I was helped to my feet and managed somehow to walk to the flat. I had been here before with Jeff, and I never wanted to go to that dark place where I was afraid of someone again.

And something else had changed – our sex life. Now that I had broadened Dane's horizons in the bedroom, he became more demanding. He got obsessed with wanting to try different things. I'm all for a bit of experimentation, but not all the time. Sometimes you just want to make love pure and simple; suddenly I felt like I was having to do things to please him and not myself. I felt like I had to put on sexy underwear because he expected it. He wanted the full works: the suspenders, the stockings, the basque, the crotchless knickers. A voice inside my head said, 'Why doesn't he want me for myself? Aren't I good enough any more?'

Often when we had sex he would go on and on about wanting to have a threesome again, and asking me to go with another girl. I had no intention of doing so, but I would say yes just to keep him happy. It got on my nerves and made me feel slightly sad. I used to think, Hang on, aren't you happy with just me now? And, because his attitude to sex was starting to piss me off, I began to admit something to myself. I secretly enjoyed using the sex toys more than having him inside me. I knew how to turn myself on.

But, even though we had our ups and downs, we both loved each other too much to leave. I kept hoping that he would learn to accept my job, and in the meantime I did everything I could to prove how much I loved him. When Another Level split, I gave him every support. He was really apprehensive about telling me the news, saying that he didn't know if I was going to want him anymore. But I told him it didn't bother me at all. I loved him for who he was, not for what he did. I told him I would be with him whatever he was doing. Looking back, it's a pity he couldn't have thought the same about me. Secretly, I was glad, because I hoped it would mean that I could have even more of him to myself.

For a while, after the band broke up and he wasn't working at all, I supported him. I just wanted him to be happy. But increasingly I was worried about how aggressive Dane could be, not just with me but with anyone he thought had offended him. He had a terrible temper and was often getting into fights. On one occasion, we were out at The Ten Rooms and the rapper Mark Morrison threw his drink over me. I think he was trying to get at Dane over an argument they'd had. I wish I'd kept my mouth shut, because when I told Dane what had happened he went ballistic and ended up having a fight with him. He was thrown out of the club and then went mad trying to smash his way back in, cutting his hand in the process. When they finally let me out of the club, I tried to calm him down but he started having a real go at me, shouting and screaming at me to let him out of the car. There was blood everywhere and he kept trying to get out to carry on the fight with Morrison. Another time he got into a fight and his nose got broken, and we had to stay in for ages so that no one saw him in that state.

I don't think he realised how much I went through for him. I would have done anything for him, but he didn't like the fact that my career seemed to be going from strength to strength. Now he had lost the band and was trying to pursue a solo career, my profile was higher than his. He had been used to getting a lot of attention from the press. That had died down, and he didn't like the fact that I was in the papers more than him. He was jealous and was often spiteful saying that I was only a two-bit model. I felt hurt and insecure. I loved him more than anything in the world; why was he treating me like this?

CHAPTER SIXTEEN
POSH?

The real downward spiral in my relationship with Dane started when he began to work with Victoria Beckham. Dane was over the moon when he found out that she had agreed to record a single with him. I don't think he could quite believe that he was going to be doing a song with a Spice Girl. Very rapidly he became obsessed with working with her. I suppose he was star-struck, simple as that. It was constantly 'Victoria this' and 'Victoria that'. To be honest, it got on my nerves.

I first saw Posh in the recording studio where she and Dane were rehearsing their song 'Out Of Your Mind'. Although she was all dressed up in designer gear, I remember thinking how rough she looked without her make-up. David Beckham was there, and in contrast he looked gorgeous. She was OK to me, not overly friendly, but what really annoyed me was how flirty she was with Dane –

153

all lippy and cheeky. I thought, You wouldn't like it if I was like that with David, would you? I wasn't jealous, but I did feel uncomfortable and left out. You just can't compete with someone like her. Apart from looks, she has everything, and in that studio she had the power: what Victoria said went.

A few weeks later, she and Dane were promoting their single heavily, flying here, there and everywhere to showcase it. They worked their arses off, and even got David to go along to one of their signings to pull the crowds in. I didn't like watching Dane doing this. I could see that people were really only interested in Victoria and David, but he was blind to it and started to think he was as important as they were. He was being an arrogant fool.

I didn't feel star-struck by Victoria, but I must admit to feeling a bit of a thrill around David. He is so good-looking, has such a fit body and is so nice with it. One night in July after Dane and Victoria had performed their single at Party in the Park, the four of us went clubbing, to Twice as Nice so Victoria could look credible on the R&B scene. Dane was DJ'ing and I was standing with the famous couple. Suddenly I felt someone take my hand and squeeze it gently as if to reassure me that I shouldn't be overawed by all the hype. It was David. I looked at him in surprise, and he was looking right back at me. Imagine how you would feel if David Beckham held your hand! Victoria was standing right next to him, so I thought I'd better keep my mouth shut. She is so incredibly possessive that, if women so much as say they fancy David, she goes mad. I would have given anything for her to disappear at that moment and leave me alone with one of the world's sexiest men. But I guess I'll never really know what David was thinking. Maybe he was showing that he understood what it was like to be caught up in Dane and Victoria's desperate bid to get to number one.

There is no doubt that both Victoria and Dane were convinced they would get to number one, and they were totally gutted – especially Dane – not to have made it. They were beaten, of course, by Spiller with 'Groovejet'. They found out where they had charted when Victoria invited us up to Manchester to see a United match. Dane turned all his anger and frustration on me. I was wearing a black backless top, which I couldn't wear a bra with, to go the match. He went mad when he saw it. He was convinced everyone would be able to see my nipples (you couldn't), and made me keep my jacket on all the time. After the match he wouldn't even let us go to the players' lounge because Teddy Sheringham was going to be there and he didn't want me to see him. I felt like saying, 'He's seen me in less than this top,' but I kept my mouth shut as I knew how aggressive Dane could get. Even when we were waiting outside the ground for our car to arrive he made me cover up in case any of the footballers caught sight of me as they went by in their coach. It was a pity, because I would have liked to have seen Teddy. I still wanted him to know that I hadn't stitched him up in the press all those years ago.

But, even though Dane was being so difficult, I still tried to be with him as often as I could, depending on my work commitments. I wanted to support him as much as I could. I remember one trip to Ibiza where the whole band, including Victoria, stayed together in a large villa. My abiding memories of Posh during that time are that: she hardly ate anything, she just picked at grilled fish and steamed vegetables; she absolutely loved getting attention from the press; and she thoroughly disliked Geri Halliwell – she made that obvious by slagging her off as we went to dinner one night.

Dane wasn't the only person to fall under Victoria's spell. His whole family did, too. She was their only topic of conversation. Whenever they were with her they would be hanging on her every word, looking all starry-eyed. It was pathetic really. There was one time when we were all in a restaurant together and they were talking about the pictures they had sent to Victoria of Dane as a kid, with funny captions they had added, just because she was ill. Why the hell are you doing that, I thought. She's only got a cold. I wanted to get up and say, 'Victoria's not that special; you look stupid falling over yourselves to get close to her.' But I didn't say anything. Inside I felt angry and left out: when I was ill I had never received that kind of attention, and I was close to them.

What upset me most, though, was the dramatic change in Dane. He started to become very critical of me, picking on what I was wearing, and things that I said. I couldn't seem to do anything right. Then he started going on about my work again, telling me that I should stop it; but now he was being so unpleasant that I was determined not to give it up. He wasn't the Dane I loved any more. He didn't seem to want to be close to me. When I wanted to have a cuddle with him, he made excuses not to and pushed me away.

Rumours started about his fidelity. A story was circulating

about him having a fling with a lap dancer from one of the clubs in Ibiza where he and Victoria had appeared. Dane denied it, and I wanted to believe him, but I wasn't sure. I longed for things between us to improve. Then I found out I was pregnant.

Immediately I was confused about what to do. Even though we seemed to have hit a rough patch, I loved Dane so much that one part of me was desperate to have his child; but then I thought about other things – like Ralf. If I went ahead and had Dane's child, it really would mean closing the door on any chance of seeing him again. Then there was my career. There were so many things I felt I hadn't done yet and that I wanted to do. I thought about what it would be like not working, having to rely on someone else, and it scared me. I had grown used to a very good standard of living – when I wanted something, I just went out and bought it – and I didn't ever want to struggle.

I told Dane the news as we were lying in bed together. He was a bit shaken. 'What shall we do?' he asked me.

'What do you want to do?'

'Let's have the baby.'

Oh no, I thought. Is this really what I want?

But Dane was suddenly so excited and happy. He phoned his parents and they were over the moon; he even started talking about how we could decorate the nursery. I can't let him down, I thought. I tried to look happy, but inside I was in turmoil.

Pretty soon Dane had told everyone our news, including Victoria. One Saturday she and Dane were booked to do *SM:tv* and I went along with them. In front of Dane,

Victoria said, 'Congratulations about the baby.' But later she took me to one side, and I assumed she was going to give me a bit of friendly advice about the pregnancy. Instead she said, 'Is this really what you want? Don't tell Dane I'm telling you this, but if I were you I would think carefully about having a baby, because they take up so much time and can really get in the way of your career.'

As it turned out, she needn't have bothered giving me any advice, because things deteriorated so much between Dane and me that I began to realise that I couldn't possibly have a baby with him. Much as I didn't want to admit it, the truth was that he didn't seem to love me like he used to. The relationship that I had thought would last for ever was falling apart at the seams. I began to wonder seriously how much longer I would be with Dane. Did I really want to be a single mother? I'd already seen what he was like as a father – he hardly saw his son – and, when I told him I was pregnant, he hadn't asked me to marry him. Perhaps if he had, things would have been different. It was becoming clear that he was no longer so committed to me. It was an agonising time; and then I found out something else.

I received a phone call from a friend of mine who works at the *Mirror*. I remember hearing the words she had to say and not really taking them in. I felt giddy and sick. They had pictures of Dane. Pictures of him kissing another woman. That woman was Sarah Bosnich, whose marriage to the then Manchester United goalkeeper, Mark Bosnich, had broken up. It had apparently happened when Dane and Victoria had been in Magaluf, a trip I couldn't go on. I was devastated.

Inside I was screaming, 'No, it can't be. Not Dane.' I know how the papers can get things wrong, so maybe it wasn't true. But pictures can't usually lie. When I confronted Dane, he denied it. I didn't know what to think. I so wanted to believe him, and I tried to carry on as normal, but it wasn't easy. Then he told me that he and Victoria had to go to Amsterdam. 'Take me with you,' I pleaded. I knew that Victoria would be taking Sarah Bosnich along, and I couldn't bear the thought of anything happening between her and Dane. I begged him to let me come, but he said it wasn't possible. Usually he wanted me to go with him, so it seemed very suspicious that he didn't this time. I was furious and hurt, and now I was convinced that there was definitely something going on between him and Sarah.

I was an emotional wreck. I knew I couldn't have the baby with our relationship in the state it was. I didn't feel strong enough. Having an abortion wasn't a decision I took lightly – I don't think any woman does – but sadly I knew it was the only thing I could do. When I told Dane I couldn't have the baby, he was still so wrapped up in his work with Victoria that he didn't try to stop me. I sat at the clinic for the consultation prior to having the termination feeling more alone than I ever had in my life. Everyone else was with their boyfriends, but it seemed to me that Dane had decided that doing a television show was more important than supporting me. I felt numb with grief. I couldn't believe how much Dane had changed from being a wonderfully warm, loving person who wouldn't let anything hurt me, into this man who only cared about appearing on television. In desperation I texted him saying that I wished he was here with me, that I felt really hurt. He just replied, 'Don't be like that.'

From then on, things completely fell apart between us. Having the abortion was like sounding the death of our relationship. I was instantly filled with regret for getting rid of the baby; but Dane had changed, and at that time in my life there was no way I wanted to be a single mum. I am still haunted by that baby, but there is no way I could have kept it.

Even though I felt so unhappy, I had to carry on working. I had a shoot booked with the *Star* – just for swimwear, nothing too revealing. Dane found out about it and went into one of his mad, aggressive rages. 'If you do that shoot,' he shouted, 'that's it! Our relationship is over.' I didn't believe he was serious, and in any case I was feeling so hurt and confused by his behaviour that I wasn't going to be ordered what to do. So, without telling him, I went ahead and did the shoot.

The day my pictures appeared in the paper he called me. 'That's it,' he said. 'We're finished. I don't want to know you any more.' I was stunned. How could he throw away our relationship and all that we had gone through over a few pictures? He couldn't mean it.

Frantically I said, 'Please let me see you. Please, it can't be over.'

'It is,' was all he would say. I felt like my world had caved in.

I begged him to let me see him one last time. Reluctantly he agreed to let me pick him up from the Sanderson Hotel where he was doing a shoot with Victoria. I was in such a state I don't know how I managed to drive there. As soon as I saw him I could tell from his face it was over. He got into the car beside me, but he wouldn't look at me and he wouldn't touch me. I was crying hysterically, pleading with him not to leave me. He just kept saying, 'It's over, Kate.'

'No it isn't!' I screamed back. 'It can't be.'

I drove us back to our flat and begged him to come inside. I felt that if I could get him there and hold him in my arms he would change his mind. But he refused, and when I tried to embrace him he pushed me away saying, 'Don't touch me.' I couldn't bear it. However bad things had got between us, I still loved him more than anything else in the world. He tried to get out of the car but I wouldn't let him. I was so desperate to be with him that I said I would drive him back to his mum's.

When we arrived, he simply got out and slammed the door without saying a word. I sat there sobbing, hoping that he would come back out and tell me it had all been a mistake. I waited and waited, but he didn't come. Eventually I left.

I truly believed that Dane was the love of my life. I was devastated that I had lost him.

CHAPTER SEVENTEEN

FALLING APART

I opened the door to our flat and collapsed sobbing to the floor. I couldn't – wouldn't – believe that our relationship was over. As I lay there I thought, If I can't be with Dane, I don't know if I can go on. I picked myself up and staggered to the bathroom. I opened the cabinet and grabbed a bottle of pills. I wanted oblivion, and it wanted it now. I started shoving pills into my mouth, washing them down with water. It was making me retch, but I kept forcing them down. If I take all these, I thought, then he'll realise how much I love him and how much I want to be with him, and he'll come back to me.

I don't know how many pills I had taken, but suddenly my heart started racing wildly. I felt faint, dizzy, out of control. I was frightened. I crawled to the bedroom where I managed to pick up the phone and call Sally. She was horrified when I told her what I'd done. I wasn't making any sense and was crying hysterically. I curled up on the bed clutching a photograph of Dane and me. The room was spinning and I was slipping in and out of consciousness. I could still hear Sally on the phone asking me if I was all right. I tried to speak, but I couldn't. I blacked out.

The next thing I knew, the doorbell was ringing and ringing. I tried to drag myself off the bed, but my body wouldn't obey me. The bell kept on ringing. Somehow I crawled to the door and opened it. Two paramedics were standing there. Immediately they started examining me and questioning me about what I'd taken, but by now I couldn't speak. I was still holding on to the picture. They tried to ease it out of my fingers, but I wouldn't let go of it.

Then Sally arrived looking frantic with worry, closely followed by Dane who showed no emotion. He didn't even come up and comfort me. If I thought I could change his mind, I was wrong. I was rushed to hospital in an ambulance, which I later discovered Dane had called, but if he still felt anything for me he wasn't showing it.

At the hospital, they hooked me up to a heart monitor, gave me some kind of injection and made me drink charcoal to neutralise the drugs. Sally was sitting by the bed, holding my hand and trying to soothe me. Dane was standing in the corner.

'I'm sorry,' I pleaded with him. 'I love you.' I said it over and over again. But he said nothing. Eventually I saw Sally mouthing at him, 'Hold her hand', and he came over and did that. But even in my out-of-it state, I could tell that he didn't want to be there. Eventually my mum turned up. I was so glad to see her. I just wanted her to tell me everything was going to be all right, even though I knew it couldn't be. Dane had left me, and he wasn't coming back.

My world had fallen apart. The overdose was just the start of it. In the weeks and months following our break-up I hit absolute rock bottom. I couldn't eat; I couldn't sleep; I cried all the time. I couldn't believe it was over between us. It would have been easier if I could have hated him, but I didn't. I still loved him.

Mum wanted me to move back to Brighton, but I didn't want her to see how upset I was. So I decided I'd move in with Sally. First, though, I had to get my stuff from the flat I had shared with Dane. I made sure he was out, but it was still like torment going back to what had been our home, where I had been so happy. Numbly I packed up my things. I had arranged for all my furniture to go into storage. Then I cleaned the flat from top to bottom. By the time I had finished, and my furniture had been moved out, the whole place looked as if I had never been there. As soon as he opened the door, the fact that I had gone would hit him straight away. I suppose I was hoping that when he saw that he would realise just what he had done, and come after me.

I was an emotional wreck; not only that, when we broke up I was left with nothing. He kept the flat because he owned it, but I had seen it as my home. Now I was living out of suitcases and sleeping on Sally's floor. He kept the car which we had bought together – in fact, he still owes me about ten grand for it. His mum even kept my dog. My horse had been stabled near where we lived; now we had split and I'd moved to the other side of London with Sally, I couldn't look after him and had to pay someone to do it for me. Not only had I lost Dane, I had also lost his family who I had been so close to. I felt like my life was in ruins.

Dane had his singing to keep him busy, but I knew I couldn't just stay in London and pretend nothing had happened. In desperation I booked a holiday to Ayia Napa. The plan was that I would take Sally with me, but then she found out she had a booking that she couldn't get out of. I knew I would be totally miserable on my own, so the night before my flight I was phoning everyone I knew to see if they could come away with me. A model called Ebony, who was more of an acquaintance than a friend, said that she could come. I barely knew the girl, but I thought she'd do.

All the time I was away I thought of Dane. I went out clubbing every night, but it was no good. The sunshine and blue skies did nothing to cheer me up. I only wanted him. We were still texting each other, and I was begging him to come back to me – how he must have loved that. But he just told me he knew I wouldn't change, that I wouldn't give up my job. He seemed to be hinting that if I only would then we could be together. But I knew he was only winding me up. He didn't mean it. And, even though he had left me, he was still jealous and was convinced that I was flirting and eyeing up other men. Ebony seemed OK at the time, but of course she went on to do some story about me being disturbed and jealous – just one more person who had betrayed my trust.

Back in London I put on a brave face, but inside the pain of losing Dane was killing me. I couldn't bear to stay in and think about him. I had to go out all the time. Every time I went out I secretly hoped that I would bump into him. I pretended that I was having a laugh, but it was all an act. If anyone ever asked me if I was OK, I would say, 'Of course I am.' But I wasn't. Someone only had to mention his name and I would want to cry. Only my closest friends realised how I felt.

The only way I could get through a night out was to drink. Before Dane I never had a drink problem, but now I was on my own I really hit the bottle big time. Whenever I went out, my main aim would be to get as drunk as possible so that I could forget my broken heart. It never worked. Even when I was totally off my head and practically falling over, I still remembered him and the tears would come. Every time I had a drink, I would text Dane and tell him how much I wanted to be with him. It was such destructive behaviour. Most of the pictures of me coming out of clubs looking drunk were taken around that time. I didn't care about anything. I just wanted the pain to stop. I was spiralling out of control.

Just to add to the torment, I think Dane still loved me too. Friends would tell me that they would bump into him in clubs and he would talk about me, saying that he still loved me and that if only I would give up my job we could get back together. I didn't believe him; but I knew one way to get close to him. I texted him saying I had a surprise, and he agreed to meet me.

I spent ages getting ready, putting on my full vamp make-up – all dark smokey eyes and sexy lipgloss. Then I slid on some black fishnet stockings, a tiny black thong and a black lacy suspender belt. I finished off the outfit with high heels and a mac. I walked into the lounge where Sally was lying on the sofa. 'I'm going to see him,' I told her.

Sally looked at me in disbelief. 'You're mad. He's using you.'
'I don't care, I just want to be with him.'

I left the flat and drove to Dane's. When he opened the door, I let the mac fall open. He pulled me inside. All I wanted to do was to be close to him, to have him hold me in his arms, but he didn't show me any affection or warmth. We just had sex. When I went home, I felt empty and sad.

But I did it again and again and again. Because I loved him so much I was blind to the fact that he was just using me for sex. Every time we met up I thought he would change his mind, admit that he loved me and that we could get back together again, but I was deluding myself. And, even though we met up for sex, he was being nasty to me. He would try and stop me getting into clubs and parties that he was going to. He accused me of stalking him when we both turned up at the same events, and then wrote a bitter little song all about me called 'Shut Up And Forget About It'. I couldn't understand why he was being so vindictive.

Then I found out that he was seeing Sarah Bosnich. It was a blow. He had been unfaithful to me after all. He hated my work, but in the end it had given him an excuse to finish things with me. I couldn't bear the thought of him being with anyone else, touching them, making love with them. I carried on my cycle of self-destructive behaviour, of drinking and not eating. I grew alarmingly skinny. I looked a mess.

To add insult to injury, a kiss and tell came out in the papers by the lap dancer who claimed to have slept with Dane when we were together. He had always denied her story but, when I phoned to confront him, this time he admitted it was true. He was laughing about it. He didn't care.

One night I was out clubbing and I received a text from Dane saying that he was with Ebony and she was trying to pull him. He also said that she had slated me. 'What kind of friend do you call this?' he asked. It was almost like he was criticising me for trusting her. I couldn't bear the fact that he seemed to be taunting me. I was drunk and I saw red. I convinced myself that Dane was getting off with her. By the time I got home, I felt ready to explode with jealousy. I had to know whether they were together, so I told Sally that I was going to drive over to Dane's flat. She told me not to be so stupid, but I wouldn't see reason. I still had the keys, and I told her I was going to let myself in, catch them at it and then beat the shit out of Ebony.

Eventually Sally realised that nothing was going to make me change my mind and so she got in the car with me. God knows how we got there, we took it in turns to drive and I'm sure we were both over the limit. It's not something I would ever do again, and I know there's no excuse for it, but at that moment in time I really wasn't thinking straight.

As soon as we arrived at Dane's flat I called my friend Jodie who lived nearby and told her what I was going to do. She said she would be right over – I think she was hoping to see a big punch-up. I kept looking up at Dane's windows. The curtains were shut but the lights were off. Perhaps even as we were waiting out here, he was shagging her. I felt sick. As soon as Jodie turned up I got out of the car, leaving Sally behind as she was too scared to come in. I could hardly get the key in the lock, my hand was shaking so much. We crept inside, banging into each other as it was so dark. I led the way to the bedroom. We waited outside for a minute, trying to hear something, but there was nothing. Then, with my heart pounding, I pushed open the door and switched on the light. There was nobody there. I sat on the bed and put my head in my hands. What was I doing here, breaking into my ex-boyfriend's flat?

I didn't know whether I was relieved or disappointed not to have taken my anger and frustration out on Ebony. But where the hell was Dane? A horrible thought came into my head: maybe he was at her place. We waited for a couple of hours then headed back home. I knew I couldn't go on like this, being eaten away with hurt and jealousy. But I hadn't reached rock bottom yet.

That came on the night I was supposed to be presenting an award at the Dance Star Awards. As usual I hit the wine. I got drunk very quickly, and one part of me did wonder how I would be able to get on the stage and speak, especially as mine was the last award and I had started drinking at seven. But I just had another drink, then another and another. Dane was at the awards as well, and that was fuelling my drinking. I couldn't bear the fact that he looked as if he was enjoying himself when I still felt so terrible. From time to time I would look over to where he was sitting; he just looked back at me and shook his head as if to say, What are you doing to yourself?

Eventually it was my turn. I was just about to get up and stagger to the stage when the organisers came up to the table. I have no recollection of this, but they apparently told Sally that I couldn't possibly present an award, and they wanted me out of the building as soon as possible to prevent a scene. I could just about stand up and walk, and they practically frogmarched us out of the building and into a car. It would have been humiliating if I could actually remember anything about it; as it was I stumbled into the car and blacked out.

If that wasn't shameful enough, worse was to come when we got home. According to Sally I was drunker than she had ever seen me before. I staggered into the flat needing a wee, but I never made it to the bathroom. I went into Sally's room, sat on the edge of her bed and wet myself there and then, thinking it was the toilet.

When Sally told me what had happened the next morning, I was horrified. The fact that I had been so out of it suddenly seemed scary. What was I doing to myself? I couldn't go on like this – where was it going to end? After apologising to her, I promised myself that I would never let myself sink so low. I knew that I couldn't go on drinking like this just to forget Dane, even though I was so cut up about him. I had to find another way of dealing with it. At that moment I made a promise to myself: I would never again let a man bring me so low.

Dane was not coming back to me; that much was clear. However painful that was, it did have some advantages. Career-wise it meant I was free to pursue all my modelling ambitions. I started to put out feelers about appearing in *Playboy* – something I'd always wanted to do and which Dane had vetoed. I also went ahead and modelled for the calendar he had stopped me from doing, and because I was so hurt by his rejection I made it far raunchier than it had been originally. Then it was time to think about my boobs again. Dane loved them as they were, but after two operations I still wasn't happy with them. It wasn't so much the size as the shape: I wanted a bit more uplift. But he had put his foot down about me having any more surgery. Now I wasn't with him any more, I was free to do what I wanted.

Looking back, I think I was also desperately trying to reinvent myself, trying to get over the pain of rejection. So in November 2000, two months after we split, I booked myself in for boob job number three. Of course, I received loads of press about it – most of it negative – but I didn't care. And, while journalists were quick to criticise, the offers to show off my new boobs came pouring in. I threw myself into a frenzy of work and partying. But my heart still ached for Dane.

CHAPTER EIGHTEEN

A BIT OF ALL DWIGHT

'So can I buy you a drink?' I looked straight into the eyes of the stylish footballer and let him take my hand. I could tell by the look on his face that he fancied me.

'Yes,' I said. Why the hell not?

I was on the rebound big time. I just wanted to get Dane out of my head. That's the only possible explanation for why I ended up in the arms of my next lover. It's a relationship I totally regret, even though it gave me the most precious thing in my life – my son. It never should have happened. It wouldn't have happened if I hadn't been so messed up about Dane. But it did, and now I'm stuck with Dwight Yorke for life.

I find it difficult writing about him because he is the father of my child and for my son's sake I don't want to fall out with him, even though I think there have been times when he has treated me like dirt. Dwight's not a bad person; it's just that we never should have got involved. We weren't right for each other, and we never will be.

Before we actually met I had known for a while that he fancied me, but I never dreamed anything would happen between us. At Sol Campbell's birthday party, I had been chatting to one of Dwight's mates who told me that the footballer had the hots for me. He insisted on calling Dwight from my mobile to let him know he was with me. I think it was just a way of getting Dwight's number in my phone, but I never called him because I just wasn't interested. Back then I believed I would be with Dane forever.

A year later, things were different. I had a broken heart and needed distraction. The distraction I chose was a famous striker with Manchester United, was five foot ten and had a superb body. Oh, and he was a serial womaniser who was incapable of being faithful to any one person, but I didn't know that then.

We met at the London nightclub Attica in November 2000. I was there with my mates doing my usual thing of trying to forget Dane by drinking and pretending that everything was fine. Dwight sauntered up to me, took my hand and asked me if I would like a drink. He came across as a right smoothie, and really I should have run a mile. But I didn't. He was one of the first guys to flirt with me after Dane, and it did feel good to have a man pay attention to me. When you've been rejected, you feel that no one is ever going to like you again, so it's reassuring when you discover that someone does. I should have realised that Dwight was only after a quick shag with Jordan the glamour model, that he was never going to be interested in getting to know Katie.

But I wasn't thinking straight. I found out later that he had planned to meet me all along – or at least someone similar. He had a match down in London and had asked Ryan Giggs to tell him what clubs he should visit to meet someone like Jordan. Well, he got to meet the real thing.

It's not even as if he was my type: I'd never been into black men before. But Dwight's smooth talking won me over. And, while I don't think he's particularly good looking, he has got a certain way about him, a certain charisma and style which did attract me. So I flirted back. After Attica we went on to Emporium, and when Dwight kissed me I didn't resist; we ended up embracing passionately in the club. Later that night I dragged him to McDonald's but he wouldn't come in at first, saying he didn't eat that sort of food. 'Fine,' I told him. 'Wait outside.' Eventually he wandered in, but he didn't order anything.

It was taken as read that he would come back to my place. When we got home he ignored all the people we were with and went straight upstairs to my bedroom. I found him lying naked in bed waiting for me. I stripped down to my underwear and got in next to him. It was obvious he wanted to have sex with me straight away, but I wouldn't let him; he had to be satisfied with kissing and cuddling.

In the morning he had to be in town for a meeting and I told him I would give him a lift in. To this day, even after all our ups and downs, he still says that it was really nice of me to drive him. It's something I would have done for anyone, but maybe he wasn't used to people doing him favours. We swapped numbers but I didn't have any expectations about seeing him again. To be honest, the night we had spent together had left me feeling a bit cheap, and I regretted the fact that we ended up in bed even though we had only just met.

To my surprise his manager phoned me later that morning and asked me if I wanted to meet Dwight in the evening. It seemed odd that Dwight wasn't asking me himself, but I thought I might as well see him. I didn't think I had anything to lose. I took my friend Vanessa along and met up with Dwight and his friend Connor at their hotel. I felt a bit self-conscious after the night we had spent together, and I decided to play it cool. After what I had been through with Dane, I wasn't going to rush into anything. We had a couple of drinks and went out for dinner at a very nice restaurant – a definite improvement on McDonald's. I started to relax, and flirted the night away with Dwight.

After the meal we returned to the hotel. I knew what Dwight would have in mind, but I had no intention of spending the night with him. So, when Vanessa said she wanted to go home, I said I'd give her a lift. I could tell Dwight really wanted me to stay, but I just gave him a quick kiss on the cheek and said goodbye. As I was driving home, Dwight called me – I knew he would – and asked me to go back to the hotel and spend the night with him. I refused. You're not going to try it on with me, I thought. I'm not that easy to pull. If someone is that keen, and really likes me, they should wait. Dwight was obviously used to getting his own way because he kept on at me, but I resisted.

After that night we began to see each other, but it was a relationship like no other I'd had before. I just couldn't tell how serious Dwight was about me. Ralf aside, I'm used to relationships that are passionate right from the start. I wasn't sure where I stood with him, so I carried on partying, clubbing and drinking.

But, before things had a chance to progress with Dwight, I met another footballer. What is it with me and footballers? We seem to be irresistibly attracted to each other, like moths to the flame! Who knows how things might have turned out if I had met Frank Lampard at a different time in my life? As it was there was never going to be anything other than a casual flirtation; the circumstances were all wrong. I met him out clubbing, and, to be honest, I think he was probably as wild as me. We drank and flirted the night away, and I ended up going back to his house with a group of friends. I stayed and he really tried it on with me. I fancied him a lot – well, he's a good-looking bloke, isn't he? – but kissing was as far as it went. When he was drunk, he was one of the lads, and I needed more than that. Sober he was a different man, and I would have enjoyed getting to know him. But we never got it together during the day; we met up clubbing a few times, but that was it. Ironically, when I was pregnant I saw Frank again and he said that if I wasn't having a baby he was convinced we could get together. It's a bit too late for that, I thought, but I couldn't help feeling regret that this hadn't happened before. I'm sure he would never have treated me as badly as Dwight did.

But Dwight was the one I ended up with. He became more persistent in his pursuit of me, and although I carried on partying I started to think of him as my boyfriend. My friends all tried to talk me out of seeing him. They didn't think he was my type; they also knew about his reputation and were worried that I would get hurt. But I didn't listen. I didn't want to be on my own any more, and I was attracted to him. Moreover, if I had another boyfriend I hoped I could stop thinking about Dane all the time. Secretly I hoped that he would feel jealous now I was with someone else, that he could experience some of the pain I had felt.

The trouble was, I hardly ever saw Dwight. I would go up and visit him at the weekend, and sometimes I'd go up midweek. I'm sure that if I had seen more of Dwight I would have fallen for him, because that's what I'm like in relationships. Once I let myself have feelings for someone, that's it: I'm committed one hundred per cent. But with Dwight I did keep things back, because he was so different from all my other boyfriends. I just didn't get the impression that he wanted me around all the time. He obviously wasn't used to having a girlfriend and, although that's how he referred to me, I know for a fact he would see other women when I wasn't there.

Emotionally I wasn't getting what I needed from our relationship; it wasn't great physically, either. You'd think after all the practice he'd had Dwight would be an amazing lover, but there was definitely room for improvement. First of all there was his kissing technique. I always think that, if a man's a good kisser, nine times out of ten he'll be good in bed. By a good kisser, I mean someone who knows how to use his tongue to turn you on – not ram it down your throat, or slobber all over your chin, or dart it in and out like a lizard's; someone who leaves you wanting more, not reaching for the mouthwash. Dwight wasn't a terrible kisser, but he didn't impress me. Maybe it was because my barriers were up, and I didn't want to be swept away with passion and let my feelings show. I desperately didn't want to get hurt again. But I gave him the benefit of the doubt. Over a month after I started seeing him we finally slept together.

I had gone up to his house in Alderley Edge, Cheshire to spend New Year with him. I had this feeling that this might be the weekend when we finally made love and I kept wondering what he would be like as a lover, and if I was doing the right thing. Maybe this would finally help me get over Dane, but did I really want to get involved with someone like Dwight? I was still afraid of getting hurt.

It would have been romantic making love for the first time on New Year's Eve, but Dwight had a match the next day and had to abstain. The following night, though, there was nothing stopping us. I finally had sex with the footballer the fans call the King of Pornography on his king-sized waterbed. I was hoping for a mind-blowing shag which would once and for all get Dane out of my head, but I'm afraid it didn't happen like that. It was OK, but it definitely wasn't great sex. I couldn't help comparing it to the sex I had with Dane, where we knew exactly how to turn each other on. Dwight was very selfish in bed. He only seemed to care about his own pleasure. Whether I was enjoying myself or not didn't really seem to concern him. He wasn't into a lot of foreplay, but to give him his due he did try different positions; it's just that they all revolved around him.

I had no complaints about his body: he had a fantastic six pack, gorgeous muscular legs and quite a big willy, which I did find a turn-on. As you already know, Dane was less well endowed in that department, so of course Dwight's would seem big to me. But it is definitely true what they say: it's not size that counts, but how you use it. Dwight had the extra inches, but the chemistry between us wasn't that strong. There didn't seem to be much feeling on his side. I couldn't help thinking that this was just a shag for him, and I think emotion needs to be there for sex to really take off. He wasn't a bad lover, I just got the feeling that he didn't really care about me. He liked my body well enough, especially my boobs, but the person inside didn't really matter to him.

Once I've slept with someone, I want to feel that there is a relationship there. I want to know that the other person is committed to me, that he feels something for me as a person, and that it isn't just about sex. I thought that, as Dwight had been prepared to wait, that was true for him too. Thinking about it, though, he was probably still sleeping with other girls when he started seeing me, so me keeping him waiting wasn't that much of a big deal for him. I was just the icing on the cake.

Apart from the unaffectionate sex, it was clear pretty early on that Dwight was not going to be the love of my life. I fancied him, but I hadn't fallen in love with him. I never really felt that I could be myself with him, and as a result my defences were always up. Looking back, I think he just liked the thrill of being with me – but only me as Jordan. People close to me always call me Kate or Katie – Jordan is who I am when I'm working, and Dwight knew this. But quite often he would call his mates in front of me when we were in the car and say, 'I'm with Jordan at the moment.' I think I was a bit of a status symbol for him, something to brag about to the lads in the changing rooms. He loved the fact that I was a glamour model and had appeared on the cover of all those glossy magazines; but he had no idea how to appreciate Katie.

He used to really have a go at me if I wasn't all dressed up and in full make-up all the time. He'd say things like, 'Can't you look more like a lady? You're with a man now.' He was a typical footballer who wanted a trophy bird on his arm, all Gucci-ed up in high heels, designer clothes and perfect make-up. But I'm not like that. Away from work, I like to dress casually in my combats and trainers. I don't even like to wear make-up during the day. He started to make me feel self-conscious about how I looked and about my body. I felt like I had to be on show all the time. He even told me I was fat. I should have told him where to stick it there and then, but I didn't. Even when I was in the early stages of pregnancy, I tried to hold my stomach in so he wouldn't accuse me of putting on weight.

Our relationship was superficial. I was used to getting totally involved in my boyfriends' lives, meeting their family and friends and really getting to know them. Dwight wasn't like that at all. I just couldn't get close to him. He didn't seem like a very deep person, or maybe he didn't show that side of himself to me. We got on best when we were on our own in his house – if we were away from other people he would be a bit more affectionate. But we never talked about things that mattered, about how we felt about each other. Conversations were all at the level of what we were going to do, what we were going to eat and what film we were going to see. When we were out he was different – a lot more arrogant and full of himself.

The other thing that really got on my nerves was the fact that he was so dependent on his manager for everything. Dwight seemed incapable of doing anything for himself. They booked his flights, his hotels – I honestly reckon he wouldn't even know how to post a letter by himself. I sometimes wondered if his manager told him what to think!

But I didn't want to be alone, so I stayed with him. I'd always had a boyfriend since I was fifteen; I was still hurting over Dane; but most of all I think I stayed with him simply because I didn't want him to reject me. Even though the relationship was going nowhere, I clung to him like an idiot, terrified of being left again. I wanted to make him want me.

I kept hoping that things would get better between us, but they never did. I was always the one making the effort to see him. I'd be the one who would fly up to Manchester at the weekends; he'd never come and see me. It is true to say that I did love going to the matches to watch him play football – it's such a fantastic atmosphere. It was everything else that went with it that I didn't like ...

CHAPTER NINETEEN

FOOTBALLERS' WIVES

Saturday afternoon, Old Trafford. The roar and the chants from the crowd are deafening. I made my way to my seat in the special stand and people surrounded me. But I felt alone: I was an outsider.

'Hi, how are you?' One of the wives had clocked me. Immediately I could feel other players' wives and girlfriends looking at me, giving me the once-over, checking to see what I looked like, what I was wearing, what I was doing. It's a clique up there. They might have said hello, but it sounded false, as if they didn't really mean to welcome me. They were all typical footballers' birds who looked as if they spent their half their lives shopping for designer clothes and the other half getting made up. They made me feel so uncomfortable. I didn't want to be like them, and it was clear that they thought I didn't belong.

Dwight did not try to make the situation any easier for

183

me. After a match he was always the last one out of the changing rooms. I'd have to sit in the lounge for ages waiting for him to come out, and I hated it. I don't know what he was doing with himself with all his creams and lotions. Honestly! Men think women take a long time to get ready, but Dwight took the biscuit. Admittedly he would come out looking good, and he always smelled fantastic – he's probably the most hygienic person I've ever been out with (there you go, Dwight, I *can* pay you compliments!) – but, when he finally emerged from all his preening, he never showed me any affection. He wouldn't hug me or anything, so I would end up feeling just as awkward with him there. I couldn't help comparing his behaviour with Dane's. Whenever I used to go to clubs with Dane when he was DJ'ing he would always make sure that his friends looked after me. He would always know if I felt insecure somewhere. Dwight had no idea. He was never there when I needed him.

It was February 2001. I had just watched the match between United and Arsenal and was walking into the players' lounge, looking forward to seeing Dwight. Suddenly I heard singing: 'Who let the dogs out?' It was the queen of footballers' wives and her sidekick, and it seemed like Victoria Beckham and Nicola Smith were directing the song at me. Then they broke off their singing to make loud barking noises and laugh. I couldn't believe what I was hearing. Dogs? They were the dogs. At the time they seemed to me like a couple of bullies at school who pick on the new girl.

I was so angry I could have punched their lights out.

Frankly I might have being doing Victoria a favour – her features could do with a bit of rearranging. As for Nicola Smith, I expected as much from a nobody like her. She has never forgiven me for having a fling with her then boyfriend Teddy Sheringham, but I was only eighteen at the time, and he had never let on that he was in a relationship. Fortunately I was with my friend glamour model Michelle Clack, and she took me off to the ladies to calm down, otherwise there might have been some serious damage. When I lose my temper, I lose it big time. I was so tempted to go up to the pair and tell them exactly what I thought of them, but I decided I would keep my dignity. I think they were the ones who showed themselves up for what they were: a couple of cheap Essex girls.

I had never been anything but nice to Victoria. All that time she was working with Dane, I always treated her with respect, even though I didn't particularly like her and thought she was full of herself. And, even though I partly blamed the fact that Dane and I split up on his working with her, I never said anything nasty about her. She even called me 'vile' in her documentary. I just don't understand what her problem is with me. I'm not being big-headed, but I can only imagine that she's jealous of my looks.

Dwight couldn't believe it had happened. He wasn't angry for me, just surprised. I told him I hadn't said anything because I didn't want to embarrass him. That was it as far as he was concerned. As for me, I just thought, Stuff them, I'm not going to be bullied like that. Nobody was going to stop me from watching my boyfriend play football.

My weekends with Dwight would always follow the same

pattern. After football we would go back to his house and chill out. Like him, Dwight's house was stylish and, although it was big – it had six bedrooms – it did feel homely. It was all done out tastefully in creams and whites and I felt relaxed there. The only thing I didn't sample was his Jacuzzi. Frankly I had heard too many stories about him shagging other women in there, and I really didn't want to add to the numbers.

We would usually end up watching sport or a movie. Then we would go out to a restaurant for dinner, either locally or in Manchester. Although Dwight is well known for his expensive tastes, he never took me anywhere particularly posh. I think I cooked for him just once after he started saying, 'Let's do more things together at home.'

'Fine,' I said. 'I'll make dinner.' Like we weren't always staying in! But even then he kept trying to tell me what to do. The problem was, he couldn't even work his own cooker. I don't think he had ever cooked for himself in his life.

All in all, it was pretty dull being up there, and I was often bored. I couldn't wait to get back home to go out with my mates and have a laugh. I did try and come up with ideas for doing different things: one day I even suggested a trip to Alton Towers, just to have some fun, to do something – anything! But all Dwight wanted to do was stay in. He was obviously saving his energy for when I left.

He was always really cagey about taking me out clubbing in Manchester. I reckon he had probably been with so many women up there that he didn't want to bump into them with me. On the few occasions we did go out together, he just stood at the bar and eyed up all the other women. It was so insulting. 'Please don't do that in front of me,' I said to him on one occasion. 'Go off and do what you have to do.' And, without any embarrassment on his part, he went off and chatted up any women who happened to have caught his eye. I couldn't believe it. I was only saying it to test him – I didn't actually believe that he would do it. Another time we were out together in a restaurant and he spent the whole time pointing out the waitresses he'd been out with, and the ones his friends had slept with. I don't quite know why he felt the urge to tell me – it's not like it impressed me in any way.

As he never bothered to visit me in Brighton, I saw even less of Dwight when I got my new puppy. He refused to have the dog in his house. Smurf wouldn't have done any harm, but there was no arguing with Dwight. He probably didn't want any dog hairs on his perfect cream sofas, not that he'd have been the one cleaning them off. Then he got all upset when I said I couldn't come up and see him one weekend because I had to look after the puppy. He just didn't understand that you can't leave a puppy on its own. We had this ridiculous phone conversation when he said, 'Who are you choosing – me or the dog?' I should have chosen Smurf there and then and knocked the Dwight thing on its head. I sometimes feel that my relationships with animals have been far more successful than my relationships with men!

Fortunately I had my career to think of. I wasn't just some footballer's bird who did nothing but think of ways to spend her man's money. I was going places. In March 2001 I was off to LA for my test shots for *Playboy*.

CHAPTER TWENTY

LA-LA LAND

From the moment I started modelling, it had been my dream to appear on the cover of American *Playboy*. Being in that magazine says that you've made it, and people all over the world are going to know who you are. It would also be a chance to work with some of the most talented people in the business – the best photographers, stylists and make-up artists. I would be modelling for the photographers who had made stars of women such as Pamela Anderson, Carmen Electra, Anna Nicole Smith and Victoria Silvstedt, and I wanted some of that magic to rub off on me. And, of course, I would get the chance to meet the man himself: Hugh Hefner.

So in March 2001 I flew to LA for a test shoot to see if I had what it takes to be in the magazine. I remember telling Dwight what I was doing and he told me that he didn't know what *Playboy* was. Pull the other one, Dwight!

I had flown over with the photographer Jeany Savage, her

assistant James and my make-up-artist friend Sally as we were going to do a shoot for the *Star* later that week. I was glad to have them with me for a bit of moral support. We were staying in a hotel near the Playboy mansion; I couldn't wait to see where Hef lived and to meet him, although I was nervous because I so wanted him to like me. We spent our first day chilling out and getting over the jet lag, and that night we were invited to Hef's mansion for dinner and a movie – he holds private screenings every Sunday night.

As we drove up the long drive I felt incredibly excited. I had been anticipating this moment for ages, and I wasn't disappointed. There were exotic gardens, several swimming pools and even signs saying 'Playmates at Play', which really made me smile. There was no doubting where we were. Finally we pulled up outside the mansion. It was time for me to make my entrance.

I wanted to make an impression on Hef and had spent hours deciding what to wear. I needed to look sexy and confident, but not too over the top. In the end I wore a pair of tight jeans, which I had customised by bleaching them and then ripping holes in the knees and backside, a white, low-cut, cropped top and high ankle boots. My hair was pulled up in a ponytail, and I went for natural-looking make-up.

We rang the bell and a maid answered the door – fully dressed, I was relieved to see. Inside there was an enormous hallway, all marble floors and glittering chandeliers, with a massive red-carpeted staircase. The walls were covered with pictures of Hef and his famous guests – film stars, pop stars, you name them they were there – and of course his bunnies. I felt another tingle of excitement: soon I'd be meeting him myself.

We were shown into the dining room and it was much more laid back than I had pictured, homely even. I had imagined loads of naked women walking around, and possibly orgies taking place behind closed doors, but it wasn't like that at all. Maybe Sunday was Hef's night off.

Then Hef walked into the room surrounded by his bunnies. He has seven girlfriends who live with him – a different one for every night, I wondered. Pretty good going for a man in his seventies. I had thought that he might be loud and a bit lecherous, but he was the complete opposite. He was charming to me, a perfect gentleman.

It did feel totally surreal sitting down to dinner with him and his girlfriends. They all look incredibly alike with long blonde hair, all-over tans, perfect teeth and silicone boobs – real-life Barbie dolls. I was expecting them to be a bit bitchy towards me, but they were very friendly as well, and, although they all looked like Barbie, they weren't dumb blondes by any means. We were also joined by Thora Birch, the actress from the film *The Hole*. It was a great night and I hoped that Hef liked me, but the real test would come the next day when I did my audition shoot.

I got up early in the morning. Back home I have a bit of a reputation for turning up late for shoots. I never set out to be late, it's just something that happens – but I knew that I couldn't be late for *this* studio session. I was going to be a model model!

The shoot took place in the Playboy studios, and it was in a different league to other studios I've worked in. The corridor leading up to it was covered in pictures of playmates, and it did make me laugh to see how glamour-modelling fashions have changed – or, to be more graphic, how pubic-hair fashions have changed! In the seventies a full bush was all the rage, but over the years the quantity of hair got less and less until today it's either all off, or there's a minimal landing strip. I'm in the all-off camp, in case you were wondering.

I remember walking into what seemed like a film set and feeling pretty nervous, almost like I did when I first started modelling. But, just like all those years ago, I was determined to succeed, so I kept my nerves to myself. Everything was on a bigger scale to what I was used to. When I worked with Jeany, she only ever used three lights. Over in LA the lighting was much more sophisticated, and the photographers had literally hundreds of lights to choose from.

I'm used to having quite a few outfits and shoes to choose from when I do a shoot, but nothing like this. The dressing room was like a dream come true for me, an Aladdin's cave of hundreds of pairs of gorgeous shoes, piles of sexy lingerie and loads of outrageous outfits that I adored, like tiny pink dresses, micro minis and sexy corsets.

My next surprise came when Alexis, the make-up artist, started on my face. She put on more make-up than I've ever had on in my life. When I looked in the mirror I thought it was far too much. I was used to the way Sally did my face, and whenever I've done a shoot with her I always feel I can go out with the same make-up on. There's no way I could have done that with the LA make-up. But then I saw how it appeared on camera and I had to hand it to Alexis: it looked fantastic.

I'm always a bit unsure of new photographers, mainly

because I hate being told how to pose and what to do; new photographers never want to trust you to do your own thing. Arny Freytag, one of the top glamour photographers in the States, was taking my test shots and at first he insisted that I did what he told me. But after a while he could tell that I really knew what I was doing, and he let me do my own poses. After just a few rolls of film I felt totally at ease with him and started being cheeky; we had a great time together. I'm used to working with Jeany and it made quite a change having a man to flirt with and boss around. I felt honoured that he was taking my pictures as I knew he was used to working with stars like Pamela Anderson and Carmen Electra.

I had to pose in the nude. The positions were all tasteful: no spread legs, graphic crotch shots or anything like that. As it was for *Playboy*, for the first time ever I showed off my pink heart tattoo which usually only my boyfriends get to see. Arny thought it was very cute.

I was having to show more of my body than I ever had before, and while I was posing I did feel very conscious of all the people in the studio. There seemed to be loads of them, what with the photographer's assistants and lighting men. I knew they were there to do a job, but I said that I didn't want anyone walking past me while I was in some of the more revealing positions. Basically, I didn't want people leering up my bum – as far as I'm concerned, my bits are my business. Just because I'm a glamour model and have gone topless and shown off my bare bum and my pink heart tattoo, it doesn't mean that I want to go all the way. I like my poses to be provocative and tasteful at the same time.

I was on such a high when I finished the day. I really had the feeling that the photographer was pleased with me. Alexis the make-up artist told me she thought I would definitely be back; she wrote 'You're a star' on a Polaroid and gave it to me.

I had absolutely loved the whole LA experience, and the lifestyle. I felt much more accepted out there for who I was. People aren't bothered about what surgery you've had done. Boob jobs are just part of life out there, in fact you're probably unusual if you haven't had anything done. It made such a change from Britain. I was almost tempted not to come home at all, but I knew deep down that I would miss my family and friends too much, and what about my boyfriend Dwight? To be honest, I hadn't really thought that much about him while I was away as I'd been too busy but, as I got on the plane to fly home, I suppose I was looking forward to seeing him again.

CHAPTER TWENTY-ONE

MONTE CARLO MISERY

Back home, I got the call I'd been praying for. Hef had seen the pictures and wanted me on the cover of American *Playboy*. I was over the moon.

I really wanted Dwight to share my excitement, but he didn't seem to understand why it was such a big deal – or if he did he didn't show it. I was starting to feel frustrated. We had been together nearly seven months, but I didn't feel our relationship was developing at all. I still felt I didn't really know him, and as a result I kept saying to myself, Don't let your barriers down, don't give too much away.

If he had made more of an effort to come down to see me, or if he had asked me to go up and spend more time with him other than at weekends, I'm sure things might have turned out differently between us. But Dwight seemed happy to let things cruise along as they were. Maybe he was incapable of letting his feelings show, or perhaps he just didn't really feel that much for me outside of the bedroom.

I'm such an optimist that I still thought our relationship might improve with time. So in May 2001, when Dwight said he would take me away for a week so we could spend some time together, I was surprised and a bit hopeful. Finally we might get to know each other better.

The plan was to go to the Laureus World Sports Awards in Monte Carlo for the weekend, and then go on to Cannes for the rest of the week. It sounded great – two classy, luxurious locations in the sun. But, as soon as we arrived at our hotel, things started to go wrong. I was looking forward to spending some time relaxing in our hotel and then hitting the town. Dwight had other ideas. When he was asked to play golf with some of his footballer mates including David Ginola and Ryan Giggs, he immediately agreed. He did ask me if I minded, and I replied, 'Do what you want. I can't tell you what to do, we're not married.' But inside I was fuming. This was our first chance to spend some quality time together, but rather than being with me he wanted to play golf with the blokes he saw all the time anyway. It was obvious I wasn't happy about his decision, but Dwight just ignored my feelings and went off, leaving me to entertain myself.

In the press I'm always portrayed as this outrageous, up-front party girl, but sometimes I can be quite shy. I really don't like being in unfamiliar places on my own; it makes me feel insecure. So, rather than explore Monte Carlo, I waited in my hotel room all day for Dwight to come back, passing the time by phoning my mates and my mum and watching a bit of television. It was hardly the trip I had imagined.

I felt terrible anyway. I had just had liposuction done on my thighs and I was in total agony. I'd also had collagen injected into my lips, and they were throbbing like hell. Whilst I don't for a second regret any of my boob jobs, I definitely wish I hadn't had the liposuction done. My surgeon Dr Prakash told me that I definitely didn't need it, I just needed to exercise. But I knew I was too lazy to go the gym so I insisted. It cost me six grand and didn't make any difference at all. And it was so painful! After the operation my legs were black and blue. I remember going to the toilet and seeing all these tiny little holes in the tops of my legs with blood oozing out of them, and I nearly passed out. As for my lips, I won't be having them done again – I didn't end up with trout pout like poor old Leslie Ash, but they were definitely too puffed up for my liking. In future, if I want bigger lips I'll go for the lipliner.

Eventually Dwight came back. 'Thanks a lot for leaving me on my own all day,' I said. He just looked at me as if he didn't know what the problem was. It was time to get ready for the awards ceremony. I was always so conscious of my appearance when I was with Dwight, and I had agonised over what to wear that night. In the end, after searching everywhere in the shops for something he would approve of, I'd had something specially made for me. It was a pale pink silk trouser suit, which hopefully made me look enough of a lady for Dwight's tastes, and which still made me feel like me. I had also bought a pair of incredibly high Gina shoes that I could hardly walk in. For the party after the awards, I was going to please myself and wear a silver rubber catsuit.

During the awards Dwight stayed by my side, but at the party I barely saw him. I felt totally abandoned and fed up. Fortunately I'd met up with a girl called Jessica who seemed really nice. I was grateful to have the company as Dwight was off doing his usual cruising around, eyeing up other women. I ended up spending quite a lot of the night with her, having a few drinks and a bit of a laugh. She even came back with me to the hotel to help me get changed into my catsuit. I needed her to zip it up – I couldn't do it myself as the liposuction made it hard for me to bend my legs. Then throughout the night she'd come with me to the loo and help me get out of the suit. I thought she was a great girl.

I might just as well not have been there for all the interest Dwight took in me. He flirted outrageously with anyone who would let him near them – Rachel Hunter to name but one. At one point I went up to the bar because I saw him talking to a couple of girls and he suddenly moved away.

'Do you know that bloke?' I asked them. They giggled and said he had just bought them a drink. What they went on to say totally stunned me. I felt as if I had been punched in the stomach when they revealed that Dwight had asked them if they fancied having a threesome with him. When I told them that he was supposed to be my boyfriend they were horrified and said, if he was one of their boyfriends, they'd get rid of him. I was gobsmacked. I couldn't believe how disgusting he was. Is this what he usually got up to when he was on his own in Manchester? But, if I thought that was the lowest he could go, I was wrong. There was much worse to come.

To try and forget about him, I started to get drunk – anything to get through the night. I couldn't believe Dwight's attitude. The next day was going to be my twenty-third birthday. What was I doing here with this man who obviously didn't have any respect for me at all?

Suddenly, out of the corner of my eye, I saw this gorgeous bloke staring at me. I looked straight back at him and before I knew it he was in front of me. He was tall and handsome with the most amazing blue eyes. Immediately he started talking to me, saying how good I looked in what I was wearing, all the usual kind of chat-up lines. But I didn't care, I needed to hear nice things after Dwight's outrageous behaviour. We flirted and danced together and he said he'd love to take me out in London.

'I'd like that,' I said. 'But I probably won't be able to as I've got a boyfriend.' Even as I said the words, though, I thought, Have I really? When he gave me his number I took it. I wouldn't normally have encouraged anyone like this, but I was so angry with Dwight.

When he told me his name I couldn't believe it – he was called Dwayne. It completely freaked me out because it was like a combination of Dane and Dwight. And I thought to myself, I've just met a guy who is absolutely drop-dead gorgeous, with this name. Could he be my destiny. I took Dwayne's number and that was that. After what happened next, I wished I had stayed with him.

It was getting late, but the night was far from over. Eddie Jordan, who I know really well from my work with the Formula 1 team, invited a group of us back to his boat to carry on partying. As we all piled into the Bentleys waiting to take us to the jetty, I saw a blonde girl who I didn't recognise. 'Who are you here with?' I asked her, just making conversation.

'I'm with Dwight,' she replied.

'Oh, right,' I said. Even though I was stunned, I thought, I won't say anything. I'll sit here and watch what happens. Dwight must have thought I was stupid, but I knew exactly what he'd been up to behind my back. It didn't matter how much I'd had to drink – I still knew what was going on. On the outside I looked as if I didn't have a care in the world; inside I was burning up with anger.

When we got out of the cars and waited for the speedboats to come and take us to Eddie's yacht, Dwight was talking to some bloke and I found myself sitting next to the blonde girl again. I'm not being bitchy but she looked like an absolute tart; she wasn't even pretty. 'So how come you're with Dwight then?' I asked her.

'He invited me to the boat so we could get to know each other better,' she replied.

I'd heard enough. I couldn't sit here and watch what was going on any longer. 'Do you know who I am? Believe it or not, I'm supposed to be his girlfriend.' Her jaw practically hit the floor.

Suddenly I couldn't take any more. I was furious. I stood up, and Dwight finally noticed I was there. I walked over to him. I felt totally humiliated but I was determined not to break down in front of him. 'Right then,' I said. 'I've met your latest bit and I'm going to leave you both to it. I hope you have a fantastic time getting to know each other on the boat.' And before he had a chance to reply I stormed off.

It was dark, and I had no idea where I was. As I stumbled along the beach trying to find my way back to the hotel I hardly knew what I was thinking. I just knew I had to get away. My Gina heels, which I had worn to impress Dwight, were killing me, but I barely registered the pain. I was so shocked that he could treat me like this. There I was in the middle of this beautiful place, hours away from my twenty-third birthday. I should have been loving every minute, I should have felt like one of the luckiest girls in the world. Instead I just wanted to go home.

Somehow I made it back to the hotel. I curled up on the bed, feeling numb. The whole night felt like a bad dream. I was tormented by the thought of Dwight being with that woman. I kept imagining what he was doing with her. I doubted they were making polite conversation. I couldn't believe that anyone could treat me so badly. Suddenly I remembered the handsome stranger Dwayne and I thought, Sod it. I will call him when I get home. I'm not taking any more shit from Dwight.

I barely slept that night. The next morning was another gorgeous day. Happy birthday to me, I thought as I ordered breakfast for one. Dwight hadn't bothered to come back that night. He didn't turn up until eleven o'clock. I pretended to be asleep as he got into bed and started cuddling me. He stank of booze and God knows what else, and looked totally hungover. 'Happy birthday, babe,' he said.

I decided to play it cool, even though I was fuming. I thought I'd let him sweat, and wonder why I wasn't starting up a row about his behaviour. But I gave him too much credit – he wasn't capable of thinking anything, because a few minutes later he was snoring.

An hour later, there was knock on the door and I was handed a huge bouquet of red roses with a card saying 'Love from Dwight'. To be honest, I felt like throwing them at him. But I didn't. I calmly put them in a vase and got back into bed.

What the hell was I doing? There I was in Monte Carlo with the sun shining outside and everyone else out having a good time, and here I was stuck with this bastard. Finally he woke up and said, 'I'd better go and get your present now.' He made it sound like it was such an effort. And so he went out again, leaving me alone in the hotel room. I should have left there and then, but I felt so alone. I was miles away from home, away from my friends and family, and I didn't feel strong enough. I just thought, Grit your teeth, get through this week and then dump him when you get home.

Eventually Dwight came back with my present. It was a watch. I'd like to say it was massively expensive – I thought I deserved it because he certainly had a lot of making up to do. Later I found out that it cost him a couple of grand. It might sound like a lot, but it's peanuts to someone like him. I wasn't really interested in presents, though. I kept waiting for him to say sorry for how he had behaved, but he acted like nothing was wrong.

We were getting ready to go to Cannes when Dwight took a phone call from his manager. Jessica, who had seemed so lovely the night before, had actually been doing a piece on us. She was one of the 3am Girls from the *Mirror*, whose job, if you can call it that, is to spread gossip about celebrities. Apparently her story was all about Dwight propositioning other women, including her (nice one, Dwight), for threesomes; how I was included in his proposals – like that's ever going to happen; and how drunk I was, so much so that she had to help me get dressed. I had liked her and trusted her. Would I ever learn?

Dwight just laughed and acted cocky, as if it proved he was some kind of stud. I felt really upset and betrayed, but I knew there was nothing I could do about it. The drive down to Cannes was tense. We hardly said a word to each other. I looked out of the window at the stunning blue sea and the scenery and thought, I hate you so much for what you've done to me.

That night I decided to make myself look as sexy as possible. I did real full-on make-up – all smoky eyes, big mascara lashes and loads of lipstick. I put on my tightest jeans with a little bikini top and a tight denim jacket, which showed off my figure to maximum effect. Dwight's eyes nearly popped out of his head when he saw me. As we walked down the street together, I could tell all the men were eyeing me up. Dwight kept pulling me next to him, desperate to make it obvious that I was with him.

Once we got to the bar, I thought, Right, I'm going to wind you up now and give you a taste of your own medicine. I made sure I had a few drinks inside me, and then started dancing extremely provocatively, making sure I was getting plenty of attention from the men in the bar. Dwight couldn't handle it at all. He tried to stop me dancing, saying that I was making an exhibition of myself and had all these men ogling me. When that didn't work, he started going on about how I was really different when I'd had a drink, and how he dreaded to think what I was like when he wasn't with me. He just didn't get it at all.

In the end we cut the trip short and came home. Dwight never once apologised. He obviously thought that taking me out for a couple of meals was going to make up for things. But I can't be bought that easily. In fact, I can't be bought at all. On the flight home I had pretty much decided to leave him. No one was going to get away with treating me like this.

I knew that Dwight was going away to Cape Town with Mark Bosnich as soon as the football season was over and I decided to wind him up. 'I've had a really good time with you,' I told him, 'and when you go away as far as I'm concerned you're free to shag as many women as you like, but just make sure you use protection. I know you'll probably do it anyway, and I'm just telling you that I don't mind.'

As I had anticipated, he was totally gobsmacked. For a minute or two he didn't know what to say, then he replied, 'You're not like a normal girl, letting me go and do this.'

'It's fine.' I shrugged. 'I don't care.' And I didn't. I thought the relationship, if you could call it that, was over.

CHAPTER TWENTY-TWO

BUNNY GIRL

I lay back in the huge marble bath, luxuriating in the hot water and perfumed bubbles. This was just what my jet-lagged body needed. I was finally here in Hugh Hefner's mansion getting ready for the most important shoot of my life. I was so excited, but I couldn't help wondering if anyone was spying on me as I bathed – the walls and ceilings were made of smoked-glass mirrors. I had the feeling that anything could happen here. But I'd poured in so much bubble bath that even if anyone was out there watching they wouldn't have seen much. I might have been about to take everything off for *Playboy*, but I was being paid a lot of money to do it and I wasn't going to give anyone a free viewing!

I got out of the bath, quickly wrapped myself in a large fluffy white towel and walked into my bedroom. I'd imagined an exotic boudoir, all red and pink velvet with black satin sheets and a mirrored ceiling. But it was nothing like that at all. It was a large airy room, tastefully decorated in cream, with a gorgeous four-poster bed. In other words it was completely normal; well, normal for a millionaire's mansion.

I lay on my bed for a while and wondered why no one had come in to see if I needed anything. I was absolutely starving. Eventually one of the bunnies popped in. She told me that all I had to do was dial 0 on the phone, ask for anything I wanted and it would be brought to my room. That's what I call service! I picked up the phone and ordered macaroni cheese, chips with melted cheese on them and a hot chocolate with whipped cream. I'm afraid healthy eating and me just don't go together.

I carried on stuffing myself throughout my stay. The bunnies couldn't believe the kind of food I ate and how I was able to stay so slim. They barely ate anything, and what they did eat was totally fat free. At breakfast they would all be picking at their egg whites and I'd be tucking into porridge. Then they would go off to the gym and work out for hours. The only time I ever went to the gym was to use the sunbed. Maybe one day I'll need to start working out and getting into yoga and pilates, but that day hasn't come yet.

I loved staying in the mansion. I had a stunning view from my bedroom window of the massive swimming pool and the beautiful grounds. One day I looked out to see loads of gorgeous girls sunbathing and playing volleyball. I couldn't help smiling: it looked like Barbie village! The bunnies gave me a guided tour of the place. As well as the swimming pools, Hugh also has the biggest Jacuzzi I have ever seen in my life. It was set in a cave and very discreetly lit. I had a go in it during the day, but I gave it a miss during one of Hef's legendary parties. I could just imagine what people got up to in there. Then there was the games house in the garden. In one room were lots of fruit machines and a large snooker table, all very innocent and above board. Then you went through a mirrored door into what I can only describe as a shag pad for his guests. All the walls and ceilings were mirrored; there were cushions everywhere to recline on; there was a large double bed, and the thickest carpet I have ever trodden on – a proper shag pile! In case you're wondering, I didn't go in there during the party, either.

I had been nervous that Hugh's bunnies might not like me. But I needn't have worried. Although they form a real clique, they were lovely to me and we hit it off straight away. Although no strangers themselves to cosmetic surgery, they were totally fascinated by my boobs. They told me they looked fantastic, and couldn't get over how big they were, and how natural looking. I took it as a real compliment: they've seen enough of these things to be real connoisseurs!

Now all I had to worry about was the shoot. I was thrilled when I found out that I was going to be photographed by Stephen Wayda, the photographer who made Pamela Anderson a star. She has always been a bit of a heroine of mine. I love the way she looks, and I was looking forward to Stephen working some of his magic for me.

It was going to be the most intensive shoot of my life, lasting four days. The shoots back home take a day at the most, and I often feel that they could probably get all the shots in a couple of hours. But, as this was for *Playboy*, I wasn't going to complain. If they wanted me for four days, they could have me.

When I got to the studio I loved the set they'd built for me. It was like a mini London, with the skyline as the backdrop, a black cab and a real old red phone box for me to pose in. There was also a piano and chandelier – very classy. It looked fantastic. Back home I often just had a plain background to pose against; here it was like being on a proper film set.

I knew that I would have to do a lot of nude poses, but I was only prepared to do ones that were tasteful. So yes, there are pictures of me totally naked, but my legs are firmly together. In one shot I'm sitting down with my legs apart, but I have my hand placed strategically. Stephen did try and persuade me to do some poses with my legs apart, but I refused point blank. He said that they would be tasteful, but I wouldn't give in. He wasn't unpleasant about it – I suppose they like to push their luck – but he was never going to convince me. Those bits will always stay private.

I can honestly say that I don't think I've ever worked so hard in my life. People might think it's easy being a model, but they should try holding a pose, making sure they're breathing in and looking sexy at the same time. All this takes place under hot spotlights, and you're surrounded by loads of people making you feel self-conscious. But, even though it was hard work, I loved every minute, and I had a great working relationship with Stephen.

I thought the pictures were stunning: sexy, yes, but not

porn – and very me. There are shots of me looking seductive in a phone booth, naked except for a tartan corset and fishnets, a diamond choker and leopard-skin heels; or posing against the piano, all long blonde hair, golden tan and pouting lips. The first shot has me topless and wearing a gorgeous pair of black French knickers trimmed with diamonds; in the second shot I've pulled them down to reveal my pink heart; and in the third shot they're off altogether and I'm completely naked. Then there's an ultra-sexy shot of me on all fours, gazing at the camera completely naked except for the diamonds round my neck. The cover shot has me naked except for a silver basque, a fishnet body stocking and a diamond belt with the word 'foxy' hanging from it. But that's all there is on show because my hand is preserving my modesty and that's where the page ends! I loved the headline: LONDON'S LEGENDARY BAD GIRL, JORDAN. I was exactly where I wanted to be, and it was a great feeling.

Alongside my *Playboy* shoot, I also had to find time to be filmed for a BBC documentary about me. It was going to be a fly-on-the-wall look at my life – showing me at work and at play. I hoped it would reveal the real me – that people would see that I wasn't the bimbo the tabloids had made me out to be. Richard Macer, the director, might disagree, but I think I was pretty laid-back about letting him interview and film me. I certainly didn't make a fuss about how I was shot. I wasn't a control freak like Victoria Beckham who, for one of her documentaries made sure she was filmed in perfect make-up, with very flattering lighting. Mind you, if I had her looks, I'd probably make sure I had more say over how I was shot. Miaow!

After the shoot I was free to do what I wanted. During the day I'd hang out with the bunnies in the house or by the pool, or go shopping. Hugh was holding one of his parties while I was there, and I was looking forward to it. These were the nights when the place would be packed with film stars, rock stars and models. There would be lots of incredible-looking women walking around either completely naked or wearing very little.

I hit the shops with the bunnies in order to get the perfect outfit. I had no intention of going around naked or in a bikini, but I can't pretend I was wearing very much. I went as an angel. I had a tiny pink dress with a plunging neckline so my boobs were practically popping out. It was so short it barely covered my bum, and was completely see through except for some pink fur in crucial places. I wore bright pink fluffy wings and incredibly high heels – pink of course. I might have looked like hot stuff, but I spent the whole night worrying about people looking up my skirt, and my feet were killing me. I decided that, if I ever go to one of Hef's parties again, I'll go in a pair of silk pyjamas. I'll still make sure I look good, with full-on make-up, but at least I'll be comfortable and not be obsessed with whether my bum is wobbling about. Also I'd look a bit different – I did find it slightly freaky the way all the women looked the same. I like to stand out.

The bunnies were all expected to sit with Hef, but I was free to go where I wanted. Everywhere I looked there was a famous face: I saw Chris Rock the comedian, some of the members of Limp Bizkit, some *Baywatch* girls and NSYNC were there. I recognised lots of people, but I wasn't interested in going up and talking to them. I spent the night chatting to the bunnies and had a long conversation with Jennifer Lopez's ex-husband Chris Judd. I had a great time, as I'm such a party animal, but no one lured me into the Jacuzzi or the shag room. I was dressed as an angel and I behaved like one – well, just about.

The three weeks in America went by in a flash. Yet again I was tempted not to come home. All the bunnies told me that I should stay out there, that I was just like an LA girl. Hef even asked me to stay on and be one of his girlfriends, which was quite an honour in its way as I would have been the only brunette bunny he'd ever had. But I had to turn him down – tactfully of course! That kind of life just isn't for me. I'm much too independent. I could never do what someone tells me, or only look a certain way, and all his girlfriends are identical. They're expected to go everywhere with him, and although they are free during the day they can't go out at night on their own. I couldn't handle someone being so over protective, and I just know I'd break Hef's rules straight away.

I was thrilled, though, when Hugh told me that I was going to be massive in the States. But I never let myself get too excited: I'm used to people making promises to me, and now I just wait and see what happens.

In terms of my personal life, what was I going home to? I hadn't spoken to Dwight for a while. After Monte Carlo, as far as I was concerned I was a single girl again, free to do what I wanted and see who I wanted. I hadn't said anything to Dwight about how I felt, I just allowed things to drift between us. Anyone else, I'm sure, would have realised that something was wrong, but not Dwight.

When he flew to Cape Town, I flew to Kosovo on another morale-boosting mission to the troops out there. I was staying with the 2nd Royal Tank Regiment. It was a good distraction as I didn't want to brood over how Dwight had treated me. That's where I met a particularly cute soldier called Joe White. He was one of the lads chosen to have breakfast with me, and he caught my attention straight away with his good looks and warm personality. We started all the flirtatious eye contact that I love, and I spent the rest of my trip pestering the officers who were looking after me to bring him to me. I think I drove them mad. I'd use their radio and say, 'Where's Joe? Go and get him for me!'

I even demanded to be smuggled into his room one night. I had to tiptoe to his barrack with one of the officers. It was like being in a film, sneaking somewhere I shouldn't, trying to avoid being found out. It took me so long to get there that by the time I arrived he was fast asleep. I slipped into bed beside him, but we only cuddled, nothing more. Two hours later I had to creep back to my room.

When I returned to London we stayed in contact by e-mail. Then, when he was back in this country on leave, I invited him and a group of his squaddie friends out clubbing with me. But as soon as I saw him again, I was disappointed. He was much too short! I need a man who is taller than me. I knew this was one encounter that definitely wasn't going any further, nice as he was. He stayed the night with me, but we only kissed – I think he might have touched my boobs, but that was that. I was the one in control. I never had any intention of having sex with him, I just wanted someone to flirt with for a while, and he fitted the bill perfectly.

Of course, my night out with soldier boy found its way into the papers, and only then did Dwight bother to call me. Unusually for him he sounded in a state. He wanted to know if it was true, was I seeing someone else? Great, I thought. It's only now that he rings me, now that he feels under threat. I told him to get lost, but he kept calling. Finally I admitted that I had gone out with a soldier. He didn't like that at all. He was getting a taste of his own medicine, and it wasn't a taste he liked. But I refused to feel guilty. As far as I was concerned we had split anyway, and I'd only been having a bit of fun – something I needed after all the humiliation Dwight had caused me with his constant womanising.

But still he kept calling me. Finally I agreed to meet up with him again. What was I thinking of? Maybe I was still on a high from LA and wanted to celebrate with someone; maybe some part of me still believed that I could have a relationship with Dwight. Looking back, I realise I was still hurt from Dane's rejection. I couldn't walk away from Dwight because I wanted him to want me. What I should have realised is that actually I deserved much better.

But, after we met up in Birmingham where I was working at Max Power, a car show, we decided to give our relationship another go, even though it had 'do not resuscitate' written all over it. Predictably, though, he and I had different ideas about what 'giving it a go' meant. I knew from the trip to Monte Carlo what he was capable of, and there had been a number of kiss and tells throughout our brief time together. He denied them all, of course, but they each described his house, his bedroom and his performance in bed a bit too accurately. He was linked with loads of different women, but there was one name that kept coming up: the television presenter and model Gaby Richens.

I knew there had been something between them in the past because he told me he had slept with her in Australia before I met him, but Dwight swore it was over. Then the papers reported that he'd been bombarding her with phone calls asking her out, or even just to come up and watch him play. When I demanded to know what was going on, Dwight denied it. In fact, he even did a piece in the *Star* saying that he loved me, and that he really wanted our relationship to work, something which he had never done before. Even his manager phoned me and said, 'I've never seen Dwight like this, he really hasn't done anything.'

It was all rubbish, of course, as I found out later. And it wouldn't have mattered, except for one thing: during our brief reconciliation I had fallen pregnant.

CHAPTER TWENTY-THREE

OH BABY

As I watched the blue line appear, I couldn't believe it, at least I didn't want to believe it. It was like some sick joke. At that time I'd only ever had five lovers in my life. I'd been in love with four of them. The only one I didn't love was Dwight. How ironic that he should be the one to get me pregnant.

I did the first test on the plane going over to Majorca with a group of my closest friends. As I stumbled out of the loo looking totally shocked, they didn't need to ask what the result was. I know that pregnancy tests are nearly one hundred per cent accurate, but that didn't stop me doing another one as soon as we arrived at the villa. I willed the second line not to show, but instantly it appeared in the little window. There was no denying the result.

I was in a complete state. I knew my relationship with Dwight was going nowhere. I'd hardly seen him even though we were supposed to be an item again. I knew that I didn't love him, and I didn't think I ever would. I didn't even fancy him any more. I would never in a million years have chosen him to be the father of my child. Perhaps if he had shown me more respect, things would have been different. But the truth is that at that time I wished it was Dane's child I was carrying. I was still haunted by the fact that I'd had an abortion, and even though I think it was the right decision, given the state of our relationship, it didn't stop me feeling guilty and wondering what might have been. And now here I was, pregnant again and totally confused about what to do. One half of me thought, Have the baby; the other told me not to. I didn't know what to do for the best.

With a heavy heart I rang Dwight. I didn't want to speak to him, but I figured as the father he had a right to know. When I broke the news he was typically unsupportive – I don't know why I expected anything different. He just said, 'Are you sure?' I think he was shocked more than anything because ours hadn't exactly been the strongest of relationships. From our brief conversation I got the impression he didn't even believe there was a baby.

When I put the phone down I felt so alone, even though I was surrounded by my friends. Everyone kept asking me what I was going to do, but I didn't know. Nobody thought I should go ahead and have the baby. I just wanted to wake up and discover it was all a bad dream, and that I didn't have to make a decision. Why was nothing in my life ever straightforward?

When I returned home, I still had no idea what to do. I looked in the baby book I had which shows how the baby develops. I was eight weeks pregnant. Already the foetus was developing, its organs were forming and its brain was starting to grow. I knew that, every week I didn't do anything, the foetus would become more and more like a baby.

I was in torment. Dwight didn't even bother to come down to London to see me, and whenever we spoke on the phone he just told me that I should have an abortion. 'We haven't been together long enough for this,' he said. 'We can't give the baby a proper family life.' As far as he was concerned, it was black and white: get rid of it and move on. But I kept thinking about the abortion I had with Dane's child, and about the miscarriage I'd had earlier. Could I really bear to end this life growing inside me? It might be my last chance to have a baby.

But I just didn't know if I could cope with bringing up a baby on my own. It was such a massive responsibility. And how would it affect my career? Of course, if I'd been in a stable relationship with someone I loved and who loved me back, it wouldn't have worried me so much, but I wasn't in that position. I was going to be a single parent and I needed to earn money to give my baby the best possible life. Would I still be seen as a sexy pin-up? I knew that I wouldn't be the kind to go all mumsy and earth-mother-like – nothing in the world was ever going to get me to wear a long floral dress and sensible shoes. But I did wonder what would happen to my body. I couldn't afford to look any different after I'd had the baby. Otherwise what was I going to do? I still had my dreams about becoming a singer, but even then you have to look good to make it.

After days of agonising soul-searching, I finally booked myself in for an appointment to have a termination. But on the day of the appointment I was in bits. I drove to the clinic but couldn't get out of my car. I remember gripping the steering wheel and crying. I couldn't go through with it.

In desperation I arranged to see Dane – I really needed to talk to him. Even though I'd been with Dwight on and off for nearly a year, I still had strong feelings for Dane. He might slag me off in the press, and call me a bunny boiler, but privately he was always texting me. I knew he still had strong feelings for me too. He was shocked when I told him the news and that I didn't know what to do. His immediate reaction was that I should have an abortion. It seems like a terrible thing to say now, but if Dane had said, 'Get rid of the baby, and we can try again,' I might well have done it. It wouldn't have been an easy decision, but I still loved Dane so much and I was so hurt by Dwight's behaviour. But Dane said nothing of the sort. I was going to have to face this on my own.

It didn't help that all my friends thought I should have an abortion too. They couldn't understand why I would want to have the baby when I wasn't with the father. It seemed like an easy decision to them, but it wasn't to me. My family were much more supportive, and I knew that, whatever I decided, they would stand by me.

Before I knew it, the time came for my twelve-week scan. I told Dwight about it, but, of course, he didn't bother to turn up. All the other women had their partners with them and, even though I didn't love Dwight, I still wished he could have made the effort to see his unborn child. It was amazing seeing the baby moving around inside me. Even at that early stage it already looked like a person; seeing its tiny arms and legs moving and its heart beating filled me with wonder.

Afterwards I called Dwight to tell him that everything looked OK in the scan, hinting at what he had missed out on. He said that the lads had told him they didn't think there was a baby because I wasn't showing, and that it was all a publicity stunt on my part.

Those early weeks were so difficult. Not only was I in this complete state about what to do, but I felt sick and exhausted all the time. I still had to work, though, as I had no one else to rely on. I had to put on a brave face and look sexy when all I really wanted to do was to crawl under the duvet and throw up in a bucket. Having to pretend you're not pregnant when you are is really hard. I'd be posing in a thong, skintight bodice and stiletto heels, trying to breathe in and look seductive for the camera. My boobs were killing me, I wanted to pee all the time and I felt nauseous. It wasn't a lot of fun.

A typical example was a shoot I did for *Loaded.* The location was at some castle in the middle of nowhere, and it seemed to take forever. I was melting under the lights and really uncomfortable posing in positions which wouldn't show off my bump. I felt I looked enormous and I couldn't relax. Mind you, I nearly didn't do it at all. When the magazine found out I was pregnant they didn't want to go ahead with the shoot. But I got my agent to tell them that if they pulled out I would never do another shoot with them again. They changed their minds pretty quickly after that. But it worried me. If *Loaded* were being funny about me being pregnant, what would they be like once I'd had the baby? Would I ever work again?

The weeks passed and I still didn't know what to do: should I keep the baby and try and work things out with

219

Dwight, or have an abortion and see if Dane would be there for me. I was in a terrible state. I knew that I had up to twenty-four weeks to have an abortion; I would look obsessively through my baby book and, when I saw what the baby would look like at twenty-four weeks, I just couldn't see how I could do it. I kept putting off making a final decision.

But after yet another horrible phone conversation with Dwight, I did make a second appointment to have an abortion. I told Dwight what I was going to do and he demanded I put it in writing that I was the one who wanted an abortion. All he could think about was his image. He didn't want to look bad if the story ever came out in the press. Once again I drove to the clinic feeling sick with anxiety, sat in the car park for ages going over and over in my head what to do, and drove straight back home. Did I really want to get rid of this baby just because I wasn't in a proper relationship and because the father was such a shit? It wasn't the baby's fault, after all, and in many ways I was to blame as I had forgotten to take my pill.

I felt like I was completely out of control. I tormented myself some more by seeing Dane. When I was eighteen weeks gone, Dane finally asked me if I was definitely going to have the baby. With a pounding heart I said, 'If I got rid of the baby, would you get back with me?' There, I'd finally said it.

'I'm not guaranteeing it,' he replied, 'but the fact that you're pregnant doesn't help the situation.'

You can imagine how messed up in the head I was hearing that. Should I take the chance and get rid of the baby; and if I did would Dane really get back with me?

I spoke to Dwight and yet again he put pressure on me to have an abortion. I thought I was going mad. Perhaps it would be better for everyone if I just went ahead with the termination. But just before I was due to go to the clinic for the third time, I went round to see my friend Clare who had just had a baby. As I held her daughter in my arms and saw how perfect she was, so beautiful and so helpless, everything suddenly became clear. Her tiny hand curled round my finger and my eyes filled with tears. I knew there was no way I could end the life inside me. All at once I felt incredibly calm: I knew I was making the right decision. Claire was a single parent and she seemed to be coping well. If she could do it, then why couldn't I?

I called Dwight and told him that I couldn't go through with the abortion, and that I was going to have our baby. To say he wasn't happy would be an understatement. However, when he calmed down, he promised he would come to London to the twenty-week scan with me. I started to feel more optimistic; maybe we could work things out. But on the day of the scan he rang me to say he couldn't come because he had a hangover. Two hours later he rang again to say that he couldn't get hold of the person who books his flights and so he wouldn't be able to come. I told him to book it himself – all he needed was a phone and a credit card. How could anyone be so useless? So he missed out on the moment when I discovered that our baby was going to be a little boy.

I was bitterly hurt by Dwight's attitude, but I swallowed my pride and sent him a copy of the scan picture anyway. I had already sent him a copy of the twelve-week scan, proving to him that there was a baby. I'd even sent him a pregnancy book and highlighted the part where it says that babies can hear their father's voice when they reach the twenty-week stage. I really wanted Dwight to bond with his son.

November 2001 was a difficult month. Dane wasn't speaking to me because I had decided to keep the baby; I hadn't seen Dwight for nearly three months; and, just when I thought things couldn't get any worse, I came back home to the flat I shared with Sally to discover I'd been burgled and that my car had been stolen. It wasn't so much what they'd taken as what they'd done – the whole place was ransacked – and they had scrawled abuse all over the bathroom mirror: 'Jordan you slag' and 'You bitch' were written on the bathroom wall in lipstick. It made my skin crawl knowing that someone had been through all my personal things and that they'd written vile things about me. The police thought it was someone who knew me, and that made it even more frightening. My home didn't feel safe any more.

But there was worse to come. I picked up the paper one morning to see Dwight on the front page holding hands with Gaby Richens. They'd been snapped coming out of a London club together. I was furious and upset. Dwight had blatantly lied to me. All those denials about there being nothing between him and Gaby were shown up as total rubbish. He had craftily planned this weekend with Gaby hoping that I would be none the wiser. In fact, he'd made a point of telling me on the phone earlier in the week what his plans were: he was just coming down for the match with Arsenal on Monday and then was going straight back to Manchester; he definitely wouldn't be in London over the weekend. And all the time he was planning to be with Gaby.

When I'm doing a shoot, I like to have some creative input – after years of modelling, I know what will work.

©www.celebritymediagroup.com

With Dwight on our unhappy trip to Monte Carlo. This is the satin trouser-suit I agonised over.

©Rex Features

Here I am, Uncle Sam! In Los Angeles, prior to my *Playboy* audition.

With Hugh Hefner, king of the playboys. ©www.celebritymediagroup.com

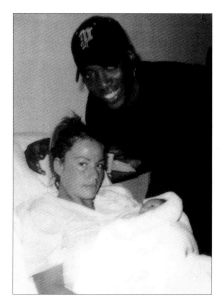

The day I gave birth to my son Harvey was the most important day of my life.

Above left: A rare picture of me, Dwight and Harvey, taken just after I had given birth.

Above right and below: A proud new mum.

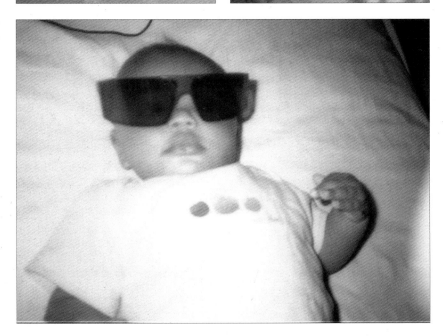

Being a single mum has not been easy, but I love every minute of it and treasure the joy that Harvey brings me.

Above: Harvey having a cuddle with his doting Aunty Sophie.

Below: With Richard Macer, who produced the three documentaries about me.

Snapped while out shopping in Brighton with Matt Peacock and Harvey.
Matt and I were happy for a while, but our differences soon brought
the relationship to an end.

©Bigpicturesphoto.com

If I hadn't seen the paper I probably never would have found out about his betrayal. For once the tabloids had done me a favour. I didn't love him, but I was still bitterly hurt. I was pregnant with his child, and he was out with other women without a care in the world.

When I confronted him, he did his usual denial routine, saying that they just happened to be coming out of the club at the same time and that after that they went their separate ways for the night. He must have thought I was completely stupid.

I had kept the fact that I was pregnant secret for such a long time that I decided I couldn't deny it any more. And so it came out in the press that I was having his baby. I didn't care, I just wanted Dwight to feel bad, even though he was never going to feel as bad as me. When he was asked about it, he denied all knowledge of the baby. Nice one, Dwight. Let's hope your son doesn't find out about that when he's older.

A few days after the revelations about me being pregnant came out, it was Dwight's thirtieth birthday. Before I knew about him and Gaby, I'd had a diamond-cross earring made for him, and even though things were so rocky between us I felt I should make the effort to go up to his party. I was having his child, after all. I couldn't bear the fact that there was so much hostility between us. But when I phoned him to let him know I was coming up to Manchester, I couldn't believe his reaction. 'No,' he said. 'I don't think that's a good idea.'

'What do you mean?' I screamed back. 'It's your birthday. I'm supposed to be your girlfriend and you're the father of my child. Why don't you want me to come?'

He answered me coldly. 'My manager doesn't think it's a good idea.'

'It's *your* birthday, not your manager's!' But I was wasting my breath. He kept insisting that he couldn't go against them. I was getting more and more angry until finally I lost it. 'Fuck you, then,' I said. 'What's the point of us carrying on? You can't keep your dick in your pants for five minutes anyway.' I ended the conversation by wishing him a shit birthday.

That's it, I thought, there's no point in making any more effort with this man. It's finished. From now on, I've got to accept the fact that it's just me and my baby.

CHAPTER TWENTY-FOUR

ALL BY MYSELF

In my heart I've always been quite old fashioned. I had always dreamed of getting married first and then starting a family; now that was never going to happen, and I had better get used to it.

Although I'd been abandoned by my baby's father, there was one place I could count on for support – my family. They were all so protective and caring which made up for a lot. I knew that whatever happened they would stand by me. Because of the burglary they had been on at me to move back to Brighton where they could look after me. Normally I'm very independent, but in this instance I took them up on the offer and I moved back home. I needed somewhere I could feel safe, secure and loved. I had also recently bought a house in the country just outside Brighton. It was going to be home for my baby and me so I needed to oversee all the building work. I was going to live there with my son, my dog and my horses. I don't need men, I thought. They always let me down.

I really hoped that having this baby would make me stronger. I've always been someone who craves love from men and I have never felt happy unless I've been in a relationship, but I thought that, once the baby was born and I had someone to love and who would love me back, things would be different. From the moment my son was born, he would be more important than any man.

I just didn't understand men, especially Dwight. I had always let him do what he wanted; I had never taken anything from him; and he still treated me badly. He had a nice house, he had the flash cars, the money, the playboy lifestyle, but there is more to life than material things. He was missing out on something that could have been good.

Fortunately, because I had been so successful in my work, I didn't need a man. I hadn't asked Dwight for any money, nor had he offered any. It did seem odd to me that a millionaire footballer might not want to contribute towards his son's upbringing, but for now I was happy to go it alone.

But, of course, I wasn't going to be allowed just to get on with it. As soon as it came out that I was pregnant the press were on my case. Once the initial feelings of nausea and tiredness had gone, I was ready to go out again and have fun. I'm just not the type to sit at home and knit. I was never going to do anything that would put my baby's health at risk – I don't smoke, and if I went out I would have one glass of white wine and then go on to mineral water – but the tabloids delighted in getting pictures of me coming out of clubs, looking, they said, the worse for wear.

Well, you try looking your best when you're getting in or out of a car and having a whooping great flash going off in your face – you're bound to look a bit bleary eyed, but that doesn't mean you're drunk. I was never drunk when I was pregnant. Then they launched into this whole health-scare thing about how I was too thin and I wasn't looking after myself. I was perfectly fine. Not everyone has to pile on the pounds when they're pregnant. My midwife was happy with how my pregnancy was going; I've got a small frame so I'm never going to get enormous. I put on weight where it mattered – my bump.

In fact, I hardly went out at all, but whenever I did the tabloids made sure I was photographed. I was even set up when I went out for a night at Stringfellows. A photographer approached me and asked if he could take some pictures for publicity for the club, saying that they were just to go on the walls. Foolishly I agreed. The next weekend, there they were in a tabloid, the headlines making me out to be a terrible mother-to-be for daring to go out and have a good time. They even suggested that I had been drinking and had just snatched a bottle of water for the photos. It was all rubbish. I hadn't even had the baby, and already I was being judged. When I was six months pregnant I went to a health farm for a quiet weekend with two close friends, and another guest sold a completely made-up story about me. They claimed that as soon as I arrived I ordered champagne, that I got drunk, shouted and started fights. It was all a pack of lies, but somehow because it's about me the papers think they can get away with printing it.

The papers also went hysterical when it came out that I was planning to give birth live on the Internet, although I will admit that with hindsight it probably wasn't my greatest idea. Actually, my manager at the time came up with it; now I've given birth I'm extremely glad it wasn't beamed to the whole world! I think it might have dented my glamour image a bit. But at the time I was serious. I do think that giving birth is one of the most beautiful and natural things any woman can do. I've always been talked about for my looks and my big boobs, but if I'd gone ahead with the project I'd also have been remembered as the girl who shared the birth of her baby with the world. Of course, it would have made a lot of money as well, but I would have used that for my son. In the end it didn't matter because I changed my mind.

I wanted to give my little boy all the love in the world. I was determined to give him everything I could. It made me want to go further in my career. I wanted to prove to all those people out there that I was capable of bringing up a child alone and being successful. I knew I couldn't work for long while I was pregnant because once I started to really show I wasn't going to be doing any glamour modelling – there's only so much digital retouching they can do! In the end I was lucky because I managed to work up to six-and-a-half months. Mainly I was doing shoots for the *Star*: I'd pose in positions where you couldn't see my belly and they'd get the old airbrush out. And I was reassured when I continued to appear in the lads' mags. When the *Loaded* shoot was published, I thought I looked pretty good. Even though I was five months pregnant by then, I was probably the only one who could tell; clever camera angles, a lot of breathing in and digital retouching had seen to that.

Now I was pregnant it seemed like the ideal time to pick up with my singing ambitions. For years I had wanted to work on my singing, but modelling had always got in the way. I started to have singing lessons again, and although I'm not a bad mover I invested in some dancing lessons too. Getting back into music was a good distraction from all my other problems. I discovered that when I was in the studio I could forget about everything and everyone else. At last I had a bit of space for myself.

First of all I had to find the right song to showcase my talents to the record company. I wanted a song that would really suit my voice. I also wanted something stylish. I definitely didn't want to do some cheesy song with a tacky video of me in a bikini. I knew it would take a while to get things going, but I was prepared to put in the work. If someone would only give me a chance, I knew I could prove that I had what it took to be a singer.

When it comes to music I'm a big softie. I like romantic ballads – anything by Luther Vandross, Alexander O'Neil or the Backstreet Boys does it for me. I really wanted to sing something along those lines, a song into which I could put my emotions and express myself. Of course, I know I will always get slated in the press for my singing ambitions, but it will be water off a duck's back. I think I have the talent to succeed, and I'm determined to go for it.

The problem I've always had is finding someone to manage me who understands my modelling commitments and who can get things moving for me in the music world.

Lots of people have made promises to me, but little ever came of them. My solicitors found me a new manager in 2000 who claimed he could get me a record contract but that didn't work out.

A year later I had a new manager, Dave Read. Sam Bond had been the nicest modelling agent I could hope for but I needed someone extremely proactive. I also needed someone with vast experience in dealing with the press. I heard good things about Dave from my friends Gary Lucy and Dean Gaffney, whom he manages. I met up with him, liked him and appointed him as my manager. I immediately introduced Dave to Sam because the last thing I wanted was any bad feeling between them. I hate it when people around me don't get on, and fortunately they were fine. After a while, though, I left Sam to go with Dave; it was easier having one person looking after my interests. Dave promised to raise my profile even further, to get me more modelling jobs, more club PAs and to get me a record deal. It seemed like my professional life had never been more exciting.

On the outside things looked great, but inside I was an emotional mess. The pregnancy hormones probably made everything worse, but I was very up and down. I was still reeling from the way Dwight had treated me, and I felt uncertain about the future. I don't think anyone ever willingly becomes a single parent: the responsibilities are frightening and I tried not to think about them.

I needed reassurance. I needed to feel loved. I wasn't going to get that from Dwight. In desperation I started to see Dane again, but it wasn't love he could give me, only sex. And, even though he had used me for sex before I started seeing Dwight, I let the same pattern start up again. I would phone him up and suggest erotic possibilities, things that I knew he couldn't resist. Once more I would go round to his flat dressed in sexy lingerie, his fantasy girl. All I wanted was to hold him, to have a cuddle and feel loved, but I knew the only way I could get close to him was if I offered sex – and adventurous sex at that. I suggested we film ourselves having sex. One time I filmed him in the bath, then he filmed me undressing for him, and getting into the bath, then we moved into the bedroom and filmed ourselves having sex. And all the time I just wanted him to say he loved me. Now I can see that I was degrading myself, that it was no way to find love, but at the time it didn't seem odd having sex with Dane, even though he wasn't the father. It would have felt odder being with Dwight after all his infidelities; I had already decided there was no way he was ever going to get close to me in that way again.

But it was doing my head in. Although I enjoyed the sex, it wasn't enough for me, and I think if Dane was really honest with himself he would admit that too. As I got bigger, Dane couldn't handle it. He said it hurt him seeing me like that, having another man's child. He told me it felt strange holding me. Increasingly I felt self-conscious when we had sex, especially if we were filming it. I just didn't feel sexy with my bump showing. But there you are: I did it to please him, as a way of getting close, but it wasn't enough. I'm an all-or-nothing girl and these half measures were doing me no good at all. Although Dane was prepared to have a physical relationship with me, he didn't want anyone else to know about us. I was his little secret, but I wasn't someone who could be kept in the shadows, on hold for when he fancied sex. I needed to be with someone who wanted me one hundred per cent, because that's what I can give in return.

God knows how long this emotional torment would have dragged on; but fortunately I met someone else, and suddenly casual sex with an ex-boyfriend stopped being part of my life ...

CHAPTER TWENTY-FIVE

POP IDOL

It was a Saturday night in January 2002. I was getting ready to go out and the television was on in the background. Suddenly I saw him and I had to stop what I was doing and sit down. My make-up could wait: this bloke was gorgeous! He had jet-black hair, huge chocolate-brown eyes – the kind that melt your heart – and a body that could melt everything else. And judging by his performance on stage he had loads of talent. He was Gareth Gates – wannabe pop idol and teenage heart-throb – and right now he was doing something to a girl in her twenties who really should know better.

Immediately after the show I was on the phone to my mate Sally. I knew she was going to be doing the make-up for a shoot of the *Pop Idol* contestants, and I was desperate to see if she could somehow introduce me to Gareth. Being a top mate she promised to do all she could, and I didn't have long to wait. A few days later she was working with Gareth and she mentioned that she knew someone who really liked him and wanted to meet him. When she told him it was Jordan he was gobsmacked and said he would love to meet me. So far so good. He immediately gave Sally his number and said to call him as soon as possible.

When I saw Sally she gave me the piece of paper on which he had written his number and signed his name with a kiss – a good sign, I thought. Over the next few days I kept getting it out of my bag and thinking, Shall I call him now? Every time I thought about picking up the phone I felt butterflies in my tummy. I really wanted to call him. It had been a long time since I fancied anyone, and I *really* fancied him. He hadn't mentioned the fact that I was pregnant to Sally, and I was hoping that he might not know. I thought that if I wore the right outfit we could meet and he might be none the wiser.

I finally decided to call him when I was in the car with Sally. She kept on saying I should go for it, and eventually I plucked up the courage to dial his number. Then I bottled out and made Sally speak to him first. 'Guess who I'm with,' she said, 'and she really wants to talk to you.' She handed over the phone and he sounded really sweet. To my excitement, we arranged to meet that week.

At that stage all the *Pop Idol* contestants were staying in the Marriott hotel on the Edgware Road in London. They were pretty much chaperoned all the time, but Gareth just told them he was going to meet a friend. Sally and I were waiting in my Range Rover just over the road from the hotel. Fortunately I have blacked-out windows so there was no danger of anyone spotting us. As we sat there I started to feel more and more tense, and kept asking Sally whether she thought he would turn up. But finally I saw him walking towards the car. My heart was thumping – there he was! As he got into the car and sat next to me I suddenly came over all shy and coy, which is not like me at all. He was much taller than I had realised, and was even better looking in real life. He had really nice lips, cute freckles and gorgeous dimples when he smiled. He leaned over and kissed me on the cheek. 'It's great to meet you,' he said.

'It's great to meet *you*,' I replied. I had that fantastic bubbly feeling inside you get when you fancy someone. At that time I had absolutely no idea he was only seventeen; he seemed so confident and sure of himself. By the time I did find out, it was too late: I was in too deep for his age to matter.

Because we didn't want to be seen together in public, Sally said that we could use her place to meet. So we drove all the way to Hayes near Heathrow and then sneaked into her one-bedroom flat. It felt like we were kids again, skiving from school, and it made us all a bit giggly and silly. We spent that first afternoon just chatting together on the sofa. We sat really close to each other; occasionally our arms would touch. We kept looking at each other as well – there was obviously a strong attraction there. I think we might even have held hands like a pair of innocent teenagers. He kept giving me compliments, saying how pretty I looked and what a fantastic figure I had. All the time I was doing my best to breathe in so he wouldn't notice my bump! I was worried that he might stutter so much that I wouldn't be able to understand him, but it was fine. The only problem I had was with his Bradford accent – sometimes I didn't have a clue what he was saying.

He told me he had always wanted to meet me, but he never dreamed that someone like me would be interested in him. I kept thinking that any second he would ask me about the baby, but he didn't. I had chosen my outfit really carefully: I was wearing tight bootleg jeans, high-heeled boots and a low-cut black top which disguised my bump as much as possible by drawing his attention away to my other assets. Maybe my cunning plan had worked.

The afternoon went by much too quickly, and all too soon I had to drive him back to his hotel; but he promised that we would meet again soon. What a cutie! I couldn't believe how well we had got on together.

After that we saw each other as often as we could, and we spoke on the phone and texted each other all the time. It was hard for him thinking up excuses to get away from the hotel, but somehow he managed it. He made me feel really good about myself. He was so loving and complimentary – he was always touching me, stroking my face or my hair, or holding my hand. He may have only been seventeen, but he could certainly have taught Dwight a few things when it came to making a woman feel appreciated. He was also a great kisser. I always thought Dane was the best kisser I'd ever had, but Gareth definitely beat him in that department. I felt like a teenager again when we spent hours snogging on the sofa. It was such a gorgeous feeling.

For once I broke my golden wait-a-month-before-I-sleep-with-a-bloke rule. After two weeks of all this heavy petting, I thought it was time we went further. I really fancied him, and I also thought that if we left it any longer my bump would be too obvious and we'd never be able to make love. Gareth assured me that he wasn't a virgin, and that he had slept with a girl back home. But I can definitely say that I took his virginity.

It was on a rainy afternoon that I decided to move things on. I shut the blinds and borrowed Sally's duvet to make the sofa more comfortable. There was a music channel on television in the background, but we weren't interested in that. Together we converted the grey sofa into a bed. Our little love nest.

After we had taken our clothes off it soon became clear that Gareth was very inexperienced. He didn't seem to know where to put his hands or what to do with them. I tried to help him by guiding them to places where they would actually be able to do something. I was very complimentary about his body, which I was pleased to discover was pretty fit, even though it wasn't a man's body yet – he needed to fill out a bit. I had no complaints about the size of his willy. It was all right – it wasn't the biggest or the smallest, just average. We snuggled up under the duvet and I have to admit I wasn't feeling at my sexiest with my bump, and I thought it might put him off. But he didn't seem to notice – I guess he was too busy concentrating on his performance.

We first tried making love in the missionary position. It wasn't particularly comfortable for me, but I thought I would give him a chance before I took over. After a few misses he managed to get inside me and off he went. It was all a bit rushed and fumbled – he wasn't able to build up any kind of satisfying rhythm – and it was over very quickly. So all in all it was not particularly pleasurable for me, but I didn't mind. Oh well, I thought, he'll get used to it and learn how to hold it in. The earth hadn't moved for me, but practice makes perfect ...

Two afternoons later found us making love again. This time I thought I would do it my way. I took control of the situation by going on top; I hoped to slow things down and at least make him keep going for longer. It was better for me this way but then we hit another problem: his willy kept on slipping out and, whereas a more experienced lover would have been able to pop it back in with a minimum of fuss, Gareth kept apologising and drawing attention to what had happened, saying, 'Oh no, what have I done? I'm sorry.' Then he would manage to get it back in and would be at it again like a rabbit. Poor boy, he didn't really have a clue.

It was a bit of a turnaround for me sleeping with such an inexperienced lover. I've always slept with men who knew exactly what they wanted in bed, who knew how to do all the things to turn a woman on and who were able to teach me a thing or two. Gareth had a lot to learn, but I didn't mind being his teacher. I know it wasn't the best sex in the world, and I'm sure he'll look back and think the same, but I didn't want to scare him by doing too many different positions. He was also a bit innocent when it came to the facts of life. After we had made love a few times, he finally asked me about the baby. It didn't bother him in the least that I was pregnant, but he was concerned that he might be able to get me pregnant again. I made a big effort not to laugh, and explained to him that was impossible.

I know some people will think that me having sex with Gareth when I was pregnant was shameful, but I didn't find it so. Just because you are pregnant, it doesn't mean you go off sex, and in any case I had strong feelings for him. Every time we met we ended up in bed, and it definitely brought us closer. I was prepared to forgive his inexperience as a lover because I liked him so much and really enjoyed our time together. When we were apart we were always texting and phoning each other, and because he was so short of money I bought myself a new Orange phone so he could use his Orange mobile after 6pm and not get charged. He would send me messages calling me his 'princess' and his 'honey', and very soon after we met he told me that he loved me. I would get text messages like, 'I love you with all my heart, honey. I love you more than anything. Have a good night, be good, love you, sweetheart. Gareth.' And he would say to me, 'Just remember when you go out clubbing that I'm your boyfriend. Don't go chatting anyone else up.' It was all very flattering; but I didn't give my heart away so easily any more. I had been so emotionally battered by my experiences with Dane and Dwight that I was more cautious. Inside, though, it felt good to hear Gareth say these things.

Best of all, now I had started seeing Gareth I suddenly felt free of my destructive dependency on Dane. I realised that he had used me and I vowed I would never let it happen again. It was too damaging. I felt like I was turning away from the darkness and walking into sunshine again.

Having Gareth as a lover certainly put new interest into Saturday night television. He would phone and text me during the breaks saying, 'Watch the next song. I'll be looking at the camera and thinking of you.' It was so exciting. I'd be sitting there, willing him to do well. He was pretty confident that he would win the competition. He might have come across as being modest and shy because of his stutter, but he was actually incredibly ambitious. I didn't mind that; in fact, I thought it made him more attractive.

Another time I was watching *Pop Idol* on ITV2 and he was relaxing backstage; on top of the pile of magazines in front of him was me on the cover of *Loaded.* It was really weird watching him watching me. After the show we spoke and he told me that Darius had been slagging me off and that he had defended me. He said it was very hard not letting on that he knew me.

Gareth came second in the competition, and his future was assured. On Valentine's Day he was in America recording 'Unchained Melody'. He sent a dozen red roses to Sally's flat – he couldn't risk sending them to my house – and he called me to let me know the flowers were from him. I remember thinking how sweet it was that he was so excited about his new white Hugo Boss suit and his snakeskin boots which he was going to be wearing in the video of his song. I thought the suit looked pretty good, but the boots were revolting. I didn't tell him that, of course; I wouldn't have wanted to hurt his feelings.

It was very romantic, and all the more so because we had to keep things secret. I didn't try and think of the future; I was happy to enjoy what we had for the moment. Occasionally, though, I did wonder what I was doing with someone so much younger than me. I thought that especially when he went home to see his family and phoned me from his bedroom, whispering that he couldn't talk for long as his mum was making his tea. Then it would dawn on me that I was seeing a teenager who still lived at home. His mum probably still bought his boxer shorts – boxer shorts which I would be ripping off him next time we met, and it wouldn't be to wash them. It was all a bit strange, but I liked him too much to care about his age.

Gareth was absolutely paranoid about anyone finding out about us, in particular his management and the press. He knew that his management would go mad because they were so busy promoting him as the lad with the squeaky-clean image who would appeal to teenage girls. And as for the press, well, of course, they would have a field day. I could just imagine the headlines: I would be portrayed as some kind of cradle-snatching man-eater and, while *I'm* used to it, I knew Gareth would be devastated. So I completely sympathised. I told him I didn't mind keeping our relationship quiet for as long as it took to get his career off the ground. I also didn't want any negative publicity coming out about me being pregnant and seeing him, so I did everything I could to ensure that no one found out about us. I really hoped that one day we could be open about our feelings for each other, that our relationship could develop, but, because of the circumstances, the only friend I confided in was Sally. No one else knew, not even my manager or my mum and dad.

But, of course, the press found out, and that was the beginning of the end for me and my pop-idol lover. We never saw each other in public; we always met in Sally's flat and she would go out and leave us alone. We never even went out for a drink together, and the only meal we shared was a Burger King takeaway in my Range Rover. So I was hugely excited when I found out we could both stay at the same hotel when the Brit Awards were on, the plush Conrad London in Chelsea Harbour. I had a ticket to the Brits, but Gareth wasn't allowed to go so we decided that we would stay in the same hotel and I wouldn't go to the awards. I begged my manager to get me a room on the same floor as Gareth. When he asked me why, I just said I had heard that that was where the best views were – as if I was going to be looking at them!

As soon as I arrived at the hotel, I couldn't wait for the day to pass so that we could be together. Gareth was busy rehearsing and I had lunch with Dave, my manager at the time. It was a real effort to seem normal when I was so excited about seeing Gareth. Later that day Dave phoned me and said, 'You'll never guess who I've just seen arriving at the hotel – only Gareth Gates.' He knew that I fancied Gareth, but, of course, he had no idea that he was already my lover. I had to act like I was really surprised; inside I was thinking, 'Yes, he's here!'

That night I made sure I was looking my very best. I took extra care over my make-up and my outfit. I wanted everything to be perfect. I wore my blue cowboy boots with pink stars on, and a little pink towelling skirt with a matching pink jacket. Underneath I was wearing Trashy lingerie from LA – a pink lace bra and pink lace French knickers. I really wanted this to be a night to remember. It was going to be the first entire night I could spend with Gareth, and I wanted to enjoy every minute. At around six o'clock, Gareth finally called and said he was free to see me. I ran to his hotel room. As soon as he opened the door we fell into each other's arms, kissing passionately.

He had been given quite a fancy suite with a large bedroom and adjoining living room and bathroom. He had his keyboard set up, and a hi-fi. He was listening to Britney, and he kept dancing round the room showing me his new moves. He told me he had just received a call from Kerry, wife of Westlife's Bryan McFadden, inviting him out to dinner, but he had turned them down saying he was busy rehearsing.

For once we didn't need to rush anything, so we decided to have a meal together. I had been too nervous to eat much at lunchtime, and now I was starving. We ordered scampi and chips from room service and then, because Gareth had no wine in his room, I said I would go and get a bottle from mine, just so we could have a glass together to relax. Unfortunately, when I was sneaking back along the corridor with the wine, I got snapped by a hidden camera. We found out later that it was hidden in a box of tissues on the table in the corridor. We had one night together before all hell broke loose.

Gareth's performance was definitely improving. I was just getting into the swing of things, and Gareth was just getting into his stride, when suddenly he leaped off the bed clutching himself and screaming, 'My dick, my dick, look, it's bleeding!' It bloody well was, too – a lot. He was practically hysterical; I suppose any man would be to see their tackle in such a state. I tried to calm him down. We could hardly call for a doctor, or go to casualty, so we had to stop the bleeding immediately. I found some cotton wool in the bathroom, discovered the first-aid kit his mum had packed up for him – I don't imagine she thought it would be put to this use – and got some Vaseline. Then I wiped away the blood to try and see what had happened. I reckoned his foreskin was a bit tight and it had ripped slightly – I'm just guessing, mind you.

Carefully I rubbed some Vaseline into the cut as I thought it might stop the bleeding. Poor Gareth took it all very badly. I laid him down on the bed next to me and cuddled him – our dreams of a passionate night of sex were well and truly shattered. But still it was lovely lying in each other's arms, and the double bed was certainly an improvement on Sally's sofa.

But, just when you think nothing else can go wrong, it always does. First thing in the morning, after lots of kisses but nothing else as Gareth was still too sore, I crept back into my room. I was looking forward to a hot bath, a day's shopping and to seeing Gareth again that night. Then I got the phone call from my manager. The *Sun* was going to be running a story that I'd spent the night with Gareth; they had a picture of me walking along the corridor towards his room. I knew I had to deny this: Gareth would be devastated. So I lied to Dave and said it was complete rubbish. I hadn't met Gareth – I'd like to, because I did fancy him, but I hadn't. I felt really bad lying to Dave, but there was nothing for it. I had to protect Gareth.

As I predicted, Gareth was very upset, and his management was furious. He was just starting out, so I think he was terrified that they would dump him. He called me in a panic and said, 'Please, deny the story. I'm in real trouble.' I reassured him and told him not to worry, I would definitely deny the story. Then he had to convince his management. Fortunately they believed him. Because we had both denied the story, there was a strong chance it would all blow over soon.

Gareth and I were both booked to stay another night in the hotel and, even though the press thing had happened, we still desperately wanted to see each other. It would have been torture staying in the hotel and not being able to be together. His management, however, insisted on moving him out of his room and into a top penthouse suite. The only way you could get to the suite was in a lift where you needed a special pass. Gareth said he didn't dare risk coming down to collect me in the lift. How on earth was I going to get up there without anyone seeing me? But I just had to see him. I worked out with my friend Claire, who was staying with me in the hotel, that the only way to do it would be to go up the fire escape. I phoned Gareth to say we were coming up, and he promised to meet us by the door to his suite.

As I put my hand on the door of the fire exit, I was convinced I would set off the alarm. Claire and I counted to ten and then I pushed it open. Nothing happened. We walked up a couple of flights of stairs. At any moment I expected someone to stop us and ask us what we were doing. Finally we reached Gareth's floor. There was another fire-exit door. Again I was sure that the alarm would be triggered, but I opened it and nothing happened. Gareth was standing in the doorway to his suite. I rushed into his room with Claire and we all collapsed on the sofa. I introduced him to Claire. Gareth and I were both in a state of shock, saying we couldn't believe the press had found out about us. I told Claire that I would call her later that night so she could come and meet me at the fire exit, and then she left us alone together.

First of all we had to talk about what had happened. Both our stories matched, and that was the main thing. Gareth was still very twitchy though. He really felt he couldn't afford to let the truth come out, and he genuinely thought his singing career would be ruined if the press found out about our affair. He kept saying over and over again that we had to deny it. He said that singing was what he had always wanted to do, and he couldn't bear it if he was stopped from realising his dream. He was also worried about his parents finding out – I think they were both quite devout Christians, so he said they would go mad if they found out about me. I totally sympathised with him. I told him that in the world we were both in it was really hard to trust anyone, but I swore he could trust me. I would never betray him to the press.

We made love that night – he was still sore, but he really wanted it and I did too. Then we lay in each other's arms talking about how we felt and he said he loved me. I had to leave at around 2am. I felt so sad saying goodbye. I wondered when we would be able to see each other again.

I was right to be sad, because after that night everything changed. It was the last time I saw him. We kept in regular contact by phone and text, but gradually his calls started to sound more and more distant. I understood that he had a lot going on, what with coming second in *Pop Idol* and getting a record deal sorted out, but whenever I asked him if we could meet up he always made excuses, saying he was really busy or that his mum and dad were with him and it would be difficult. Things were not right, I could tell. But I had plenty of things in my life to occupy me. I was still busy with my singing lessons, and getting things ready for the baby. And I was still doing the odd shoot – it's amazing how they can airbrush things out – so it's not like I was waiting for him to call.

Then I read about him being linked to two of the *Pop Idol* contestants – Hayley and Zoe. I immediately texted him to ask him what was going on. He denied it, of course, but I was angry. Why the hell had he insisted on keeping me a secret if he was seeing these girls? I almost felt like going to the press then, but I kept my mouth shut. I still wanted him to know that he could trust me.

When he went back home after *Pop Idol*, things became even worse. He phoned even less and when he did he didn't sound like himself at all. Whenever I did call him to find out what was going on, he barely spoke. Then I got a series of text messages from him ending the relationship: 'Over the next year or so I'm going to be so busy, it's so hard meeting you so early in my career, it's dangerous and being so young is difficult.' 'Kate, you're the most honest and trustworthy person I have ever met, please understand this is all so hard for me because I love you but it's for the best.' 'Kate, this is too hard for me, it's my first-ever relationship and it's just come at the wrong time. I couldn't have said this over the phone.' His family, of course, was in the next room.

I was gutted. I really didn't need any more rejections in my life. I was with him at an important time in his life, and then suddenly he dumped me. He had always said that once he got his record deal then we might be able to be open about our relationship, but, when the deal came through, our relationship was over.

Did I love him? I don't know. I was very fond of him and I did fancy him – maybe it was my pregnancy hormones. Also at that time I did feel very low: I felt abandoned by Dwight and tormented by Dane, and all I needed was love and protection. So I probably could have fallen in love with Gareth if we had carried on seeing each other because he was so charming and good looking and said all the things a girl wants to hear. To be honest, though, I thought it was all too good to be true. I knew there was no way it could last; it was too perfect. How sad that I was right.

Even though I was hurt by the way he had treated me, at the end I kept my promise. I didn't tell anyone about our relationship, apart from my two closest friends. I would still send him a text every now and then and once, just before I had Harvey, he texted me from the airport on the way back from LA telling me not to worry about giving birth, that he was sure I'd be fine. But after Harvey was born he changed his number and didn't contact me.

After that I would think of him every now and then; I would wonder what he was doing and whether he still thought of me. He had seemed so into me that I couldn't really understand why he had changed. Part of me hoped that he would get in touch again; we had become close and it seemed sad that he had turned his back on what we had. I did feel down about it for a while, but I had to be strong. I had so many other things going on in my life; I couldn't wait around for a seventeen-year-old to call me.

CHAPTER TWENTY-SIX

SINGLE MUM

I had hardly seen Dwight during my pregnancy; he took no interest in the fact that I was carrying his son. I didn't want to get back with him, but I couldn't help feeling let down. I was also angry that he hadn't offered to contribute anything financially. I didn't want to fleece him, but I thought it was only right that he paid something towards his baby. I knew I'd get nowhere talking to Dwight, so I went to my solicitors.

As soon as he received their letter stating that we would be asking him for maintenance, he was straight on the phone to me. 'Couldn't we sort this out between us?' he asked. 'Do we have to go down this road, involving solicitors?' He was concerned that it was all going to end up in court and there would be loads of publicity.

I pointed out to him that if he agreed to be reasonable there wouldn't be any publicity. I just wanted some security for my son.

251

'People ask me why you're having my baby,' he told me. 'And they think it's because you're after my money. They think you chose to have a baby with me because I'm worth more than all the other men you've been out with.'

I was furious. 'I don't care what other people think! They're wrong. I'm not a money-grabber. I've never asked you for anything, you know that. I've got my own money, I don't want yours. This is about our son.'

But, as on so many other occasions, I felt Dwight wasn't really taking in what I was saying. His number-one priority was himself. Selfish through and through, all he could think about was that he might have to reach into his pocket. It's not like he couldn't afford it – he probably earned around forty grand a week, and good luck to him. All I wanted was for him to do right by his son.

I didn't make any promises about not using solicitors. I thought I would wait and see what happened. Dwight decided to turn on the charm. He came down to Brighton and took my family and me out for dinner, twice. He impressed them, but he didn't impress me. It would take more than this to make up for his treatment of me.

But I knew I couldn't shut him out of my life altogether. I wanted my son to know his father, even though Dwight wasn't going to make it easy. His attitude to the birth was a prime example. First of all he said he wouldn't want to be there because he thought it would be a disgusting sight. I couldn't believe that he could think that of something so natural and beautiful. Then he changed his mind and asked if he could be there. I knew I wouldn't feel comfortable being in labour with him in the room, but I had no problems with him waiting outside. I would never want him to be able to say to our son that I hadn't let him be there. Secretly I hoped that, when he saw his son for the first time, he would finally show some emotion, that it would hit him that he was a dad. After all, who couldn't fail to be moved by seeing their baby for the first time?

Despite his suggestion that we could sort out the question of maintenance ourselves, he made no effort in that direction. He even changed all his phone numbers and wouldn't give them to me. When I asked how I was supposed to get in touch with him, he told me I could call his manager – as if he was going to be there at four in the morning when I went into labour! It was stress I didn't need.

In March 2002 when I was seven months pregnant, Dwight invited me and my friend Sally to his place in Cheshire for the weekend. Was this his way of trying to bring us closer together? If it was it turned out to be a disaster. When I arrived at his house after an exhausting five-hour drive, he wasn't even in. He had gone out clubbing and had left the key for us to let ourselves in. As Sally and I settled into the house we kept finding notes left by Dwight's various women. I even found one by the sink in the bathroom when I was cleaning my teeth. It said, 'Thank you for a lovely weekend, for my pink necklace. Sorry about the press stuff, love G.' Had he left them lying around deliberately so that I would read them? And if he had, why? Did he think I was interested in him in that way? I thought it was very immature.

When he finally rolled in at three in the morning, he got into bed with me. All I wanted to do was sleep, but he kept putting his arm round me and trying to have a cuddle. He was the last person in the world I felt like doing that with. I couldn't believe his nerve.

The next evening he took us out to an Italian restaurant in Manchester. He made a big deal of telling us to dress casually in tracksuits, then he put a suit on. After the meal it became clear why. 'I'm going out to a club,' he said. 'You can't come, you're not dressed correctly.' I asked him how we were going to get back to his house and he told me to take his car. It was the perfect end to a terrible weekend – I ended up lost and was stopped by the police for speeding.

The next morning I left without saying goodbye. On the journey back to Brighton I texted him: 'You were rude, arrogant and that was the worst weekend of my life.' I don't understand why Dwight bothered to ask me up at all if he was only going to treat me like that. But then, I have never understood what makes him tick. Our values and outlooks on life were poles apart.

After that, we had no contact until the week before the baby was due. When he finally phoned it was again to talk about the solicitors, asking me not to go down that route, that we could sit down and sort things out together. I said to him, 'You haven't rung me for seven weeks, since I last went up and saw you, and then you were a right bastard to me, and showed me no respect. How can you talk about us being able to sort anything out?' He apologised, but then he went on about the solicitors again. In the end I said, 'You're going to have a son in a week. Do you want to be at the birth or not?'

He replied that he did, but when I asked him for his numbers again he still wouldn't give them to me, telling me to ring his manager. What possible kind of relationship could I have with him when he behaved like this?

A few days later he called again. This time he said he was in London and that he might drive down to see me. I asked him why he was in London and he said it was to see me, but he couldn't commit to a day. I knew there was no way he had come down especially to see me, and sure enough he had been invited to the Beckhams' World Cup party. In the end he said he would come down on Saturday during the day. But he didn't ring, so I made other plans. I arranged to go out for dinner with Gary Lucy, Dean Gaffney and a couple of friends. I wasn't going to hang around waiting for Dwight. Finally my phone rang at half past eight just as I was getting ready to go out. It was Dwight telling me that he was on his way to see me. I told him that I now had plans to go out because he hadn't bothered to ring earlier, but he was welcome to come along. He refused, saying we had important things to discuss and he wanted to see me on my own. It was only when I put the phone down that I wished I'd said to him that he'd had nearly nine months to show an interest, to talk things through. Why leave it until four days before I was due to give birth?

I suggested we meet another time, but he said he couldn't because of the Beckhams' party. He was also going to be busy in the week working for a children's charity, and that made me want to laugh. He was doing that, and he wasn't even taking responsibility for his own child. So I tried to shrug it off, and ended the conversation by saying, 'I'm sure if I was in labour you'd come down.' But I wasn't sure at all.

Like all expectant mothers, all I could think about was

the birth. As the day grew closer I felt a mixture of excitement and nerves. This was a time in my life when I needed to feel looked after. I am very independent, but I could have done with some support from Dwight. Then, on 16 May, the day before my due date, he rang again. He said he had to see me: he had something important to tell me which he could only say face to face, and would I travel up to London and meet him?

I was speechless. I can't imagine there are many other men who would expect a woman in my condition to travel all that way. But reluctantly I agreed. Perhaps it was going to be something that would affect my son's future.

As usual I couldn't have been more wrong. After Dwight had dragged me to NikeTown to get his free trainers, he told me that he was flying to Australia the next day to teach football for a week, so he wouldn't be there at the birth. He said it was good money and he couldn't refuse. I couldn't believe he put earning cash, which he definitely didn't need, above being at the birth of his son. Our baby hadn't even been born, and already Dwight was proving himself to be a worthless father. As I drove home, physically and emotionally exhausted, I thought, I *am* going to get him to pay maintenance for this baby. It was the least he could do.

CHAPTER TWENTY-SEVEN
HELLO HARVEY

On Monday, 27 May 2002 at 1.15am, I met the most important person in my life, all eight pounds seven ounces of him. He was perfect. Hello, Harvey Daniel Price.

When I first saw him, I just couldn't believe how beautiful he was. A lot of newborn babies can look really wrinkly and scrunched-up like little old men, but he didn't: his skin was smooth, his features perfect. I couldn't get over how gorgeous his lips were – so red and cute, definitely not like his dad's! I was also surprised by how white he was. It sounds funny, but I was expecting him to be darker with loads of Afro hair!

He didn't cry at all, but just seemed peaceful and laid back. It was wonderful holding him in my arms; I couldn't believe he was finally out in the world. Here was this new person and I was responsible for him. It was an incredible feeling. And such a relief! Harvey was ten days late and I had to be induced. I was terrified because, even after all the surgery I've had, I still have a complete phobia about needles, but, within an hour of being given the drugs, my contractions started. It was bearable at first, in fact I was playing cards with my mum, my stepdad Paul, my brother, his wife Louise, my sister, my manager and Sally. Then the pain got worse and worse, especially when they broke my waters. I wanted an epidural but they thought I was doing OK without one. Later, when I asked again, they said I was too far gone. So it was just good old gas and air for me.

I never wanted to have a caesarean – I'm certainly not too posh to push. I wanted to have a natural birth, and I'm really proud I managed it. I did it on the NHS, and the room *was* a bit ropey: the window was broken and people kept coming in and tying a sheet over it to stop it banging, which I thought was quite funny even though I was in agony. The birthing pool wasn't working, so I was in and out of the bath trying to cope with the pain – I bet you don't get that at the Portland. But I never complained. I think the staff thought that I would play up and be all demanding and starry, but I didn't care what the room looked like so long as they were there to deliver my baby safely.

Everyone was great, really supportive and caring. Everyone except Dwight, who was back from Australia by this time. I had been in the hospital since nine in the morning, and my mum had been phoning him all day to say that I was about to give birth, but Dwight didn't turn up until eleven at night. I think he was hoping that, the later he left it, the more likely it was that everything would be over and done with and he'd just be presented with a perfect little baby in a Babygro. He also seemed shocked to see me in so much pain, but that didn't make him sympathetic. At one point he turned round to my brother and asked him if the noise I was making meant I really was in that much pain, or whether I was making it up. My brother was outraged. 'What do you think?' he said. 'She's in agony, can't you see?' Then Dwight came into the room and tried to give me the gas and air, and told me how to breathe. I told him to get out! How dare he tell me what to do when he'd only just got there? I was doing fine without him, thanks.

Giving birth has to have been the most painful experience of my life, and the most undignified – I ended up on all fours pushing Harvey out. But I suppose there were some funny sides to it as well. Because my contractions weren't coming quickly enough, the midwife made me go for a walk; but because they wanted me to be where no one could see me, just in case someone sneaked a photo, I had to walk up and down the fire escape. It was fine walking down the stairs – it was on the way up that things really started hurting. Then in the bath I had a hair crisis. I knew I was going to look terrible by the time Harvey made his appearance, and I thought, at least if my hair was all right, I wouldn't look so terrible in the first photos my family were bound to take. So I kept telling the midwife not to get water on my hair when she sponged my face, because I really didn't want it to go curly. I know it sounds mad, but I wasn't thinking straight at the time. How vain was I?

When Harvey was finally born, my mum ran out to Dwight in the waiting room and tried to get him to come in and cut the cord. He refused, saying he couldn't stand the sight of blood, so my stepdad Paul did it. I would have thought most fathers would have been dying to see their son as soon as possible, but not Dwight. My mum only took Harvey out to him once he was all clean and wrapped in a towel.

Dwight didn't come in to see me until half past two, over an hour after I'd given birth, and the first thing he said to me was, 'You look really rough, minging!' What the hell did he think I was going to look like after all those hours of labour? And then he asked, 'Are you still doing the *OK!* shoot?' Never mind about his son! At this amazing time, all he could think about was himself. Then he saw a baby's bottle next to me, and started having another go about how I should be breastfeeding Harvey. I really didn't feel I had to justify my reasons to him, and I was so tired I could hardly speak. I just wanted him to go so I could rest with my baby.

The next morning he came back to the hospital with a huge bunch of flowers and a teddy, but I'm sure he only did that because he knew the press were going to be outside. He didn't even hand me the flowers – he just dumped them down on the bed – so he had obviously only brought them for the cameras. Then he managed to have yet another go at me. As I was getting Harvey dressed he noticed some black marks on his back – they're called Mongolian blue spots and are quite common with dark-skinned or mixed-race children. Dwight immediately jumped to the conclusion that I had bruised Harvey somehow, and was so quick to blame me. I don't know what I had expected – maybe I had some naive hope that he would be different when he saw his son, but it obviously wasn't going to happen. We even argued about whether Harvey should wear a little cotton hat or not. I wanted him to wear it to keep warm, Dwight thought he didn't need it. Was there nothing we could agree on?

I stayed in my room because I didn't want to draw attention to myself, but Dwight went walking round the ward with Harvey, showing off like a proud dad. I wondered how long it would last.

I left the hospital at ten the next day, but before I did I had an upsetting moment. I was watching morning television and there was a discussion about what was in the papers. The conversation turned to Jordan's new baby, and they started slating me. I was used to getting abuse, but somehow now I had Harvey what they were saying was much more hurtful. I couldn't wait to get home.

I found life with Harvey surprisingly easy. I'm used to babies, because when my sister was young I used to look after her. Everyone else was amazed at how I took to motherhood, but I was so happy with my beautiful son. I kept looking at him and thinking, God, he's really mine! I felt so protective of him. I loved holding him and breathing in his wonderful newborn smell. My mum had bought me a baby book and every day I took Polaroid pictures of him to put in it; they change so quickly at that age and I didn't want to forget any of it.

The midwife couldn't believe how together I was; I didn't get the baby blues or anything. The only downside was the agony I was in down below! I could hardly bear to sit down for two weeks. Ten days after I'd had Harvey I did a shoot for *OK!* and I really don't know how I got through it. It's bloody hard trying to look good when your nether regions are throbbing like hell! But I was so proud of him, and I wanted to show him off to the world.

I couldn't relax; there were so many things to sort out. Even though I was fuming with Dwight, I had to involve him in some decisions about Harvey. I had already decided on the names – Harvey after my granddad and Daniel after my brother – but I kept having to call Dwight to remind him that we had to register Harvey within six weeks. But he kept putting me off. I felt frustrated by his attitude; didn't he want to be recognised as the father?

Finally he came down to Brighton. We were on our way to the town hall to register Harvey together, and Dwight's mobile rang. It was his manager. The next thing I knew, Dwight was telling me that he couldn't register Harvey because his manager had told him not to. They said they wanted him to take a DNA test to see if he really was the father. Apparently they were concerned because Harvey looked too white.

I hit the roof, and we started arguing furiously. He said he had to go along with what his manager said; I told him not to be so stupid. I felt so humiliated and hurt. I knew Dwight was the dad, and it wasn't something I was proud of. I wanted Dwight's name on the certificate for Harvey's sake. I didn't want there to be a blank space where his dad's name should be.

In the end we didn't register Harvey that day, but we did do it a few weeks later when I'd just about given up hope. But Dwight wasn't going to make it easy. Once again we were on our way to Brighton town hall and we started arguing. Out of the blue Dwight said that he didn't want Daniel as a middle name, he wanted Elverson. I said that he had no right to make demands, as he hadn't been around when I was pregnant. I told him he could have Elverson, but I wasn't dropping Daniel. Dwight replied that in that case he wouldn't register Harvey, and he got out of the car.

By that stage I'd had enough. I was about to go into the building and register my son without him when Dwight called me on my mobile. He said to wait for him, but when he turned up there was no apology; in fact, he didn't say a word. The atmosphere was so tense between us, I remember saying, 'You could hear a pin drop.' When the registrar asked us what names we wanted I said, 'Harvey Daniel Price.' I then turned to Dwight and said he could still have Elverson, but he just shrugged. The registrar must have picked up on the bad vibes between us; she asked Dwight if he was sure he didn't want to include his name, but he just shook his head and said nothing.

We had arranged that he would look after Harvey in the afternoon, but by now he was in a right mood and said he couldn't. Here we go, I thought. Every time we argue, he's going to take it out on Harvey.

A week later my solicitor called. He told me that Dwight had taken his DNA test and they were waiting for Harvey to have his done. Apparently Dwight had done it that afternoon in Brighton when we registered Harvey. So, if we hadn't argued, he would have taken Harvey with him to the hospital, though whether he would have been able to test Harvey without my permission I don't know. All I know is that I was furious. I phoned Dwight and asked him what the hell he was up to, what was the point of registering Harvey as his and then having a DNA test? He said that he could apply to have his name taken off the certificate if Harvey turned out not to be his.

'This is our baby we're talking about, not a toy!' I shouted back at him. I told him if he really didn't think Harvey was his then I didn't want him coming down and seeing him. Dwight told me that he did believe Harvey was his, and it was his manager who wanted him to have the test.

'If your manager told you to jump off a cliff, would you?' I asked him. I felt totally drained by this constant arguing which got us nowhere. It was no big surprise that Dwight was turning out to be a disaster as a father.

CHAPTER TWENTY-EIGHT

THE BOMBSHELL

Apart from Dwight, things seemed to be going well for me, and I was loving being a mum. Miraculously my body had gone back to a size six without me having to do any workouts at the gym or live off steamed fish and boiled rice! I was getting ready to go out to Los Angeles to promote my first *Playboy* cover. Richard Macer had been filming a second documentary about my new life as a mother for the BBC. The first one had been well received and I thought it was great they wanted more. Life was looking pretty good. Then Harvey had his six-week check with the midwife and everything changed. She told me she was worried about him. She asked me if he followed me with his eyes – that's what babies are supposed to do – and I said not really. She explained that Harvey should have been fixing on my face and smiling what they call a social smile, and he wasn't. She told me that I must take him to the doctors as soon as possible to get him checked out.

I just couldn't imagine there could be anything really wrong with him. I remember thinking, Oh, it won't happen to us, he's probably just a bit slow. After all, no one in my family thought there was anything the matter with him, and my mum and my nan have had loads of experience with children, so they should know. Harvey seemed like a very happy baby, just a little quiet.

It was at the doctors that I started to feel really anxious. He shone lights directly into Harvey's eyes, but he didn't react at all. He told me there was real cause for concern and that Harvey must see a specialist. Straight away we went to the hospital in Brighton. There they put drops in Harvey's eyes which must have hurt him because he cried and cried and normally he never did that. It was agony watching them doing it, knowing that my baby was in pain. Then again they shone lights into his eyes. I could tell something was really wrong by how serious they looked. I was gripped with panic and anxiety and I was praying that everything would be all right.

But it wasn't. Finally, after an agonising wait while they did all their tests, they dropped the bombshell. My son was blind. His optic nerves had failed to develop and he would probably never be able to see. It was the most shattering moment of my life. I broke down and cried. I felt as if my world had been blown apart. I wished more than anything that what they had said was not true. I was desperate to get a second opinion, but at the famous Moorfields Eye Hospital in London they confirmed my nightmare. Harvey was blind.

I couldn't help thinking it was somehow my fault. The first thing I asked the doctors was if my lifestyle was to blame for what had happened to Harvey. I was worried because I had used sun beds when I was pregnant, and I thought that maybe the ultraviolet light had caused his blindness, even though I had been assured that they were safe to use. I could just imagine what the press were going to write about me: they had already criticised me for going out when I was pregnant; now they would really stick the knife in. But the doctors told me it was nothing to do with anything I had done. Harvey's optic nerves had failed to develop in the womb, and they don't know why. It's such a rare condition there's only a one-in-a-million chance it can happen. Why did the arrow have to point at my baby?

They told me that there was nothing they could do. Harvey's blindness was permanent. They said that there was a very slight chance that some small part of his sight might develop when he was older, but it was very unlikely.

I kept shutting my eyes and wondering how my son was going to cope with all that darkness. It seemed so frightening. How would he be able to make sense of the world? What kind of life would he lead? I felt so sad thinking about all the things he would never be able to do. I thought of all the things I loved doing as a child – all the sports like swimming and riding. All those things would be closed to him.

It was only gradually that I realised that he doesn't know any other way, that he doesn't know what it is like to see. He will experience the world differently to me, but it doesn't mean he'll be scared by it. I knew that I would have to be strong for him; I would be no use at all if I fell into a depression; I couldn't give in to grief. But there were times, and there still are, when I feel terrible sadness for him. I worry how he will get on in life, knowing how cruel the world can be to people who are different.

Even though I had my family there, who were brilliant, I did feel alone. I longed to have support from Harvey's dad. But, when I phoned Dwight to break the tragic news to him, he was anything but supportive. 'It's your fault,' he said. 'You must have done something when you were pregnant and that's why he's ended up blind.' I couldn't believe he could be so hurtful, insensitive and wrong. It was bad enough having total strangers write terrible things about me in the papers, let alone hearing any of this from Dwight. I knew he was wrong – the doctors had assured me that I wasn't to blame – but his comments still hurt. But that was Dwight through and through. The tragedy which could have brought us together had pushed us even further apart.

I was trying so hard to hold things together and be strong, but, not long after I learned the terrible news about Harvey, I did lose it. I found it so painful seeing the way my friend Clare's daughter looked at her and smiled, whereas my son couldn't. He was never even going to be able to see my face. What made it even more painful was that Clare only knew she was pregnant six weeks before giving birth, and so she was out all the time clubbing, drinking and smoking – and yet there she was with a perfect baby. I never did that. Yes, I went out partying a few times, but I never got drunk. I was always careful and looked after myself.

One Saturday night I was beside myself with grief. I met up with Clare and set out to get drunk, trying desperately to drown my sorrows and blot out the pain I was feeling. But the alcohol didn't make me forget – if anything it made me feel worse. All I remember saying to Clare over and over again through my tears was, 'Why me? Why my baby?'

CHAPTER TWENTY-NINE

THE ONLY WAY IS UP

When you've hit rock bottom, the only way has to be up. I couldn't sit around crying all day, even if I wanted to. What good would I be to Harvey then? He was going to need me more than a child who could see, so I had to pull myself together and be there for him one hundred per cent. Thank God I had my family near me to help. At first, like me, they were devastated. It hit my mum especially hard, but I kept telling her that we had to be strong for Harvey's sake and get on with it.

It was hard, but we helped each other. My mum and I started to find out more about Harvey's condition. Inevitably his development was going to be slower than other children. Eighty-five per cent of all early learning is visual, so it would take him longer to crawl and walk and he would be slower at talking. But already he was starting to respond more. Suddenly he was smiling when I touched him or talked to him, and it was wonderful. Yes, he was blind, but he still had his own personality and I loved him more than anything in the world.

Of course, I had the press to deal with. There were lots of stories about Harvey, and many of them were sympathetic; but there were still plenty which asked if it was somehow my fault that he had ended up blind. I wondered if these journalists ever thought about the impact of what they wrote on the people concerned. I tried to ignore them, but it still hurt me. Sometimes I felt I only needed to read one more horrible comment to push me over the edge. Why wouldn't these journalists believe what the specialists had said, that Harvey's condition was one in a million and I had not been responsible for it?

I stayed with my family until Harvey was three months old, by then my new house was ready for us to move in to. But I ended up having to make it into a virtual fortress, with a huge fence, an entry-phone system, CCTV, alarms and panic buttons directly connected to the police station because I had a stalker. Fortunately I never came face to face with the man but, when the local paper printed my parents' address, which is where I was staying when I was pregnant with Harvey, he bombarded me with letters claiming he knew me, that we were having a relationship. I could just about handle that, but then he took to turning up at the house, which really freaked us all out, especially my mum who had the misfortune to open the door to him on several occasions. We had to get the police involved, and go to court and get a restraining order for two years. Now he can't come anywhere near me, but that wasn't

Happy snaps from our family album.

Above: With Danny on his wedding day.

Below: Me, Mum, Danny, Louise and my stepdad, Paul.

Above: Girls' night in! *From left to right*, Mum, Sophie, me and my friend Sally.

Below: My nan, Essie and Grandad, Harvey, with baby Harvey. Sadly, my granddad died a couple of months after this picture was taken.

Above left: My mum, Amy, enjoying a day at the races.

Above right: My nan with Harvey, aged 18 months.

Below left: My sister, Sophie, soaking up the sun in Spain.

Below right: With Paul and my ex-boyfriend, Scott Sullivan, preparing to be harnessed at a zip-run in aid of the Royal London Society for the Blind.

©Sean Clark

Not the kind of horse I usually ride, but in my line of work I do all kinds of weird and wonderful things for the camera. ©www.celebritymediagroup.com

Above left: With my good friend Dean Gaffney, who used to play Robbie in *Eastenders*. ©Rex Features

Above right: With Gary Lucy, star of *Footballers' Wives*, in which I made a cameo appearance. ©EMPICS

Below left: Happy Birthday to me! On the way to my 'Pimps and Prostitutes' birthday party. ©Rex Features

Below right: With Scott Sullivan, before I disappeared to the jungle.

©Rex Features

My former pop idol Gareth Gates.

©Rex Features

Being in the jungle was a tough challenge, but I loved it. ©Rex Features

Above: Yuk! The final stage of the Bite to Bite Bushtucker trial – the dreaded fish eye.

Below: Overcoming my fear of deep water so that we would all eat that night.

Above left: With the man of my dreams just after he came out of the jungle.

©Rex Features

Above right: Working hard to make sure my book became a bestseller!

©Getty Images

Below left: With my two gorgeous boys at the Disney Channel Kids Awards.

©Getty Images

Below right: Proudly displaying my bump at the 2005 British Books Awards – my book was nominated for Biography of the Year.

©Getty Images

enough for my mum. Her house didn't feel safe any more, and the family moved.

Throughout my anxiety about Harvey and security, my work kept me sane: I don't think I could have coped without it. I made sure that I was so busy I didn't have time to sit at home worrying about Harvey. I had modelling assignments lined up, and I got back into doing PAs in clubs. Whenever I could, I took Harvey with me so I knew he was safe. I wanted to earn money even more now for Harvey's sake, so I could give him everything he would need. Dwight still hadn't given me anything.

My first big glamour shoot after Harvey was born was with *Loaded*. I wanted it to be completely perfect so that people would see I hadn't lost my figure and that I was still at the top of my profession. It was probably my girliest shoot ever, which was just how I wanted it: I posed in tiny pieces of pink lingerie, gorgeous long pink suede boots, pink leather bracelets and lots of diamante jewellery. I even went topless to prove my boobs hadn't sagged. When the pictures came out I was extremely pleased. I thought they looked classy and sexy, and I don't think you could tell I had just had a baby. I especially liked the front page which said: JORDAN – STILL BRITAIN'S NUMBER ONE SEX KITTEN. I was back doing what I loved, and it felt great.

On the way back from the shoot, I decided to give Dane a ring. Since I'd had Harvey we had been sending each other flirty texts, and I thought I would love him to see me looking so good. Now that Harvey had been born, and my head was clearer, I realised that he had taken advantage of me when I was at a very low point, and just used me for sex. His cruel treatment had killed any love I had left for him, and I was planning to take my revenge. I was going to shag his brains out one last time, make him realise what he was missing, and then never have anything to do with him again.

I arranged to drop by at his flat. Richard, the documentary maker, had been filming me during my shoot for *Loaded* and was travelling back with me. He had access to most areas of my life but this bit was going to stay strictly private. I told him to wait for me in the car, but I didn't say who I was seeing or where I was going. I was dressed to kill in tight low-cut jeans, you could just see my pink lacy G-string peeping out – I knew Dane would appreciate that – and I was wearing a short white jumper which showed off my flat brown stomach. As I had anticipated, Dane was *very* pleased to see me.

As soon as I got through the door, the first thing I noticed were his girlfriend's shoes lined up against the wall. They must be living together. Don't worry, darling, I thought. You're welcome to him. I didn't feel guilty. I just wondered how many women he had been with when *we* were together.

Dane came on to me straight away, and we quickly tore off each other's clothes and started having sex. I revelled in seeing the desire in his eyes. He really wanted me. I made sure that the sex was passionate, intense and totally satisfying – for him, at least. I definitely wanted to make it an experience he would remember for a long, long time. I felt like a slag, but I wanted to torture him. All the time he was touching my body I was looking round the bedroom trying to see what other signs there were that he was living with his girlfriend. I don't imagine Dane gave her a second thought as he lay on the bed with me.

After we had finished, Dane was all over me, asking me to call him soon. I just replied, 'See you later.' I was cool as anything, and promised nothing. I wanted him to feel cheap, to realise that I had just used him for sex. I wanted him to feel like I had felt so many times before. I walked away knowing that that was the last time I was ever going to have sex with him, knowing that he still wanted me. It was a very satisfying feeling. I had been through hell for him, but now I had the upper hand.

After that he kept calling me, desperate to meet again and have sex. He even suggested we stay in a hotel so his girlfriend wouldn't find out. But I'd had enough. Hopefully that one final time made him realise what he had lost. I didn't need him any more. Finally I was free.

After that Dane became even more bitter and twisted about me. He still tries to get me barred from events that he's going to; whatever I do he criticises it and puts me down as a two-bit model. In 2003, we both ended up taking part in a celebrity football match for charity. By now, I was being filmed for a third documentary about my life and how I wanted to break into music. When Richard went over and asked Dane what he thought about me wanting to pursue a music career, he just said, 'Kate's a cunt.' And yet, when we bumped into each other at a party and I got talking to him and his girlfriend, he whispered that he was still in love with me. In front of other people he makes out he hates me and is vile about me. But I bet if I

273

phoned him up and said, 'Let's have a shag,' he would. I always used to think that I would have feelings for him forever, but he has killed them.

CHAPTER THIRTY

BACK TO LA-LA LAND

Now that I'd been strong enough to walk away from Dane, I should have had a break from men altogether; but me being me it wasn't long before I met my next lover. I don't regret many things, but I do regret ever letting this bloke into my life. Unfortunately I allowed myself to get swept away by his boyish good looks, but, believe me, the novelty soon wore off. My toy boy was a nineteen-year-old tanning-salon assistant. The only good thing I have to say about him was that he has the biggest willy I've ever seen. It's a pity he didn't have a clue how to use it. He ended up selling two of the most vile kiss and tells about me, even though he promised, for Harvey's sake, that he would never go to the press. For that I will never forgive him, although I have done my best to forget him.

I should have known better than to get involved with Matt Peacock. But I'd just had Harvey, I was on my own and I'm the kind of woman who needs a man in their life. I knew as soon as I saw Matt that I could easily get him round my little finger. I know that sounds terrible, but I think I'd had enough of blokes walking all over me. From now on I was going to call the shots.

We met in July 2002 at Max Power, which is a big car show at the NEC in Birmingham and is aimed at boy racers who like fast cars and models. I've been doing it for several years, and usually it's a laugh. I have to go along to the different stands, pose with the cars, pose with the punters, sign autographs, go on stage and play games. Usually I dress quite casually because I can't be bothered to totter around in a short skirt and high heels all day, but on this occasion I wore a tiny pair of shorts, a skimpy top and high heels just to prove I still had my figure.

I was signing autographs and having my picture taken with the fans when I caught a glimpse of him. From a distance he looked great – tall, good looking, tanned and blonde. I sent my little sister Sophie over to him to ask for his number; the cheeky sod told her he already had a girlfriend, and only gave Sophie his friend's number. Typically that made me want him more, and for the rest of the day and night I kept thinking about the handsome stranger.

The next day he was at the show again. I thought I'd give it another go, so I sent Sophie over yet again. This time he did give her his number. Aha! I thought. Gotcha! All the way home I texted flirtatiously with him. When I asked him how old he was, he told me he was twenty-two. That was a relief – I had been worried that he was younger than that – but, of course, he had lied to me.

Two days later I invited him down to London to go out for

dinner. He brought a friend with him and we went out with a group of my mates, including Tony and Ross who do security for me every now and then. They didn't think much of Matt, and they told me so. They also said that he was only after me because of who I was and what I could give him, but I couldn't see it at the time. I fancied him and that was all that mattered to me, even though at the back of my mind I wondered if he would end up going to the papers.

I ignored everyone, asked him down to my house for the weekend and the relationship, if you can call it that, took off from there. He told me that his tanning salon had said that he could take off as much time as he wanted. Within a couple of weeks he was staying with me practically all the time. At first I didn't mind – it was nice having someone to put their arms around me and tell me everything was OK – but it wasn't long before Matt seriously started to get on my nerves, and I began to wish I'd never met him.

The photo shoot I had done with *Playboy* the year before was about to be published, so at the end of July I was booked to go back to Los Angeles to promote it. More importantly, I was going to take Harvey to some eye experts to get a second opinion about his condition. I was hoping for a miracle, but I knew in my heart of hearts that there was probably nothing they could do.

It was weird going back to LA after everything that had happened. A year before, I hadn't a care in the world – nothing to worry about and no one to be responsible for. What a difference a year had made. Now I was the single mother of a son who was probably going to be blind for life and who would always be dependent on me. But I couldn't show the sadness I felt: I had a job to do, and I had to put on a front and appear happy. It wasn't easy, but I had to do it. At the airport my mum, Harvey and me were greeted by lots of American paparazzi. I hid my true feelings behind my shades and put on the biggest smile I could. I knew I would have to be acting a lot over the next week, so I'd better get used to it.

It was great to see Hef and the bunnies again. There were some new ones – Hef obviously likes a bit of variety – but everyone was lovely to me, paying me compliments about how good I looked and how much weight I'd lost. I knew I had got thinner: stress and worry about Harvey had made food the last thing on my mind. However, I did find it difficult dealing with the way they kept saying that they couldn't believe that Harvey was blind because he didn't look it. I know they meant well, but I wanted to scream out, 'Stop talking about my baby! You don't know anything.' I didn't, of course; I just gritted my teeth and smiled. I couldn't show my true feelings.

The party to promote my *Playboy* shoot was held at Hollywood's British-style pub, Ye Olde King's Head. I turned up in a white stretch limo wearing a white cropped top with a plunging neckline, a tiny denim mini and thigh-high denim boots. Then my performance began. I flirted with Hef and posed for saucy pictures with the other models. I chatted, drank and giggled my way through the night. I was playing the part of sexy glamour model to perfection because that was my job, but I couldn't stop thinking about Harvey.

Over the next few days I had to carry on with the act. I

spent most of the time with Harvey and my mum, although I did have to meet up with Hef and the bunnies every now and then. The English tabloids reported that Hef called me his 'British bad girl' but, unlike back home when people call me names seriously and with the intention to hurt me, he really meant it as a joke.

While I was out there I had to shoot a calendar using the *Playboy* team. Steven Wayda was going to be the photographer, and I knew he would do a great job as he had done my original *Playboy* shoot. I had made sure that I was completely in control of how the calendar would look in terms of the poses, the props and my outfits. I wanted to create something different and striking. This calendar was costing a lot more to shoot than usual, and the whole look was glossier, sleeker and sexier. I loved the results. I have particular favourites: in the March picture I'm lying naked on some gorgeous purple velvet, dripping with pearls; in May I'm bursting out of an enormous cake, naked except for a diamond tiara – very appropriate, as my birthday is in May; and in August I'm riding a pink horse in a pink bikini and silver thigh-length boots.

With all that out of the way, I was finally free to take my son to the specialists. I had made an appointment with one of the world's top ophthalmologists, although I was doing this for my mum as much as anyone. She still hadn't accepted that Harvey was blind; I was prepared for the worst.

It was like replaying the nightmare watching the doctors perform all these tests on my precious baby. Then they told me that some particles of light were getting through to his optic nerves, which are the link between the brain and the eye. But, before I could allow myself to feel any hope, they told me he would always be legally blind. My mum immediately said, 'He'll be able to see a little bit then.'

I had to tell her, 'No, Mum, he's blind. Blind is blind, there's no getting round that.' I hated having to keep saying it to her, but I needed her to understand. Still, though, she wouldn't give up hope, insisting that she was sure he would be able to see something.

But, as if that wasn't enough, the doctors then said that Harvey might have a growth defect. Apparently the growth problem and the blindness could be connected because the optic nerve is so close to the pituitary gland which is important in controlling growth and development. 'Please, please,' I prayed, 'let there be nothing else wrong with my poor little boy.' The doctors reassured me that if he did have a growth problem he could have hormone injections that would help him grow at the normal rate; but Mum and I were emotionally and physically drained by the time we left the clinic. I held Harvey close to me and kissed him. I would give anything for him to be able to see, but it wasn't going to happen.

Later I phoned Dwight to tell him what the specialists had said. We still weren't really talking, but I felt that as Harvey's father he should know the latest news. He barely spoke to me. He still blamed me for my little boy's blindness. I didn't have the strength to argue.

CHAPTER THIRTY-ONE

THE BIG C

Yet again I found it hard leaving LA and flying home. I knew I would take a battering from the British press for going to the States so soon after the news about Harvey, even though I had taken him to see more eye experts. I was just trying to get on with my life and be a good mum; why couldn't they understand that? Why couldn't they see that I had to work? I was all my son had; there was no man in the picture taking care of us. Harvey's welfare was all down to me.

I tried to push those negative things out of my mind and concentrate on Harvey and my work. Fortunately there was support out there for my son. He was given a special teacher who came once a month to check on his progress and to give me ideas on how to help his development. He gave me special toys to help stimulate Harvey's vision. I had to put ultraviolet lights over his baby gym, for instance, and lie him underneath. It would seem strange for any child who could see, but he loved it. Harvey was going to be different from other children, but I was starting to accept that. I thought to myself, I'm different, and now my son is. We'll always have each other. No one will ever be able to tell me what to do with him because they don't know what he needs, and I do.

Gradually my mum started to accept that Harvey was blind. Soon she was taking my attitude, and trying to make the best of things. She started collecting news cuttings about what blind people can do, which made us both feel more hopeful about his future. We began to realise that, while Harvey's life was going to be different, there were still plenty of things he would be able to achieve. It just might take him longer. I even found out that he should eventually be able to go to a normal school, to play football and run around like a sighted child can.

I also found out that I wasn't alone in having a child like Harvey. My mum and I were introduced to a group of parents who have children with similar conditions. Either she or I would take Harvey to the group once a week, depending on my work commitments. It gave us hope to see how other children were developing, and the group offered us a great deal of support and encouragement. My mum has since become good friends with some of the other parents. We also found out that, when he is older, Harvey will be able to go to a special centre for the blind to help develop his movement.

My whole family, especially my mum, was like a rock to me during those early months. I don't know how I would have coped without them. The one thing we didn't agree on was my relationship with Matt. She couldn't stand him, and thought he would only bring me trouble. 'He's poncing off you,' she told me. 'Tell him to get a job.' She couldn't understand why I was interested in him, so we ended up having a big falling out because I wouldn't listen to her. I fancied him, so I defended him. Of course, I should have knocked it on the head as soon as I returned from the States. While I was out there, his ex-girlfriend sold a story and I discovered that he had lied about his age to me: he was only nineteen. Straight away I thought, If he's lied about that, what else has he lied about? He had told me he was a model, but I didn't believe that. He had also said he was into tai boxing and made out he had taken part in lots of competitions. Later it turned out he had only been in one. He was just trying to impress me but I was blind to it. And he was much too young for me. He was a boy, and increasingly I realised I needed a man.

But, when I got back from America, I received such shattering news that Matt's age and occupation suddenly didn't seem important. In August 2001 I was told I had cancer. I think I was still numb from finding out about Harvey's blindness, because I didn't break down. I just sat there in a state of shock. I couldn't feel anything, couldn't think anything, couldn't even cry. I couldn't believe that this was happening to me after what had happened with Harvey. How much more could I take?

My manicurist Rachel had been the first to notice the lump on my finger. I didn't think it was anything at all – I thought I had knocked my hand horse riding. It was when I was four months pregnant with Harvey, and it didn't seem that important. But Rachel told me I really should do something about it. Eventually I went to the doctor, but unfortunately I couldn't see my regular GP and the doctor I saw told me it was nothing serious. Over the next few months the lump kept getting bigger and so I went back to the surgery on two more occasions, but never saw my own GP. Each time I was told the same thing: it's nothing to worry about, but keep an eye on it.

Finally, when I'd had Harvey, I got to see my GP Dr Khan. He took one look at my hand and immediately referred me to a specialist. Within a couple of weeks I had the lump removed at a private hospital. From then on I thought that was it, problem solved. I went out to LA thinking everything was fine. But when I came back I had a call from the specialist's office saying that Mr Williams needed to see me urgently. I thought they were just fussing because I'd had a private operation, so, when I drove to the clinic with Matt, Harvey and my friend Claire, my main worry was whether I would get to my hair appointment on time. I was so convinced that there couldn't be anything wrong that I left the engine running in the car while I went to see the doctor. He told me to sit down. Then he said those words that everyone dreads and that everyone prays will never be said to them, 'I'm afraid it's not good news. You've got cancer.'

That's it, then, I thought. I'm going to die. I was too shocked to speak. I sat there paralysed with fear. He told me that I had something called leiomyosarcoma, or LMS. It's such a rare type of cancer that it only affects four in every million people. In its advanced stages there is only a fifty–fifty chance of survival; luckily for me it had been spotted early on. Mr Williams said that, on a scale of nought to ten as to how serious the cancer was, I was at number three, so, whilst it was extremely worrying, it wasn't deadly. I was fortunate that the cancer hadn't got into my lymph gland because that's when it can't be controlled. I asked him if the cancer had caused Harvey to be blind, but he said it hadn't, although the fact that I was pregnant had accelerated it.

He recommended that he operated on my hand again to make sure that there was no cancerous tissue left, and that I should have a whole body scan. He warned me that if tests showed that the cancer had spread through my hand he might have to consider amputation. This type of cancer only affects soft tissue in the body and cannot be treated by chemotherapy. He was saying all these things to me, but I was having difficulty in taking any of it in. I just wanted to get back to Harvey and hold him. Even though Mr Williams had said that my cancer was treatable, suddenly life seemed incredibly precious.

I walked back to the car. 'I've got cancer,' I told Claire and Matt. They thought I was making some kind of sick joke because I seemed so calm. But the truth was I didn't know what I was feeling. I only knew that I didn't want to show my true emotions in front of Matt. The person I really wanted to speak to was my mum.

When I called her she couldn't believe it. She was very upset. I tried to underplay how scared I was, saying, 'Don't worry, I'm sure it will be fine.' I was trying to be strong for her sake, but inside my mind was racing. What if the cancer had spread? What if it was worse than they thought? What if they couldn't treat it? What would happen to my little boy? Mum brought me back to reality, wanting to know every detail of what the doctor had said, and the exact name of the cancer so she could research it on the Internet for me.

I couldn't give in to my fears. I had to get on with my life, keep busy, keep working; never giving myself time to think was my way of dealing with things. The cancer scare should perhaps have been my wake-up call about Matt, but I had bigger things to deal with in my life than a toy boy and for the time being I carried on seeing him. Increasingly, though, things were going wrong between us. The strong physical attraction I had felt for him initially was starting to wear off, and lots of other things were starting to bug me. First of all I couldn't forget what my mum had said about Matt living off me. He wasn't working so I don't know how he was supporting himself. Whenever we went out, I paid for everything. I even bought him new clothes, and when I wanted to spend the weekends alone with my mates I would give him his train fare home. He really was my toy boy. At first I didn't mind too much, but after a while it started to annoy me. I couldn't understand how he could afford to buy me presents every now and then. I'm terrible for leaving money lying round the house, and there were a couple of times when I went to look for it and it wasn't there. I'm not accusing him, but it did seem strange when Matt could afford to buy me yet another cuddly toy.

After a few weeks of him sitting round my house doing nothing, I sent him down to the job centre in Brighton. I hated being around someone who didn't work. I needed to be with a man who had ambition and drive, someone who would keep my on my toes. The fact that he was so dependent on me and did everything I said was starting to be a massive turn-off. He didn't even make up for it in bed. You might have expected that a younger man would be able to fulfil my every desire, but Matt didn't seem to know how to. Outside of the bedroom he was starting to suffocate me. He would tell me all the time that he loved me; I just replied, 'And you're gorgeous too.' I didn't love him and knew I never would. He was a bit more than a fling, but not much more.

To his credit he was very good with Harvey. He was gentle and caring with him, and had worked in a nursery before, so he knew how to interact with children. I felt confident leaving Matt to look after my little boy, but I knew I wouldn't be with him forever, so I didn't share my pain and sadness over Harvey's condition with him. I kept all my feelings locked inside.

I was booked to do a photo shoot and interview for *OK!* in Cyprus and I planned to do it with Matt. As much as anything, I did it to annoy Dwight. He was still acting like I was to blame for Harvey, and when I had seen him last he had just turned to me and said, 'I heard you got cancer.' Not 'I'm sorry, are you all right?' I wanted him to feel jealous seeing another man with me, another man holding his son. He deserved to feel it after everything he put me through. But I was putting on an act for the cameras. It looked like I was deeply in love with Matt, but I wasn't.

Earlier in the year, before I had Harvey, I had booked to go on holiday to Ayia Napa with my friend Clare, but at the last minute she couldn't come so I ended up asking Matt along. That was when the rot set in for good. A few days before we left, I had another operation on my hand. I had wanted to postpone it until after the holiday because I knew I wouldn't be able to do any water sports, but my mum had begged me not to, saying that my health came first. 'If I've got it, I've got it,' I told her. 'Just let me go and have fun.' I think I was still reeling from the shock, because I'm very glad I did have the operation.

Matt, Harvey and I were staying in a five-star hotel, all paid for by me. After what I had been through over the past few months I really needed the break, but I found it difficult to relax with Matt. He was making me feel trapped. He even asked me to marry him and said again and again that he wanted to have kids with me. Having more kids was the last thing on my mind – Matt was the last person I would want them with, and Harvey needed me one hundred per cent.

My feelings were brought home one night when I went out to dinner with a bunch of people. I was sitting at a large table with Tony and Steve, who I'd brought out for security, and Matt. Richard Macer was also there, filming a second documentary about me. I bet he couldn't believe his luck, given the eventful year I'd had so far. What with Harvey's tragic blindness and now my cancer scare, plus my turbulent love life – were things never going to settle down for me? Suddenly we were joined by two young men, one of whom immediately caught my eye. He was extremely good looking. When Matt's back was turned, I whispered to Steve to try and get his number when he next went to the gents. I would never normally do anything like this when I was with someone, but I wasn't really planning to be unfaithful to Matt. I was planning who to see when we'd split. Sure enough, Steve got his number and I thought I'd call him when I got home.

By the time the holiday was over, I couldn't bear Matt to touch me. I used every excuse in the book to avoid physical contact with him. I started to feel repulsed by him, particularly by his mouth and his teeth, which looked like he never cleaned them. It wasn't that he had changed, it was just that I could see what he was really like, and I'd had enough. When we got home Claire asked him about the holiday and he told her that the hotel rooms could have been bigger. I was fuming: he had just had a free holiday on me and he couldn't even be grateful. The honeymoon period was definitely over.

I had a wedding to go to, but instead of asking Matt I invited the bloke I had seen in Ayia Napa. He was as good looking as I remembered, but much too short; straight away I thought, No, you're not my type. He had driven to the house in his convertible Mazda MX-5 and I thought, No, thank you, that's a hairdresser's car – actually he turned out to be a chef. He came to the wedding with me, my friend Clare and one of his friends, but nothing happened and that was that.

I grew to hate Matt being at my house all the time. I would drive in after a shoot and he'd just be lying on the sofa twiddling his hair. I invented business meetings in London, anything to get away from him. When I went out clubbing in London I would never let him come with me. I started to make up excuses for where I was going at the weekend and how he should go home, but he always wanted to stay. I wouldn't let him keep any of his things in the house, even though he kept asking. Everything he did annoyed me. I hated the way he never ate properly, but just picked at his food. When we were out in my car he used to wind down his window, play the music full blast and click his fingers. Put your window up, I would think, and stop drawing attention to yourself! Friends would tell me that when we went clubbing he would walk behind me, looking as if he owned me. He was becoming an embarrassment.

Finally, at the beginning of September, I'd had enough. Rachel was doing my nails and my friend Clare was also round my house with her boyfriend, one of Matt's friends. I told Matt that he should get the train back home with his mate. He replied that he didn't want to. 'Look,' I said, 'just go. I've had enough. We're finished.'

He looked completely shocked. 'We need to talk,' he told me.

'We don't need to talk. You're going. I've had enough, I need space, and it's only going to wind me up you staying here.'

Rachel was trying to do my nails through all this and she whispered, 'My God, you're ruthless.' But as far as I was concerned that was it. I had made the decision: I wanted him out of my house and out of my life. Of course, he didn't have the train fare, and I ended up giving him the cash to go home.

I don't feel bad about what happened. I had fancied him at first and initially things had been good between us, but I always knew I wouldn't be with him for long. And, just in case you're feeling sorry for him, he never once tried to get back in touch with me once we had split up – that's how much he loved me. It was obvious that he'd been using me, that he was only with me because of who I was. The kiss and tells he did prove that. I've seen pictures of him since we split and he looks really cheap and nasty wearing the jewellery he must have bought from the money he got paid for stitching me up. I didn't bother to read his story, but friends told me about his claim that we'd had sex seven times a night. Please! He wishes he could get it up seven times a night, but I don't know any man who could – and *he* definitely couldn't. The affair with my toy boy was well and truly over. I found out recently from an actor acquaintance of mine who appeared in *Coronation Street* that Matt had gone up to him in a nightclub and briefly asked after me. Then he asked my friend how he felt being recognised, because he got recognised all the time! I thought to myself again, What a prat. Thank God I got shot of him when I did.

I didn't just have Matt's kiss and tells to put up with. Clare had put me in touch with her childminder, and she looked after Harvey a few times, probably no more than six – one of which included him staying overnight when I was working in Ireland. It was always going to be a temporary arrangement because my mum was going to give up her job and be Harvey's nanny.

Harvey always seemed happy with his childminder, and she never expressed any worries to me, so imagine my horror when Dave, my manager at the time, called to tell me that she had sold a story on me and Harvey, claiming that I was unfit to be a mother. I never read what she said. Why would I want to? I knew it would all be distorted lies. I was absolutely furious though; I wanted to go round and beat her up. My friends and family would know that her story was rubbish, but everyone else would read what she had said and believe her. I don't care what the press say about me any more – they've said everything hurtful they can possibly say – but when they write lies about my son, an innocent child who can't speak up for himself, that's a different matter ...

CHAPTER THIRTY-TWO

RETURN OF THE POP IDOL

'Don't make it obvious, but I've just seen him,' Dave whispered to me. I turned and looked in the direction he indicated. There, standing a few feet away, tall, dark and handsome, was Gareth Gates, my pop-idol lover. I hadn't seen or heard from him for months, but now he was so close I could feel the familiar butterflies starting up in my stomach. What was going to happen now? Would he say hello? I couldn't bear it if he ignored me. I summoned up all my courage and walked over to him. 'Hi,' I said.

'Hi,' he replied. I was relieved that he looked pleased to see me because I was very glad to see him again. A lot had happened since we had last met, but I still fancied him. I was desperate to carry on the conversation, but the awards were about to start and we had to go to our separate tables. I had suspected he might be here at the *Elle* Style Awards as Wella were one of the sponsors and he had a deal with them. I had made certain that I looked as sexy as possible, and by the look on Gareth's face my efforts had paid off.

Back at my table I couldn't stop talking about him, wondering what he was thinking, whether he still had the same feelings for me. I had finally confided in Dave about my affair a few months earlier – as he was my manager I thought it was only fair – but he had promised not to breathe a word of it to anyone. Now I was relieved that he knew – he could help me talk to Gareth again. I told Dave that I really wanted to speak to him and that he must try and get his phone number for me. I dared him to follow Gareth to the gents and tell him that he was my manager and that he knew about us. He wouldn't at first, but I kept on at him. Now I had seen Gareth again, I just had to talk to him.

Eventually Dave gave in to my pestering and when he saw Gareth making his way to the gents, he followed him. Well, what's the point of having a manager if they won't do what you ask them? As soon as Dave returned I made him repeat exactly what had happened – you know what we girls are like, we have to know every single detail – and he told me what was said word for word, and described the expressions on Gareth's face. Apparently, as they were both peeing side by side – how sweet! – Dave introduced himself as my manager and said that he knew what had happened between us and that I really wanted to talk to him again At first Gareth was all stuttery and shocked and didn't know what to say, but then he pulled himself together, gave Dave his number and said that I must call him.

Gareth sat back at his table. I couldn't take my eyes off him and he kept looking at me as well. The eye contact was tantalising. I was longing for the awards to be over and the partying to start so I could go and talk to him.

It was wonderful talking to him again, but not easy – we were both conscious of all the photographers, and we had to keep moving apart so they wouldn't get a picture of us together. We both said that we missed each other. I assured him again that he could trust me, and it was wonderful being with him. Now we had met up again, it brought back all those feelings. I know he's young, but he is gorgeous and there was definitely something between us – it was more than physical attraction.

In the end there were just too many people around for us to talk properly, so reluctantly I returned to my table. He promised to ring me. Meanwhile my good friend Clare had turned up. I told her she had to go and talk to Gareth and find out if he was still interested in me. She had met him at the hotel in February, and she is the kind of person who isn't afraid to do anything. So, after Gareth and I had exchanged another meaningful look, Clare went over to him.

She was gone for ages and I was desperate to find out what they had been talking about. He told her that he did still like me, and that the song 'Anyone of Us' had been meant for me, but it was still really hard for him to see me. However, he promised he would call, and it seemed as if there was a real chance we could rekindle our romance.

Then I saw him leave the awards. Disappointment swept over me as I really wanted to spend more time with him. Suddenly my mobile rang, and my heart skipped a beat: it was him. I spent practically the rest of the night talking to him. He told me how much he missed me, that he definitely wanted to meet up again and how strange it had been reading about me in the papers and not seeing me.

After that night we started texting and phoning each other regularly. I definitely had the vibe that, if only we could meet up again, we could carry on where we left off. I was in the final stages of my relationship with Matt and I was desperate to get rid of him so I could be free to be with Gareth. One time he called me at home when Matt was in the house and we were on the phone for ages. Matt wasn't happy about it, but he wasn't going to stop me.

But, before we had the chance to meet up, the press found out about our affair and ruined everything. My manager called me and said the story was going to come out. I had two choices: either I could give my version of what had happened, or I could deny it totally. Straight away I wanted to deny everything, but Dave pointed out that, if I denied it, the papers would end up writing what they wanted to, and it may well put us both in a bad light. I was devastated. I was in a no-win situation. I really wanted to keep my promise to Gareth, but I just didn't see how I could now the story had broken. I thought that at least if I gave my version of events I could protect Gareth from some of the tabloid extremes. Finally I told Dave to admit that Gareth had been my mystery man but that I wasn't going to give any more details. As soon as I could I phoned Gareth to let him know what was happening and to promise him that I hadn't gone to the press: they had found out somehow, and all I was doing was admitting it was true.

Unfortunately I didn't get to speak to him, so I just had to leave a message; from then on, whenever I tried to call him to clear things up between us, his phone was constantly on voicemail.

I was shocked by Gareth's reaction when the story broke. By now he was a successful singer and his career had really taken off so I don't understand why he denied our affair. He had always said to me that once he started to do well we could be open about our relationship. I started off feeling hurt when I read about what he had said, and then I began to get angry. I know the papers can twist things, but I was gutted when I read comments he was supposed to have made. 'It's all lies,' he claimed, 'and I don't know why she'd make all that up.' And 'As if it would be Jordan when there are so many lovely girls out there.' He was making me look stupid and it felt like everyone was laughing at me. How dare he? And why would I want to lie about having an affair with him – it's not like I needed the publicity. He even got his solicitors to send a letter to me demanding that I didn't talk about our affair. If only he had just admitted that we were lovers, then eventually the story would have blown over.

I felt bitterly disappointed by him. I know he's young, but I don't think that's an excuse to hurt someone. He also made a mistake crossing me. What he forgets is that I'm in the public eye too, and it's easy for me to put my side of the story to the press. I'm not just a dumb bimbo who is prepared to put up and shut up. So I don't feel guilty about revealing the intimate secrets of our affair. He has a girlfriend now, someone older than me, and he is completely open about their relationship. So what was the problem with telling the truth about us?

Gareth finally admitted the affair in July 2003. To me it

seemed a cynical move because he had a new single coming out and was trying to reinvent himself with more of a bad-boy image. He probably needed the publicity that he knew I would bring him. But at what price? I can never forgive him for making me look a fool. We might not be lovers any more, but we could have stayed friends.

CHAPTER THIRTY-THREE

LOVER BOY

Fortunately, by the time the press story broke and Gareth chose to deny our affair, I had another man in my life. I was on a girls' night out in Brighton. I wasn't looking for a man, and when I first saw Scott Sullivan he had such pretty-boy looks I was convinced he was gay. Luckily for me, he was straight.

It was clear from our first meeting that Scott Sullivan wasn't going to be a pushover. My friends got talking to his friends, but Scott ignored me. He came across as quite shy and mysterious, as if he really wasn't interested in me. It's an attitude guaranteed to make me want to attract him even more. We all met up again the following night. We had dinner first, then went on to a club. As I was dancing I was willing Scott to pay me some attention, but he was still resisting my charms. Look at me, damn you, I thought to

299

myself rather crossly. Everyone else has noticed me, why don't you?

It's a bit cheeky to admit this, but the first time I met Scott I was still with Matt. In fact, while I was making eyes at him, Matt was babysitting Harvey and Clare's baby. We had told him that we were going out for dinner with my mum to persuade her that he was actually OK; the truth was, Matt was definitely on his way out. I got shot of Matt pretty soon after that, and then I was free to try my luck with Scott. Eventually he gave up playing hard to get, and we became lovers.

Overall, it was one of my more stable and happy relationships. Scott was a lovely person: down to earth, funny, kind and wonderful with Harvey. Our birthdays were even on the same day, which seemed a bit like fate saying we should be together. There were so many positives. The trouble was I just had this feeling inside that he really wasn't the one for me. We were together eighteen months but it didn't feel like the relationship was going anywhere. I loved him and we were great friends, but I knew deep down there was someone else out there for me.

Before Scott met me and Harvey, he had never had any experience with babies. He had never even held one. He told me after we'd been seeing each other a while that the fact that I was a single mum nearly put him off – he just couldn't imagine seeing someone with a child. He remembers being shocked when we went out for dinner and I brought Harvey along, and wondered whether it was all going to be too complicated. But over the months we were together he grew so attached to Harvey. He was wonderful with him, loving and gentle, and was much more of a father to him than Dwight has ever been.

Ah yes, Dwight. Remember him? He just hasn't been there for Harvey as a father. He has probably only seen him twenty times since he was born. The last time he visited he hadn't seen his little boy for over two months but, instead of picking him up and hugging him as soon as he saw him, he was more interested in watching the football. However bad relations were between us, I always hoped he could be close to his son. Sadly it hasn't happened, and I don't think it ever will. Whenever Dwight does pay a visit I always have to be there because he doesn't know how to deal with him on his own. If Harvey starts crying, he doesn't have a clue how to comfort him. And yet I feel I've gone out of my way to try and get him to bond with his son. In May 2003 I flew out with Harvey to Tobago so he could meet all Dwight's family. It wasn't a happy trip. I wasn't made to feel particularly welcome, and I felt they were rejecting me. My family, on the other hand, have always tried to get on with Dwight for the sake of their grandson.

Although he has promised many times that we could come to a financial arrangement whereby he would contribute towards Harvey, at the time of writing this book we are still talking about it. The plan was that he would at least pay my mum, who has given up her job in order to be Harvey's nanny, and if there were any hospital bills he would pay half of those. Harvey needs a lot of support and special care. It is a big responsibility for me, and I can't believe that Dwight doesn't want to contribute. I find it unbelievable that, when he does see us, he is forever going on about his latest purchases – a new car or a new watch – so now I am trying to formalise the contact he has with Harvey. At the moment it all seems to be on his terms: if he feels like seeing him, he expects me to drop everything and be there. But if he wants to see his son, he has to start contributing more towards his upbringing. Harvey isn't a toy he can play with when he feels like it. My mum thinks I should have gone to the Child Support Agency right from the beginning to sort out maintenance for Harvey. I have a feeling she might be right.

Since Harvey was born, Dwight has often confided to my mum that he's still in love with me and wants to marry me; he keeps asking her how he can win me back. In May 2003 during our ill-fated trip to Tobago, he finally confessed that he loved me, asked me to marry him and presented me with a ring. He finally apologised for the terrible way he treated me, and begged me to believe that there was no one else in his life. It was all too late in the day. I don't love him. I don't think I ever could now. I can never forget how he abandoned and betrayed me. Ironically I've got him where I want him, but I don't want him any more. Of course, in an ideal world I would love to be with the father of my child, but I can't imagine being with him again. He can keep his flash lifestyle; I've only ever looked for love.

And while he claims to love me, he comes out with some blindingly insensitive comments. For instance, he told my mum that, if he married someone else and had children, they would be more important to him than Harvey. I can't believe that he could think such a thing, never mind say it. I know that he is the womaniser he always was, and I could never trust him. On one visit he left his phone behind while he played golf with my stepdad Paul and my brother, and when it rang I'm afraid I couldn't help myself. I listened to the message and sure enough it was from a girl. I carried on a text conversation with her, pretending to be Dwight, and it was obvious she knew him very intimately. After that I texted every single girl on his phone (there were twenty) pretending to be Dwight, and told them to come round to his house the next day. I told them not to text or call back, but to take a taxi which he would pay for, and to be there at three for a big surprise. Dwight couldn't have a go at me about it because he would have had to admit that he was seeing other women. I'm well out of it now. He can't hurt me any more.

Scott was so completely different from Dwight. He understood that there needs to be a bit of give and take in a relationship, something that Dwight seemed incapable of grasping. He was there for me through some very difficult times. In 2003 I found out that Harvey's medical problems extended way beyond him being blind. Tests revealed that he has an underactive thyroid, which is the main reason why he is much bigger for his age than normal; he also has a growth defect and will need hormone injections; and he has a condition called diabetes insipidus, which affects his waterworks and makes him wee a lot and be incredibly thirsty – he wakes up five or six times in the night needing water. As a result, we're in and out of hospital. Sometimes I watch him when he is playing happily and I can't believe a little boy can have so many things wrong with him. But I think Harvey's a lot like me: he seems to cope and get on with life. He has always been a happy and sweet-natured child, which seems incredible given his medical condition. I love him so much and, if someone said to me I was going to have another child with the same problems, I would definitely have the baby; it wouldn't put me off at all.

In October 2003 my grandad died, and although he had been ill for many years I was still devastated. I'm part of such a close-knit family, and when I was growing up I saw my grandparents practically every day; even when I left home I still saw them a lot. He was a lovely man and I miss him very much. He and my nan were so proud of me for making a name for myself modelling; they would always get really excited when a magazine came out or when I appeared on television. My family kept a vigil by his bed; we knew he didn't have long. I spent hours sitting with him and talking to him, holding his hand and stroking his head. I was supposed to be going to a Grand Prix ball and I've never felt less like partying, but everyone convinced me that I should go. I left the hospital to collect my dress and instantly knew my place was by his bedside. I called my mum and told her I was coming straight back. As soon as I got back to the hospital I could tell he only had a few hours left. I remembered all too well from my days spent working in the nursing home what people are like when they are about to die.

Finally he opened his eyes and stared straight at me. His eyes were incredibly blue. I smiled at him, and then he looked at my nan. He was saying goodbye. He coughed, and his breathing sounded wracked. Then it was over.

He had always believed in me, and had always wanted me to sing, so for his funeral I had a recording made of me singing 'Show Me Heaven' by Maria McKee. I also wrote a poem about how important he was to me and the family. I was so emotional as I read it out, and tears poured down my cheeks. I am usually the one who tries to be strong in the family, but this time I couldn't hide my sadness. I keep my grandfather's ashes in my house, and it comforts me to have them there.

Scott was great during that time, really loving and supportive. But I'm afraid the rot had already set in. Just the month before, he let me down badly and destroyed my trust in him. We had been out clubbing in London and were staying in my flat with a group of friends. I was feeling exhausted and a bit drunk and just wanted to crash out. Scott had different ideas and became angry when I said I was too tired to have sex with him. He went storming out of the bedroom. Half an hour passed and I got up to see what he was doing. I opened the door and got the shock of my life. He was sitting on the sofa next to one of the girls we had gone out with, wearing just his boxer shorts. They pulled away guiltily from each other. It was obvious that they had been kissing. I flew into a rage, accusing him of being unfaithful. He denied doing anything, but I knew what I had seen. I had always believed that Scott would never do anything to hurt me; now it seemed like he was just the same as the other men who had betrayed my trust. There were other things as well we were starting to fight over. First of all there was my work – it's a bit of a pattern, isn't it? Scott was fine about my modelling career. He never got jealous about the shoots I did, however revealing they were. He never minded the saucy comments I come out with in interviews; he understood that it's my job, and he knew it didn't mean that he couldn't trust me. But we fell out badly over the personal appearances I do in clubs. I admit I have a few drinks in order to give me the courage to go on stage. Sometimes I have a few too many, and that's when my outrageous side kicks in and I end up doing things which I probably wouldn't do if I was sober. I've kissed people on stage, and flashed my boobs and, of course, it ends up in the press. Those are the things that upset Scott. He argued that there was no need for me to get my boobs out – that's not what I'm there for, I'm not a lap dancer; he thought it was tacky when I behaved like that, and I'm worth more.

He had a point; but I would tell him that people had paid to come and see Jordan and that's who I had to give them. When I go on stage I can't sit there looking all coy; when I'm asked a question about my favourite sexual position, I can't say, 'Oh, I couldn't answer that!' To me it is just my job, and when I've finished I can walk away from it. But Scott found it difficult. There were times when he left me over it, and I was gutted, but I always managed to win him back, and then I thought I didn't want anyone else but him. I was tired of my work causing problems in my relationships.

The other problem in our relationship is *his* work – or rather the lack of it. I've always loved being with a man who has ambition and talent, but Scott didn't seem to mind what he did. He was happy to work for his dad, who happens to be a millionaire businessman with property and a string of garages in Brighton. He was into motocross racing, but that was more like an expensive hobby than a career. I suppose that's the down side of being brought up having everything: you don't have that burning drive to succeed.

But there was something more fundamentally wrong between us: the sex wasn't good. I fancied him no end, but in the bedroom there simply wasn't the right sexual chemistry. At first I thought it was bound to get better as we got closer, but it didn't. If anything, it got worse. I began to dread going to bed with him, because I didn't want to have sex. I loved him, but he didn't turn me on in bed. It got so bad that I could only bear to have sex with him when I was drunk. Scott wasn't stupid. He could see what was happening and he confronted me about it. I was honest and told him that I fancied him, but sexually it wasn't happening between us. As you can imagine, he was very upset. I tried to make it up by saying we should be more experimental, but inside I knew that wasn't the problem. I convinced myself that I still loved him, and that's what I told everyone.

Perhaps I should have been stronger from the start. Even as early as Valentine's Day 2003 when we had only been going out for three months, I knew things weren't right. He whisked me off for a romantic meal at an expensive hotel, then after dinner upstairs in our room he gave me several presents. One was a Burberry teddy bear. As soon as I opened the box I saw a large diamond ring on its paw, and my heart sank. I tried to pretend I hadn't seen it, but then Scott made his intentions crystal clear by going down on one knee and proposing. I said yes, but I made him promise not to tell anyone – hardly the behaviour of someone passionately in love. He was so lovely, so good looking, so perfect in many ways that I think I wanted it to work. Who was I kidding?

In November 2003 I bought a new house. I was getting fed up of people driving past and shouting abuse. My new home was off the beaten track and surrounded by fields so no one could bother me. I asked Scott to move in with me, so we could commit more to each other, but he refused, saying it was too far away from where he kept his bikes. It was hardly the response of a man who loved me. I started to question whether we really had a future together.

In January 2004 I treated him to a luxury holiday in Antigua. We had visited the same hotel the year before, and the contrast was painful. Scott wanted to go off and do his sports rather than stay with me and Harvey. Sex, which is supposed to improve on holiday, was a disaster. I didn't want to make love with him at all. I did it simply to avoid the rows.

So I wouldn't say that my mind was made up to leave him as I flew out to Australia to appear in *I'm A Celebrity Get Me Out of Here!*, but it hardly seemed like our relationship was in the best of health.

CHAPTER THIRTY-FOUR
JUNGLE FEVER

When I was a teenager, he was my pin-up and I idolised him. I spent hours lying on my bed gazing up at the huge poster of him, fantasising about what I'd say if we ever met, never dreaming for one minute that we would. I loved his dark, handsome looks, his sexy, toned body and his music. And I'm definitely not talking about John Lydon!

I had been asked to take part in the 2003 series of *I'm A Celebrity Get Me Out of Here!*, but I didn't want to leave Harvey then – he was much too young. In January 2004 the time seemed right. I was looking forward to the challenge, and it was all in a good cause: I was going to be raising money for Look, a charity for the blind. And, although I knew I would miss my son, I didn't want to go on about it, mainly because I knew it would upset me too much, and I didn't want people to think I was playing for their sympathy.

Unlike some of the other celebrities taking part I didn't see it as a career move. It wasn't like I needed to increase my profile, but I hoped that people might see a different side to me, and realise that there was more to Katie Price than Jordan, the outrageous party girl the papers love to show. I was prepared to rough it, to do the scary, outrageous bushtucker trials, to live off rice and beans. I definitely wasn't expecting to fall in love, but I did – truly, madly, deeply.

As soon as Peter walked into the drinks party before we all went into the jungle, my heart started racing and I thought, My God, I think he's the one for me! I have never felt like that before in my life; yes, I had quickly fallen in love with Dane Bowers and once thought of marrying him but there was no comparison to how I felt about Peter. Dane was just the rehearsal – Peter was definitely the real thing. I was totally blown out of the water by the intensity of my feelings for him. It really was a case of love at first sight. I was bowled over by his good looks, gorgeous body and warm personality. Please let him be attracted to me, I prayed. But I knew I couldn't let my true feelings show. I still had a boyfriend, I was going to be on a TV show watched by millions, plus my friends had all warned me to be careful around Peter. They said that he might well try to get close to me or Alex Best because it would look good on camera, so I tried to play it cool.

All the other celebs were probably worrying about surviving on little food and getting through the bushtucker trials; all I was worried about was how I was going to hide my feelings. As soon as we got into the jungle I was totally focused on Peter. Wherever he was standing or sitting, I wanted to be next to him. I just wanted to be close to him. It was insane, or should I say insania?

Peter quickly made his feelings very obvious to me and to everyone else. Within just a few days he confessed that he really liked me. It was wonderful hearing that and I was longing to tell him that I felt just the same. But it was easy for him, he was single; I had baggage. I knew as soon as I saw Peter that my relationship with Scott was over but I didn't want to humiliate and hurt Scott by giving away how I really felt about Peter on a TV show. I wanted to end things with him properly. I also didn't know for sure if Peter really meant what he had said. I had to hold back. As a result, I know it must have looked as if I was leading Peter on.

When we were alone and I thought our microphones were covered and no one could hear us (how stupid was that?) I told him that I was definitely interested in him and that I would sort things out with Scott when I left the jungle. But I also told him that I wouldn't admit my feelings on camera or to anyone else at the camp. So in front of everyone else I flirted with him, but I denied it went any further than that. I was cheeky and rude and bantered away as if I didn't have a care in the world, when really I was thinking, I really want this man. As for my comment about his manhood being like an acorn, it was just a wind-up. I could tell there was a lot more to him than that!

Underneath the banter, the sexual tension between us was electric and almost unbearable. We couldn't stop staring at each other: my eyes kept getting drawn to his amazing body and whenever we sat next to each other he would fold his arms and secretly put his hand under my clothes and stroke my skin. I kept imagining what it would be like if we were there on our own, without the cameras, and I was single. It was intensely romantic sitting next to each other by the fire, giving each other massages and going swimming together but also incredibly frustrating, knowing that we both wanted each other and couldn't do anything about it.

The night he slipped into my bed and curled up next to me it felt so right. I made him put his arm around me and I wanted him there beside me all night. But then reality kicked in and I pretended I needed to cover up from the mosquitoes. Reluctantly I made Peter return to his own bed.

We did manage one passionate kiss without anyone seeing what we were doing. I was sleeping in my bed, when suddenly I was woken up by Peter gently kissing me all over my face and neck. He had lifted up the mosquito cover and crawled under so his face was hidden from the cameras. I grabbed his hand and kissed him back. It was the best kiss of my life and I wanted more. But we had to stop.

'You know I care for you so much,' he told me. I knew I was falling passionately in love with him. He saw me looking my worst possible, and yet he was still attracted to me. Unlike all the other men in my life he hadn't met me as Jordan the glamour girl, he was seeing me as Katie. In fact, he said he hated the idea of Jordan: he wanted me for myself. When I told him not to look at me because I was a mess, he replied that he liked that shy insecure side of me. But to be honest I was dying to show him what I looked like with the braids out of my hair and with a bit of make-up on – wouldn't any girl?

Everything else about the jungle experience paled into insignificance alongside my passion for Peter. I got on fine with all the other celebs – except John Lydon. I could tell he didn't like me so I kept well away. I wasn't impressed by his constant spitting and swearing. As for walking off and saying he knew he was going to win, what a load of rubbish: he was just scared of being voted off.

And, while everyone else moaned about the food and lost weight, I stuffed my face! In fact, I managed to put on half a stone. As for taking part in the trials, I was pleased with my performance. I'm petrified of spiders and yet I managed to endure having five of them crawling all over my face. I've had panic attacks in the past when swimming out of my depth, but I managed to swim in a pond full of snakes and eels. I tried not to make a big deal about my fears. I wanted to prove myself. I tried to be strong and get through them all. I did the most trials out of anyone there and they were all difficult, but, once that adrenaline rush kicked in, I refused to be defeated. It was hideous having cockroaches, beetles and huntsman spiders poured on my head when I was wearing the plastic helmet. Just when I thought it couldn't get any worse they added a snake to the mix! The worst thing was probably the way the creatures all reacted together in a confined space, they bit me and scuttled around madly and made the most horrible screeching sound. Yuk! But it was such a great feeling once the helmet was off and it was all over.

As for the 'bite to bite' trial, I don't know who came up with that but I'd like to watch them do it! It was unbelievably gross. It would have been bad enough if the creatures were dead; as it was I had to eat them alive. I thought things couldn't get any worse than the witchetty grub, but then they unveiled the fish eye! That defeated me and I'm not sorry. Still, seven meals for seven hungry celebs wasn't bad going, was it?

I was amazed and delighted that I made it to the last five. I never thought I was likely to win, but I think my popularity started going down when it looked like I was stringing Peter along. On what turned out to be my last night in camp I was lying in bed and I overhead Peter telling Charlie that he really liked me, and Charlie replied that I had asked him to fix me up with an older man. It was true, but I'd only said it as a joke. Peter sounded gutted. I desperately wanted to throw my arms around him and tell him that he was the only man for me.

The next day he was very subdued and told me that he wanted to talk away from everyone else. We walked to the pool and then he told me what I'd been dreading. 'I've had enough,' he said. 'I don't want to know any more.'

I knew the cameras were on us and I was trying to be cocky, as if I didn't care, so I just replied, 'Whatever.' What I really wanted to say was, 'Stop! I want you! I'm in love with you!' I knew there was no point in prolonging the conversation – it was just going to lead to an argument – so I turned and walked back to the others thinking, Oh my god, please don't let me lose this man.

By the time we got back, Ant and Dec were there ready to evict the next celebrity and it turned out to be me. I was massively relieved. I hugged Peter and kissed his neck, willing him to believe in me. At last I would be reunited with my son and I could sort out my love life. I was going to end my relationship with Scott, and when Peter came out of the jungle I would be a single woman, able to show him my true feelings.

It was torment when I came out. I missed Peter desperately and I had no way of watching the show except when it was eviction time. Of course, it was wonderful seeing Harvey and my mum again but I longed to be with Peter and tell him how I really felt about him once and for all. At least I was able to tell Scott that it was all over between us. I was a single woman again, but hoped I wouldn't be for long.

In preparation for seeing Peter again, I had the braids taken out of my hair and went platinum blonde; he'd seen me looking my worst, now I wanted him to see me at my best. When we were all gathered together to watch the eviction of the next celebrity I went over to Peter's manager and told him that I really wanted to be with him. I wanted the whole world to know how I felt about this gorgeous, wonderful man who had stolen my heart. I was praying that Peter would be evicted, but was horribly disappointed when it was Charlie. I just didn't think I could survive another day without seeing him. I longed for him, body and soul.

I had to let Peter know how I felt, I couldn't bear the fact that he didn't know my true feelings. This wasn't a crush – this was the man I was determined to marry. So when I was being interviewed on ITV2, during a commercial break I ran over to the barrier with the jungle beyond leaned over and shouted out to the camp 'Tell Pete "yes"!' The production team thought I had gone mad and, yes, I was – madly in love. Romeo and Juliet, eat your hearts out.

315

Then Peter went to the bush telegraph and they asked him what he thought about my message. He said that he really had feelings for me, but that I had hurt him, and that we would have to do some serious talking. This *has* to work out I thought, I'm so in love with this man.

The next day, when he was finally evicted, I could at last see him. The first time we met, though, it was on live television, with the cameras on us, surrounded by loads of people. Immediately, we hugged and he whispered to me, 'I told you I wasn't lying about my feelings.'

I whispered back, 'I've finished with Scott, please tell me I haven't blown it.'

He simply said, 'We'll have to talk.'

I didn't want to leave his side, but he had to be interviewed by the papers and as soon as the TV show finished his management whisked him off to the hotel and I wasn't able to see him for the rest of the day or night. It was torture knowing he was in the same building as me. I even broke down and cried because I really couldn't bear to be parted from him, and it takes a lot for me to cry. I knew that I had finally found the man for me. I had travelled across the world, and met him in a bizarre situation but I just knew with every part of me that Peter Andre was the man for me.

It just goes to show that there is a right person for everyone. It's just taken me a bit of time, and a few thousand miles to find him but one thing's for sure – if this doesn't work out I'll have to become a nun! I really don't want anyone else but him.